D0443755

THE WOMEN WHO WRITE THE MOVIES

THE WOMEN WHO WRITE THE MOVIES

From Frances Marion to Nora Ephron

Marsha McCreadie

A Birch Lane Press Book
Published by Carol Publishing Group

A Birch Lane Press Book
Published by Carol Publishing Group
Birch Lane Press is a registered trademark of Carol Communications, Inc.
Editorial Offices: 600 Madison Avenue, New York, N.Y. 10022
Sales and Distribution Offices: 120 Enterprise Avenue, Secaucus, N.J. 07094
In Canada: Canadian Manda Group, P.O. Box 920, Station U, Toronto, Ontario M8Z 5P9
Queries regarding rights and permissions should be addressed to Carol Publishing Group, 600 Madison Avenue, New York, N.Y. 10022

Carol Publishing Group books are available at special discounts for bulk purchases, for sales promotions, fund-raising, or educational purposes. Special editions can be created to specifications.
For details, contact: Special Sales Department, Carol Publishing Group, 120 Enterprise Avenue, Secaucus, N.J. 07094

Manufactured in the United States of America

10 9 8 7 6 5 4 3 2 1

Library of Congress Cataloging-in-Publication Data

McCreadie, Marsha.
    The women who write the movies : from Frances Marion to Nora Ephron / by Marsha McCreadie
        p. cm.
    "A Birch Lane Press Book"
    ISBN 1–55972–251–7
    1. Motion picture authorship. 2. Screenwriters—United States—Interviews. 3. Women screenwriters—United States—Interviews.
I. Title.
PN1996.M46   1994
812'.03099287—dc20   94–18113
                                                                CIP

To Bob Keller, who sat through many never-before-seen films with me late into the evening, never letting me forget that the visual element in movies is still the one most viewers respond to.

Contents

Acknowledgments

Many thanks to the following people who gave freely of their time in interviews, as well as for their insightful, honest, often unexpected, thoughts about their work and their selves.

Nora Ephron, for giving much more than the requisite hour for an interview, and for making room in what must have been a very tight schedule in the middle of casting for her next film. And for taking it in good humor when I cornered her with my interview request in the women's room of the Loew's 84th Street Movie Complex. Also to her amiable assistant Amy for being very much on top of requests for photos, texts, and the like.

Barbara Benson Golseth was gracious in talking about her mother, Sally Benson, and in remembering bits and pieces no articles could ever record.

Albert Hackett was similarly forthcoming in talking about his wife, Frances Goodrich, and their work and life together. It was particularly touching that he showed me the study in his home where the two had worked together. And thanks for his good manners and ease in handling his own failing memory: "I can't remember when my own birthday is," quipped the ninety-four-year-old when asked about Goodrich's birthdate.

Special thanks to the daughters of Mary McCall Jr.—Sheila Benson and Mary-David Sheiner—for loaning prized photographs of their mother. And for the most frank and intriguing interview ever given by two sisters on one mother who ended up sounding like two different mothers, though the same fascinating woman.

Thanks to Catherine Turney for speaking so openly about her work, and its sometimes deleterious effect on her personal life, when she was working in Hollywood at the height of her power in the forties. And for maintaining that remarkable feisty spirit of competi-

ix

tion: "What did she work on?" was the sharp response of the eighty-seven-year-old when another writer was mentioned.

Dick Andress of the New York State Archives became a most helpful instant film scholar as he searched for specific items and scripts in the Film Archives at Albany before sending them on.

Thank you to the staff of the Museum of Modern Art's Film Studies Department for research help, especially Charles Silver, and to the staff of the Billy Rose Collection at Lincoln Center.

A tip of the hat to Jerry Vermilye for loaning photographs from his extensive collection of movie stills and for some intricate research accomplished in the twinkling of an eye. And to the scrupulous Al Marill, for straightening me out on more facts than I care to admit.

I am grateful to my women friends, Carol Calhoun, Lael French Scott, and Suzanna Turman, for always being interested in my work, and to my editor, Allan J. Wilson, who took a chance on what must have seemed an interesting but perhaps not very commercial idea.

MARSHA MCCREADIE
New York City
April 1994

THE WOMEN WHO WRITE THE MOVIES

1

The Pioneers

The directors were dunces, you know. [But] if you've got a good writer, the director has got the whole thing in his pocket.
Anita Loos, interview in
Women's Wear Daily, August 23, 1974

It is the writer's job to get screwed. Writers are the women of the movie business.
Nora Ephron, interview in New York City
October 15, 1993

There you have the two incredibly different perspectives that a span of more than sixty years makes. The importance of the screenwriter, the subjugation of the screenwriter. So which is it?

And if the downgraded position that Nora Ephron assigns to women is true, then what is valid for scriptwriters today can only be multiplied for today's women screenwriters. Except there just aren't that many.

From a position of pioneer importance with some familiar and many never-before-heard-of names breaking in, and helping create the art of cinema, to a handful of female writers listed in the current *Film Writers Guide.** There are over 1,500 men listed today, and only

---

*Ed. Kate Bales, Lone Eagle Publishing, 1988.

33 women. According to the Writers Guild of America, from the turn of the century to the mid-twenties, women outnumbered men in the screenwriting trade ten to one.

What can have happened in the intervening years? Or were there peaks and valleys of prominence of women screenwriters?

There appear, actually, to have been clusters. Clusters rising to a crescendo in the middle forties, and then a dramatic drop-off from a peak which has never re-formed since, even in an era when the hue and cry has been for better roles for women.

Of course you can answer that writers are the unsung heroes of any cinematic age. But they weren't as unheralded, or as powerless, in the early days. Their titles, or job descriptions, may have changed constantly. But they wrote, and many held influential positions. Best of all, there was the fun, the camaraderie, the chutzpah that got these young women (and a few of them not so young) into the new movie business.

They were first. That clearly had something to do with the excitement of it all. And they were opportunists in the best sense of the word: seeing something new to develop, to work with. But this was true for men, too, and so it is really quite extraordinary that it is so easy to rattle off dozens of names of important women writers in the first two decades of film: Elinor Glyn, June Mathis, Frances Marion, Anita Loos, Gladys Unger, Bess Meredyth, Dorothy Arzner (before she moved on to directing), Dorothy Farnham, Clara Beranger, Alice D. G. Miller, Sonya Levien, Lenore Coffee, Isobel Lennart, Adele Buffington, Luci Ward, Jane Murfin, Jeannie Macpherson, Claudine West, Zoë Akins, Ouida Bergere, Beulah Dix, Olga Printzlau, Gene Gauntier, Grace Cunard.

And a little later—mainly in the late thirties and forties—Ruth Ann Baldwin, Mary McCall Jr., Sally Benson, Sarah Y. Mason, Mae West, Frances Goodrich, Ruth Gordon, Phoebe Ephron, Joan Harrison, Tess Slesinger, Lillian Hellman, Catherine Turney, Alice Duer Miller, Laura Perelman, Marguerite Roberts, Helen Deutsch, Dorothy Kingsley.

Heard of any of them? Perhaps a few. But even given the relative obscurity of writers, and especially screenwriters, these are for the most part unsung if not dead heroes. But they were highly paid, regularly working professionals all through the teens, twenties, thirties, and especially the forties. Who were these women and how did they move into the industry so readily? More important, perhaps, how did they get their spunk and drive?

You can make some guesses, on the mark or not. Movies were more declassé than theater, and only a bit more on the up and up than vaudeville. Generally speaking the "out" or "under" of the mainstream attracts the nonestablishment nonpowers, here women, as their only possible venue. Additionally, in the teens and early twenties there was a freer attitude toward women being in the professions than there has been since, maybe even counting our time. Here are some possible reasons why, according to social historian Carole Klein:

> The role of women in American society had been steadily evolving, but now, as during the Civil War, many were able to put aside their traditional roles and behavior. Women began routinely dining out on their own, and many even smoked in public.
>
> As the needs of war [World War I] became more demanding, most women turned to more purposeful activities. At the war front, the country needed them as nurses, stretcher bearers, and ambulance drivers; at home, they filled the jobs in factories and offices left by men who had become soldiers.
>
> Everything about these women began to change to suit their new lives. One discovery women made very quickly was how impractical their enormously complicated hairdos were in their new, busier lives. With patriotic abandon, they untwisted the nineteenth-century chignons, removed the combs and "rats," and cut their hair short. When the very popular dancer Irene Castle was forced to cut her hair because of an infection, the look became fashionable as well as utilitarian.
>
> (*Gramercy Park: An American Bloomsbury*
> Athens, Ohio, 1987, pp. 236–37)

A more hands-on view is offered by Barbara Benson Golseth, the daughter of screenwriter Sally Benson, who said she remembered conversations from her childhood among her accomplished aunts. And that even in the Midwest where her mother grew up it was not considered at all unusual for women to be at the top of some of the most competitive professions shortly after the turn of the century.

Add this to the atmosphere of the beginning movie business: wide-open, uncompartmentalized, open-ended, with easily made lateral moves. And all in the very raw little town of Hollywood. For some of these women from the much more sophisticated San Francisco—such as Frances Marion, Anita Loos, and Lenore Coffee—it must have seemed easy pickins'. Local talent in a way, and many of them stayed for decades. Others, like Bess Meredyth and Jane Murfin, mostly actresses and writers, drifted in from the East: a pattern to be seen today. And enterprising types like Marguerite Roberts or Alice D. G. Miller came from the Midwest on their own steam.

And the third—even more startling—fact is that there seems to have been an informal but strong and highly effective networking system among women in the film business. They were friends, but they took their friendship into the professional arena in a way that our more self-conscious and liberated age, with a few notable exceptions, hasn't managed to, at least in the movie business. They wrote parts for other women. They exchanged jobs and information about jobs. They hired each other when they could. And they often worked on the same projects together: Frances Marion writing for Mary Pickford. And for Marie Dressler. Marion and Lillian Gish putting together a project. Director Lois Weber hiring Marion. Anita Loos writing for Lillian Gish, and that friendship lasting—ultimately—more than seventy years. June Mathis working on projects with Dorothy Arzner, and with Bess Meredyth. Lenore Coffee writing for director Lois Weber. Jeannie Macpherson writing for Blanche Sweet and Mae Marsh. A bit later, by-then director Dorothy Arzner using writers Mary McCall Jr. and Tess Slesinger. Bette Davis and Barbara Stanwyck requesting writer Catherine Turney. Coffee writing for Davis and Joan Crawford. It goes on. You might even say that the collaborative nature of film lent itself readily to the feeling of community that these women already had. Either because of the times or—more radically speaking—because they were women. And the esprit de corps seemed contagious.

The ubiquitous director D. W. Griffith used some of these young women first as actresses, then script girls, and then title writers. Bess Meredyth, who had been a singer on the East Coast and came to Los

Angeles for a rest and to look around, started out as a Griffith extra. Jeannie Macpherson from Boston was first an actress—a big star really—before making the full-time shift to scriptwriting. But that shrewdest of all young hustlers, Anita Loos, after a brief stint in acting (her father was in the theater business), went right to where she perceived the action was for her: writing titles and scripts for Griffith. Loos, a workaholic, though she denied it throughout her life, turned professional writer in her teens. And she was sending in sample scripts from her home, some of which sold, before the concept of a "spec" script was anything more than a twinkling in some future agent's eye.

The get up and go, the gumption of these young women—an attitude which seemingly has to be inculcated in pep talks, tirades, and pieces in contemporary magazines for today's young women— runs all through stories these women told about their beginnings in the business; perhaps embellished by time, perhaps not. Lenore Coffee said that when she would go to a movie with her mother she would always leave the theater and say to her mother, "'I could do better than that.' And Mother always said, 'Why don't you?'" In 1919 Coffee read in the *Motion Picture Exhibitors Herald* that a studio was looking for a story idea for silent star Clara Kimball Young. Coffee wrote one, the studio bought it, and she had enough business savvy to demand a credit line (and this without the benefit of a "hot agent").

Alice D. G. Miller (as opposed to the prominent and wealthy East Coast playwright Alice Duer Miller, who came along quite a bit later) also had a democratic entry into the movie business. With no connections known to this writer, the native of Milwaukee entered the film industry in 1919 reading and doing editorial work for Griffith. *Variety*'s obituary somewhat downplays her role in the 1928 picture *Two Lovers*, but the fact is that she had the sole credit for the complicated, well written, and quite innovative script. You could even make a case for Miller's heroine Leonora as being an autonomous, progressive heroine in an action film.

I guess it's not really possible to go any further in even a light sprinkling of names of women who were pioneers in the business without discussing June Mathis and Frances Marion, those supplementary alter egos of, in Mathis's case, power and innovation, and in Marion's, the creativity and compromise that so often seem to accompany longevity and monetary success in the movie business. If June Mathis is the matriarch/mastadon of the movie business,

Frances Marion is the lovely, long-lasting matron. But they are both far too complicated in makeup to be stuck in any such neat pigeonholes.

For one thing, June Mathis may have been a phenomenon of will-power, among men and women alike. And this includes today. It is said that, once she was empowered in the movie business in the early twenties, this was Mathis's persona:

> When June swept through the studio onto the sets, into the offices and dressing rooms, appearing as by magic wherever there was a problem, her fierce authority soon brought to others some of her divine fire. Short, stocky, with blazing brown eyes, brown hair curling untidily, Paris clothes that on her looked dowdy, she was a woman of indomitable will.

Mathis was born in Leadville, Colorado, of English and American parents, probably in 1892. In the information sheet she gave to Goldwyn in 1922, she listed her family as having been nine generations of doctors, lawyers, and professors, and that her great-uncle was a dean of one of England's oldest colleges. She went to school in Salt Lake City and San Francisco and she worked in vaudeville as an ingenue to help support her mother after her father's early death. Throughout her mid and late teens Mathis traveled to many of the large cities of the West to appear on stage, and later credited this with helping her learn a lot about human nature by quietly studying it and figuring out various types.

When Mathis's last play, *The Fascinating Widow*, closed in Los Angeles, she began to meet film actors and actresses, a breed somewhat looked down upon by stage performers. This is what Mathis said about that period to a film publication of the time:

> An indifference to my stage career developed. I began to meet writers and others interested in literature, editors and those who had friends or relatives connected with the writing game. Out of this grew my first real contacts with the motion picture industry. Soon I was devoting all my efforts to writing.
>
> > (two above quotes from an undated and unsigned
> > article in the Margaret Herrick Library at
> > the Academy of Motion Picture Arts
> > and Sciences, Los Angeles)

She had saved enough money for two years' leisure and she and her mother went to New York, where she took courses in literature and writing in the daytime and went to all the movies she could in the evening. Mathis started publishing stories in magazines, and she entered a film scenario competition. Her entry did not win, but it was well enough thought of that she got offers to work in Hollywood, and by 1918 she was in charge of the scenario department at Metro at the age of twenty-seven.

In addition to being a script writer, Mathis became a production executive, the first in the industry and the first, if not the only, woman to hold such a position in the history of the American film. For while there are the few Sherry Lansings and Dawn Steels today as studio heads, they are not simultaneously writing and producing their own scripts as well. Mathis was the equivalent of Irving Thalberg a decade later at MGM (though Thalberg was not a writer too). Her domain was Metro, Goldwyn, and to some extent Paramount and First Nation.

An article on Mathis, "The First 100 Noted Men and Women of the Screen" by Carolyn Lowrey in 1920, declared:

> A close association with Maxwell Karger, director-general of the Metro, has deeply imbued Miss Mathis with the art of direction and her activities are ceaseless from the inception of a story to its completion. She watches with a narrow eye the filming, cutting and titling of each production, lending aid wherever she may.
>
> (Mathis file, Margaret Herrick Library at the Academy of Motion Picture Arts and Sciences)

Other top women writers were earning as much as a thousand dollars a week in the twenties, but as a woman studio executive as well, Mathis was singular. According to Lewis Jacobs's *The Rise of the American Film*, "To her [Mathis]—and to Thomas Ince—can be credited the makeup of continuity as we know it today. Gaining a reputation for her stress on timely themes and her careful planning, she originated the writer-director combination which was to plan the film's action before any shooting began. The result was less waste, lower production costs, and a smoother, more rounded picture." (New York: Teachers College Press, 1969, p. 328). A Business Head's dream! Careful pre-preparation of the shooting script by writer and director resulted in cutting out waste while at the same time sharpening narrative continuity.

Mathis wrote the films *The Millionaire's Double* (1917); *To Hell With the Kaiser* and *An Eye for an Eye* (both 1918); *Out of the Fog, The Red Lantern,* and *The Brat* (all 1919); *Old Lady 31, Hearts Are Trumps,* and *Polly With a Past* (all 1920); *The Four Horsemen of the Apocalypse, The Conquering Power, A Trip to Paradise, Camille,* and *The Idle Rich* (all 1921); *Turn to the Right, Kiss, Hate, Blood and Sand,* and *The Young Rajah* (all 1922); *In the Palace of the King, Three Wise Fools, The Spanish Dancer,* and *Greed* (re-edit., rewrite) (all 1923); *Sally, The Desert Flower, Classified,* and *We Moderns* (all 1925); *Ben-Hur, The Greater Glory,* and *Irene* (all 1926); *The Masked Woman* and *The Magic Flame* (both 1927).

Probably the single most famous accomplishment of the seven years Mathis spent at Metro was her demand to film the Ibañez novel *The Four Horsemen of the Apocalypse.* And she also insisted that the role be given to a relative unknown named Rudolph Valentino whom she had seen in bit parts. This was no casting couch scenario, however (despite rumors), for according to an article in *Photoplay,* Valentino asked, "Who is she?" when given the news that Mathis had selected him for the role. She wrote the script, and also chose Rex Ingram as the director.

But her personal life should hardly be the point, though her association with Valentino is, ironically, that for which Mathis is the best known. It is as if the only thing that D. W. Griffith were known for was the discovery of Lillian Gish.

In any event, *Four Horseman,* which has been considered box-office "poison" because it treated the until then unpopular subject of World War I, was a big success. And Mathis had extended her influence at the studios to that of associate producer.

A hustler extraordinaire, and the first woman one, to boot, in the film business. But perhaps her longest-lasting contribution was to establish the importance, and even the form, of the shooting text. Bess Meredyth and Anita Loos were also major contributors. Just a brief look at Loos's first film, *The New York Hat,* short though it is, shows how the titles are listed, straight down the page. The description—or continuity—is briefly typed after this. The year is 1912. Then bit by bit it is possible to see in a Mathis script a fuller integration

4032

THE NEW YORK HAT

Released Dec 1/12

4032   8

A dying mother's strange trust   4

The bequest   2

My Beloved Pastor: (LETTER "A")
          My husband worked me to death, but I have managed
to save a little sum. Take it, and from time to time buy my daughter
the bits of finery she has always been denied. Let no one know.   14
                    Mary Harding

                         Afterwards

              "Daddy, can't I have a new hat?"   8

The village sensation   2

The minister recalls his trust   4

The gossips speculate   2

                       Sunday Morning

                  She attempts to explain   6

                       After Church

          Mary and the minister linked in a scandal   8

The gossip reaches the father   4

He seeks reparation from the minister   6

The Church Board investigates   4

Four foot flash of letter   4·

An unexpected trust   2

                                                    ⊕   2

                                                            80

Facsimiles of early screenplays: Above, *The New York Hat* (1912);
on the following two pages, *The Millionaire's Double* (1917) and
The Sea Beast (1926).

June Mathis script The Millionaire (?) title
1917

9

CHRISTMAS EVE

BENNINGTON ARRIVES IN NEW YORK AND DISCOVERS THAT IN FOURTEEN
YEARS NEW YORK HAS GROWN SOME.

18 Scene : Needle point in and vignette - bird's eye shot of New York
water front - shooting toward Cunard docks - showing ocean
liners.

19 Scene : Exterior Cunard pier - Bide and Stevens comes from pier
followed by porter with luggage - Stevens has Bide's seal
o vercoat over his arm - Bide wears a very smart cloth
overcoat - they exist toward taxi.

20 Scene : At curb - by taxi - Bide and Stevens enter - Bide speaks
to Stevens.

OUT IN : "GO HOME, KISS THE CARETAKER AND HANG A WREATH IN THE WINDOW
I AM GOING TO THE CLUB AND ROUND UP A BUNCH OF OLD FRIENDS."

Back to scene.

Bide gets into taxi - drives off - Stevens hails another -
puts luggage inside - drives off - FADE OUT.

TITLE : *EXT OF BENNINGTON HOUSE* AT THE CLUB.

21 Scene : Needle point in - main clubroom - long shot toward entranc
fireplace at right - Xmas tree near fireplace - Merton,
an old man with grey whiskers, is sitting by the fireplace,
half asleep - Bide enters, comes toward camera and to fir
place.- he stops - surveys tree - sees Merton - goes to
fireplace.

A-21 Scene: *Berry Enters* Close view by fireplace - shooting to take in tree -

S̶C̶R̶E̶E̶N̶P̶L̶A̶Y̶ ̶O̶F̶ ̶M̶O̶B̶Y̶ ̶D̶I̶C̶K̶

Scene 473. CLOSEUP AHAB ON SUPERSTRUCTURE

As he sees this--swings himself to the deck by the chain and goes out

Scene 474. DECK OF WHALER

On a slant-awash-lightning-horror. Ahab makes his way to the wheel.
He is almost blown off his feet but gains the wheel---

Scene 475. CLOSEUP WHEEL

As Ahab grasps the wheel, sets his face defiantly to the storm and
holds his course. He is cursing and blasmpheming God. A huge wave washes
over him but he clings to the wheel-the wild gleam to do or die...

Scene 476. GROUP OF TERRIFIED SAILORS IN STERN OF SHIP

Waves washing over the boat--- Group of terrified sailors-with one
of the mates and Queequeg ; they are watching off at Ahab (out
of scene) and suddenly the mate (Flask) looks off and sees-and attracts
the others attention to

Scene 477. MINATURE SHOT IN STORM

Ship in distress sending off rockets---(this ship is some distance ahead
of the bow of the Pequod);

Scene 478. GROUP OF SAILORS IN STERN OF SHIP

As they huddle together-the seas sweeping over them and look off at
the distant other ship

Scene 479. SHIP (PACKET) Minature JUNO

Foundering in the storm-sending up rockets

Dissolve to

of text and instruction/description in *The Millionaire's Double* in 1917, until finally one sees in *Sea-Beast*, a 1926 film by Bess Meredyth and her adaptation of *Moby Dick*, that the format—setting, scene description (as in exterior or interior and the time frame), the listing and placement of characters' names, and the dialogue spoken—are virtually identical to the film script as it appears today. In a few short years these women, in their day-to-day work in the new form, helped to evolve the basic format of a contemporary script.

This is how Mathis described her modus operandi for success in the movie business in a *Los Angeles Times* interview. It is June 3, 1923, and—showing us that *plus ça change*, etc., in the newspaper business—the picture of Mathis is headlined with the caption "Her Salary Is $75,000." The article begins:

Do you keep mental office hours? Can you turn your thoughts on and off at will? Does your brain present to the world an orderly appearance of pigeonholes tightly crammed with experiences and with facts? If you can't answer these questions by "yes," you might never be a June Mathis!

Officially June Mathis is editorial director of the Goldwyn studios; she is said to be "the woman with the most important job in the world." And the Goldwyn studios pay her $1,500 a week for doing it.

There is little doubt that she holds the most responsible position ever held by a woman. Not only the entire direction of the artistic end of one of the biggest studios in the world is on her shoulders, but she also has to make out financial estimates involving millions.

"I had all sorts of miserly instincts when I was a youngster," she said by way of explanation of her success in this branch of the work. "One summer I kept track of every drink of soda water I had, and every bit of candy that went the downward path. It was such fun that I kept it up. Who knows—I might have been doing it just to be prepared for the figuring I have to do now. I have a queer brain, you see. I train it a little and it will travel right along doing that thing over and over.

"In that way I keep mental office hours. I can come down to the office at 9 or 9:30 in the morning, but mentally I never function until 10. I can look at pictures or talk, but as far as work is concerned, I am absolutely a dead issue. Why? Simply because 10 o'clock is the hour at which my brain has been trained to start work. I read somewhere when I first started to write, that Rex Beach always started in to write at 10 o'clock, and I said to myself, 'If 10 is good enough for Rex, it's good enough for me!' And that's how it happened.

"It's the same with my creative work. My creative hours are from 4 to 6 in the morning. I wake up as if an alarm clock has rung, and start in. I just lie in bed and let my brain think things out. Then at night from 6 until 8 I do my writing."*

Mathis went on to say that she didn't find it necessary to have a study, or a special place to work, and that sometimes she even wrote at the family table with someone reading the paper out loud and the piano going strong. (Jane Austen said much the same thing.) And that she believed it possible to train your mind to concentrate to such an extent. This, she said she believed, also helped her in remembering types for her character creation and dialogue writing:

I played at every water tank from Maine to California, and from the Gulf to the Canadian Rockies. And I certainly saw life. Traveling across the United States in a car with the other members of the cast I got to know them mighty well. I watched my women friends in their domestic life, and what I saw was photographed on my brain—for, you see, I have a photographic brain, too.

My first scenario, "The House of Tears," had a scene in which a woman waits for her unfaithful husband to come home. At great length I pictured in the script her every act, how she went to the clock and wound it casually, as if she were not counting every tick of the minute hand, and told just what she did during those hours. When Edwin Carewe, the director, read it, he said, "You can't tell me that you aren't married! You have given yourself away. No one but a married woman who had waited for her husband to come home could tell what you have told."

---

*Barbara Benson Golseth said she believed her mother had a similar method of working things out in her head at night. So that it seemed to be a kind of automatic writing when she would put it on paper the next day. (See the chapter on Benson in "The Forties.")

I said to him, "I am not married, but I have watched my married friends wait for their husbands to come home." And that was the truth. Everything I saw, even to experiences such as this was stored away within my brain, so that if I had to act that part some day, I would know just exactly how to do it. I watched on the streetcars how women of certain class dressed and held their hands and feet.

And in another article, this one actually written by Mathis in *The Photo-Play Journal* for October 1917, she gives even more specific instructions:

If they [the stories] are visualized before you, before the story is told, you begin to scent their relationship and just what influence they will have on the story. [This could be seen as Mathis's own intuitive way of working toward the idea of a "backstory"—or history or background of each character—a technique recommended today for scriptwriters.]

After your characters have been introduced, unfold the story with action, leaving out superfluous scenes, carrying each incident until you reach the development of suspense, then carry the story to its climax and gently down the hill to the usual happy ending which our "fans" seem to favor. Make your characters human. Of course a great deal of this is up to the director. Don't be afraid of writing a title or a leader if it helps the story.

It is better to know what the action is about than to remain in doubt. And if your story will permit add comedy, for five reels of suffering after a day's work gets on the nerves. Like the old saying, "the voice with the smile wins," "the photoplay with the laugh gets the money."

Tellingly, Mathis has an exemplum which serves as an admonishment:

[One woman] writes a picture play. She keeps trying to better it. She polishes up scenes and situations, she adds a climax here or an anticlimax there. The main point is that she is not satisfied.

Another woman writes a picture play. She believes it is sublime. She does not view it critically—she does not try to better it. She sends it to a producer, and it is "returned with thanks." Satisfied with her own work, she believes those who have looked at it are lacking in intelligence.

Which is the successful scenario writer? My illustrations give their own answers.

So how does Mathis measure up by her own standards? In *Blood and Sand*, which she scripted in August 1922, Valentino stars as Juan Gallardo, a poor Spanish boy who is not really interested in the saddler's trade which he is supposed to take up. The only way out is the one he takes (as countless members of the underprivileged class have always done: through sports), and he becomes a famous matador in Seville. He marries his childhood sweetheart, the sweet and pure Carmen (Lila Lee), and then encounters Dona Sol (Nita Naldi), an upperclass and very wealthy vamp who throws herself at him.

Dona Sol tricks him with the ruse of a car breakdown. He is forced to let her stay overnight and is caught by his wife, who assumes the worst. She leaves him, and in this state he goes to fight what will turn out to be his last bullfight.

In adapting the novel which was not that puritanical, and for the benefit of the American viewership, Mathis has emphasized Juan's true love for his wife, and the fact that he is really being tricked by the aristocratic temptress. But there is a subtext of sexuality—vamps lying on couches, exotic tobaccos being offered, enticing but evil-looking smoking drinks—to say nothing of some double entendre dialogue. (These motifs are also to be found in *Ben-Hur*, another of Mathis's scripts.)

The proper moralistic but very melodramatic tone is struck right away in the script with its opening title:

The wide world over, cruelty is disguised as sport to gratify men's lust for excitement. From the early ages, humanity has congregated to watch the combating forces of man and beast. [In possible explanation to the American audience] To the Spaniard, the love of the bull-fight is inborn. A heritage of barbarism—its heroes embody the knights of old.

First we see a philosopher, then the use of dissolves of various human figures being thrust into different torture machines. So the sadism and the morality are mixed in right off. And in deconstructing this text, it's the kinkier visual elements which win hands-down.

Soon thereafter there is a nice integration of real documentary footage into the bullfighting scene. And it was this imaginative, seemingly modern, editing done by Dorothy Arzner that got Arzner her next big assignment, to edit *The Covered Wagon* in 1923. So here we have these two huge talents—Mathis and Arzner—working on the same project.

And in the scene when Dona Sol—the seductive Nita Naldi—first tries to intrigue the matador, she gives him a ring: "It once belonged to an Egyptian queen who gave it to a Roman conqueror for his bravery." But the titles declare, "Happiness and prosperity built on cruelty and bloodshed cannot survive." A bit later, Dona Sol, flinging herself at Juan who—vacillating between resisting and yielding though he does finally resist her snake-like and seductive movements—says, "Someday you will beat me with those strong hands. I would like to know what it feels like." Beyond Sharon Stone.

Juan is in agony at all this, telling his friend, "It is torture to love two women. There is no one like Carmen. But this other woman is different," to which his friend rejoins in flowery Victoriana, "Impure love is like a flame. When it is burnt out, there is nothing left but the blackened embers of disgust and regret."

It is visually effective when the bad woman makes Juan pick up her handkerchief in front of the good wife, leading the wife to think that an indiscretion has occurred, and so the denouement can take place in the film. It is done very quickly of course, as Juan hesitates between the two women, wavers at just the wrong second, and Carmen is devastated. It is the same kind of emotional shorthand that we see when Dona Sol takes out her lipstick somewhat callously after Juan has been killed and starts looking in the mirror while his body is being carried out. Just good cinema, of course, until you remember the year this was made: 1922.

The titles announce, while the camera pans the cheering crowd, "Out there is the real beast. The beast with ten thousand heads." And cut to the worker sweeping the sand over the blood. "Out there is the real beast." And this theme is one that will be developed further in *Ben-Hur*.

Though controversy swirls around the final filming of *Ben-Hur*, Mathis's shaping hand is still evident in the movie, which remains the

Mathis reading Dead Sea scrolls from *Ben Hur*

model for the later sound version in 1956. The structure is the same, and so are some of the most dramatic sequences: from the beating of the drums for the galley slaves to the chariot race to the image of mother and daughter lepers huddled together. It seems that Mathis's *Ben-Hur* is the most memorable of all versions of Lew Wallace's novel, especially as Esther goes into the underworld of the Valley of the Lepers to search out Ben-Hur's mother and sister, a scene with shadowy grotesque rocks and steamy lakes, ending with a leper crawling like an animal to drink from one of the fetid-looking lakes.

Many studios had been trying for years to obtain the rights to the Wallace novel, and Mathis, through her personal contacts with those who held the stage rights, got them to agree to let Goldwyn film it. Part of the deal was that she would write the script and be in charge of production and casting. The first director she selected, Charles Brabin, did not work out and eventually Fred Niblo did the direction. The continuity is by Bess Meredyth (and Carey Wilson) and perhaps Mathis extended the job tow-rope to Meredyth .

And here are some of the Mathis signposts: there is the sweet, pure Esther (May McAvoy), and the temptress figure of Iras of Egypt (Carmel Myers), whom Mathis had made much more intriguing than Esther. Iras tries to seduce the righteous Ben-Hur (Ramon Novarro), saying at first, "My heart is in the hollow of your hand," and then a bit later, when becoming impatient with his demurring (on the eve of the Chariot Race), "If you are as slow in the race tomorrow as you are in love today, Messala (Francis X. Bushman) may drive snails and win." When she first sees him there are smoking drinks being served in her lair. And a speech, too, has an overtone of S&M: upon seeing the horses Ben-Hur will drive, she says, "Flashing eyes and milk white bodies! Beauty to be tamed! Does it not thrill you?"

And like Dona Sol, Iras has no loyalty to either of her men: she is Messala's lover as well as Ben-Hur's, and makes sure he knows that it's Ben-Hur driving the chariot. And when Ben-Hur wins, she has a moment of "grief," then laughs madly. Again, there is the sense of the insatiable crowd.

A romantic, affecting image which is still used in versions of *Ben-Hur* is the moment when he is visiting his old home, sleeping peacefully on the stones, and his leprosy-ridden mother and sister come upon him. Not daring to touch him, his mother strokes the stones instead, and leaves a tear spot when she goes. They leave:

"Not a sound!" she implores her daughter. "He belongs to the living—we to the dead!" And when Ben-Hur awakes, he is heartened by the sign of the wet tear spot on the ground and seems to know it was his mother.

Some say Mathis was fired from the final filming of the movie, and some reports have it that she was glad to leave because of a controversy with the studio. Still, the masterpiece bears her name and signature style, with melodramatic lines like "I am revenged, indeed, but to what profit? My mother and Tirzah are dead! Can gold restore them to me?"

Mathis can write contemporary dialogue too, as can be seen in her very early script for *The Millionaire's Double* or *Bennington Alias Bennington* in 1917. Her concluding image for the film perfectly captures all the themes: marriage, inheritance, falsification of identity.

> FADE IN—*Vignetted marriage certificate—with the names of Bide and Constance—two oval portraits at top of certificate—that come to life in the persons of Bide and Constance—Bide points to the names on the certificate— smiles—puts his hand to his mouth—blows her a kiss—she smiles—lowers her eyes—Needle to and fade out.*

And she can be funny as well. Consider these titles:

> BIDE
>
> I'm going to take a trip to Japan—The South Sea Islands —Become a Hottentot—Anything! Pack up at once!

A bit later:

> [*Picks up a seal coat*]
>
> I won't need this where I'm going—all they wear is a kimono and a pleasant smile.

Mathis, with her uncanny commercial sense, has included all the elements that might be able to sell the film today in a "pitch" meeting: a Christmas Eve scene, a prison scene, lawyers, and a question about who is the true heir.

In fact, it was Mathis's reputation of having a very good commercial sense that got her into hot water with future generations of film scholars. She was asked to reconstruct the Erich von Stroheim masterpiece *Greed* (overlong in the opinion of the studio heads at nine hours). As the film now stands, its title page indicates: Rewritten by June Mathis, with Screen Adaptation and Scenario by June Mathis and Erich von Stroheim. (For a full visual analysis of what may have happened—as it's impossible to tell since there are missing reels—see *The Complete Greed of Erich von Stroheim* by Herman Weinberg [New York: Arno Press, 1972].)

The movie was based on Frank Norris's classic novel *McTeague* about a dentist who falls in love with a woman who has won some money in a lottery, but hoards her money to a terrible end. The corruption and tragedy that money can create is the ultimate point of the film. McTeague is played with animal-like vigor by Gibson Gowland, and ZaSu Pitts is an appealing Trina. Mathis cut the film from seven hours to two—it is said without the director's knowledge—something from which von Stroheim never recovered, either personally or professionally. According to Weinberg's book, the final editor, Joseph Farnham, was supposed to have written the titles—or more likely selected them—for the film's final version.

But the letter and spirit of the original novel has been kept at the end of the film, and we know from Weinberg's notes that anything in typescript here is from the original script. It is therefore something that von Stroheim put in, and Mathis left in.

Mathis's death at thirty-five—probably from a stroke or heart attack due to high blood pressure—while watching a Broadway play in 1927 leaves a giant Whither? as to what direction she might have taken the art of film had she lived longer. But it is still remarkable that so little attention has been given to this dynamic woman, particularly in a time when we are looking for female role models in the professions.

If Mathis was the matriarch of women in the movie business, Frances Marion was everybody's favorite aunt, even if she did arrive in 1915 from her native San Francisco with a couple of careers, and a couple of husbands, under her belt. On a poster art assignment from an advertising agency where she had been working, she decided to stay in Hollywood at the behest, she says, of her friend, novelist-

Two stills from *Greed.* Above, ZaSu Pitts. Below, ZaSu Pitts with Gibson Gowland and an unidentified actor.

274

bag on saddle of dead mule.

SHOT FROM HIS ANGLE of split open canvass bag, twenty

dollar gold pieces falling into sand.

BACK TO CLOSE UP McTeague, he looks once more at hand-

cuff and at body.

MEDIUM SHOT all in, he sits cumbersomely down, looks

stupidly around.

SHOT FROM HIS ANGLE of desert.

BACK TO McTeague he looks at bird cage.

SHOT FROM HIS ANGLE of bird cage, bird flops.

BACK TO McTeague nodding gravely.

FADE OUT

FADE IN

TITLE "O cursed lust of gold!

when for thy sake

the fool throws up his interest in both worlds.

First, starved in this, then damn'd in that

to come"

FADE OUT

F I N I S

Comparison of Mathis's screenplay for *Greed* and, on facing page, the Frank Norris novel *McTeague*.

McTeague

violence of their fall, and rolled out upon the ground, the flour-bags slipping from it. McTeague tore the revolver from Marcus's grip and struck out with it blindly. Clouds of alkali dust, fine and pungent, enveloped the two fighting men, all but strangling them.

McTeague did not know how he killed his enemy, but all at once Marcus grew still beneath his blows. Then there was a sudden last return of energy. McTeague's right wrist was caught, something clicked upon it, then the struggling body fell limp and motionless with a long breath.

As McTeague rose to his feet, he felt a pull at his right wrist; something held it fast. Looking down, he saw that Marcus in that last struggle had found strength to handcuff their wrists together. Marcus was dead now; McTeague was locked to the body. All about him, vast, interminable, stretched the measureless leagues of Death Valley.

McTeague remained stupidly looking around him, now at the distant horizon, now at the ground, now at the half-dead canary chittering feebly in its little gilt prison.

THE END.

newspaperwoman Adela Rogers St. Johns. The irrepressible St. Johns had apparently decided and convinced her (and everyone else it seems) that movies were to be the coming thing. In Marion's words:

> You see, my real ambition has always been to write. I put in every spare minute trying to write stories. Some of them I sold—for ten or fifteen dollars apiece! Not much encouragement in that, but I went on writing them.
>
> Occasionally someone would buy the picture rights of one of my stories; and as the usual price, fifteen dollars, was sometimes more than I had received for the story itself, I began to think of the possibilities in that line.
>
> Mary Pickford especially interested me. I hardly knew what her name was. To me she was "Goldilocks," a wonderful child, although she was not playing child parts at that time, but grown-up ones. I began to dream of writing picture stories in which she would play these child parts. Later, I actually did write thirteen of these stories, and they were the ones in which she was enormously successful. Everybody remembers her in *The Poor Little Rich Girl, Rebecca of Sunnybrook Farm, The Little Princess, Amarilla of Clothesline Alley, Stella Maris, Pollyanna,* and the other pictures in which she was an adorable little girl. I wrote all those scenarios. They were, of course, based on the original novels; but a scenario, even when it is built on a story in a book, may contain so much original matter of its own that the two are quite different.
>
> When I began to be interested in motion pictures I knew nothing of the technique of the screen. I never had been inside a motion picture studio. Perhaps one reason why I have succeeded is that I have a certain amount of practical sense. This practical sense warned me that the amateur cannot compete on equal terms with the trained worker. So I determined to become a trained worker. I gave up the business I had established, went to Los Angeles, and got a job at the Bosworth studios at fifteen dollars a week.
>
> ("A Girl Who Has Won Fame and Fortune
> Writing Scenarios," *The American Magazine,*
> an undated issue in the Billy Rose Theatre
> Collection at Lincoln Center)

Marion parlayed a "Jackie of all trades" job in the early days of the movie business—as script girl, titles writer, part-time actress, and continuity person (this vague term seems to mean scene organizer)— into a job as a scriptor. Through her friend St. Johns, Marion got an introduction to Lois Weber, the film director, and after seeing Marion's drawings Weber took her on as a protegée at the Bosworth Studios. While at Bosworth, Marion met the man married to Mary Pickford, and eventually met Mary Pickford. They became best friends, and it was a bonding that was useful to both throughout their lives as Pickford became the star (eventually one of many) around whom Marion would create a vehicle.

In *Off With Their Heads*, her 1972 memoir about Hollywood, Marion describes her own feelings about the inspiration for screenwriting: "...the writers of scenarios were pushed into the background, poorly paid, their talent unexploited, but the idea kept sticking in my craw like a fishbone, and I decided to try to outline a story which I would submit to Mary Pickford when she returned to California." (p. 24)

Frances Marion with Mary Pickford

And in one of the last interviews Marion gave before her death in 1973 at age eighty-six, she credited the women's friendship system as having helped her and others: "Too many women go around these days saying women in important positions don't help their own sex, but that was never my experience. In my case there were Marie Dressler, Lois Weber, Mary Pickford, Elsie Janis, Mary Roberts Rinehart, Adela Rogers St. Johns, Hedda Hopper, Bess Meredyth, Anita Loos, Ella Wheeler Wilcox who encouraged me..." And she said that women were so well entrenched in the movie business that two decades later:

Bess Meredyth, Anita Loos, and I were asked our advice on virtually every script MGM produced during the thirties. It would have been embarrassing had other writers discovered that the executives asked our opinions about their work and that we were, without credit, making revisions. When we carried the scripts on which we were doing re-writes, we made sure they were in unmarked, plain covers. But we knew male writers were complaining about "the tyranny of the woman writer" supposedly prevalent at all studios then, and particularly at MGM.

> Interview with Frances Marion, DeWitt Bodeen
> *Films in Review*, pp. 138, 142, February and
> March, 1969)

Marion had a small role in *A Girl of Yesterday* and was the lead in *The Wild Girl From the Hills*, both in 1915. A short story of hers was the basis for *A Daughter of the Sea*, but the first script for which she is credited is *Camille* in 1915. This was followed by the tragic story of the loss of *The Foundling* by fire, which was written for Mary Pickford.

Marion was not easily discouraged, it's clear; over her entire career she wrote more than 130 films, including *Humoresque* (1922); *Abraham Lincoln* (1924); *Stella Dallas* (1925); *The Son of the Sheik* and *The Winning of Barbara Worth* (both 1926); *Love* and *The Scarlet Letter* (both 1927); *The Wind* (1928); *Min and Bill, Anna Christie*, and the Oscar-winning *The Big House* (all 1930); another Oscar-winner *The Champ* (1931); *Dinner at Eight* (1933); *Riffraff* (1936); *Love From a Stranger* (1937); and *Green Hell* (1940) for a quick overview. At one point, she was paid $3,500 a week while under contract at MGM.

After *The Foundling* was written and destroyed (though recut and released the next year in 1916), Marion headed for New York where many more movies were being made than at present. Fudging her background to say she had more experience in film than she really did—and since she did not have *The Foundling* to show—Marion convinced William Brady of World Film Studios at Fort Lee, New Jersey, to let her work for him for two weeks for free, after which he could let her go if he didn't find her useful. According to *Off With Their Heads*, Marion reworked a number of poorly-done films which were "on the shelf," thereby impressing the producer and earning herself a permanent job.

During the silent era, Marion wrote five or six scenarios every year. These films were not just for Pickford, but for other major stars of the day, such as Marie Dressler (*Tillie Wakes Up* in 1917); Constance Talmadge (*East Is West* in 1922); Norma Talmadge (*The Lady* in 1925); Aileen Pringle with Ronald Colman (*A Thief in Paradise* in 1925); Lillian Gish (*The Scarlet Letter* in 1926, *The Wind* in 1928); Greta Garbo (*Love* in 1927, adapted from *Anna Karenina*); and even for Valentino (*The Son of the Shiek* in 1926).

It is certainly true that Marion has a good eye, perhaps because of having been a painter and commercial artist. This can be dynamically

Greta Garbo with Robert Taylor in *Camille*

Greta Garbo in the American (above) and German versions
(on facing page) of *Anna Christie*

seen in *The Scarlet Letter*. Showing that she understands film very well in its use of an image for a visual equivalent for emotion—and also as a foreshadowing for the rest of the film, and story—here is a nice moment early in the film script, Scene 10, when Hester Prynne shows her true nature:

SEMI CLOSE-UP AT WINDOW

Close to the window is a rustic cage with a bird in it. But a black shawl has been thrown over the cage; for the bird's song is forbidden to mount on the Sabbath. A shaft of sunlight has fallen upon the cage. Hester's face, as she gazes at the cage, becomes wistfully sad. Why should she hide its song, Hester asks herself in this moment of faint rebellion. She draws the black shawl away.

And she is able to establish character with a stroke, using the device of the mirror which has been used so many times for contemporary audiences since that it's become a visual cliche. Marion has described how Hester is tucking her hair back and binding it at her neck, making certain that no lock escape her bonnet, for it would be "unchristian." But that "when she comes to her bonnet, the eternal feminine is revealed."

INSERT: CLOSE-UP HESTER AT WALL

She regards the worsted mat. On it is inscribed this warning from the scriptures:

"Vanity is an evil disease."

Then Hester lifts it aside and sets it down. Behind it is a piece of polished metal which serves Hester as a mirror.

CLOSE-UP HESTER

She practices how she will wear her hat, and her eyes smile reflectively, for there is someone at church who may look upon her, and she would meet with his approving glance. Hester forgets it is Sabbath and smiles. It is entirely the fault of that jaunty little hat. Something stirs within her,

*springtime—a longing for life—and love, which is the
fulfillment of life. She starts! The church bells! She hears
their warnings.*

In one of the many examples of cooperative efforts between and
among women in the movie business in the early era, it was Lillian
Gish who barraged Congress and censorship groups with letters in
order to obtain the right to film the classic Hawthorne novel, which
had been banned from being filmed. The indomitable Gish did obtain
permission, and as she has said in a documentary about her life, "It
was ridiculous that a classic work of American literature, something
that was taught in our *schools*, could not be filmed." (*Lillian Gish: The
Actor's Life for Me*, directed by Terry Sanders, 1988.)

Marion successfully made the transition to the sound era, with
films such as *Let Us Be Gay* (1930, with Norma Shearer and Marie
Dressler), *Min and Bill* (1930, script by Frances Marion and Marion
Jackson), *Dinner at Eight* (1933, script by Frances Marion and
Herman Mankiewicz), and *Camille* (1937, script by Frances Marion,
Zoë Akins, and James Hilton). Many of the sound and studio films
were collaborative efforts, of course, and some latter-day critics have
accused Marion of being just an uncomplaining craftsperson at best:
She is "good-natured, optimistic and lively—and in the end curiously
self-effacing, perhaps a reflection of the conditions of her employment
[that] the writer was subservient to the studio," according to the
foreword by Gloria Swanson to *Off With Their Heads*. Or a studio
hack at worst, as Nancy Lynn Schwartz says in her book *The
Hollywood Writers' Wars*:

> There were writers who had made the voyage to Hollywood
> before talkies came in. Many of them were women, such as
> the veteran Frances Marion, darling of L. B. Mayer and
> Hearst, who wrote screenplays for Marion Davies. Her staff
> would each write a separate part of the script, for which only
> she would get credit.
>
> (p. 19)

Yet the interview Marion gave to author DeWitt Bodeen in *Films
in Review* (March 1969) shows that she knew very well what was

going on, and that she did not necessarily like the situation. Discussing the studio years at the end of the thirties at MGM, and before the Credit Arbitration Board of the Writers Guild was as strong as it now is, Marion said,

> I was beginning to feel that film writers are like Penelope—knitting their stories all day just to have somebody else unravel their work by night. . . . it was apparent that if a writer wanted to maintain any control over what he wrote, he would have to become a writer-director, or a writer-producer. Writing a screenplay had become like writing on sand with the wind blowing.
>
> (p. 139)

For a look at unalloyed Marion, see her classic 1930 adaptation of Eugene O'Neill's *Anna Christie*, starring Greta Garbo. Marion has the beginning of the play-into-film opened up to include the riverfront barge, in the standard fashion of adapting plays to films by extending the scenes beyond, or outward. Or by creating new settings, as in reel seven, page one, which is opened up to include an "amusement pier." Intelligently, Marion has kept the lines very much the same as O'Neill's when we first see Anna, with the sole addition of two "Well"s.

ANNA

Gimme a whiskey—ginger ale on the side, and don't be stingy, baby.

LARRY

Well, shall I serve it in a pail?

ANNA

Well, that suits me down to the ground.

Possibly Marion felt that the beginning "Well" to each sentence, which is not in the play, made the dialogue more colloquial.

In *Min and Bill*, this time a *comic* seaside drama, we see Marion's abilities with the "common touch," and it was a part written for her then down-and-out friend Marie Dressler, who made the most of it. Min gets to say funny lines like "Just cut out the applesauce" (the B.S.) and "I don't give an abalone if he runs the jail." Referring to a cop, she says, "Shut up and answer this guy as if he were a gentleman." There are Keystone Kop-like antics, and lots of visual gags. Min's adopted daughter, whom she generously tries to help by giving her to a wealthy, more acceptable home, doesn't want to stay there, and complains that "Things are so quiet, they don't even have a fight."

Marion, who has been quoted as saying about herself, "writing is a refuge for the shy," gave this advice in her book *How to Write and Sell Film Stories*:

If you know a studio executive, producer, director, star or other employee of standing...you may be sure that it will receive a careful reading. All these persons are seeking good stories and, as a rule, are willing to submit those of their friends, provided they are good stories. [But] Do not believe for a moment that "pull" will sell your story. Influence may get it a reading, but no company can afford to buy stories that do not offer screen value. The story editor stands or falls on his selection of material that will be financially successful when filmed. Nothing else concerns him.

Another method of selling originals is to get work in any capacity at a studio and, when you have been accepted as a trustworthy person, to offer your stories directly to the story editor. Writers have taken positions as stenographers, typists, readers, file clerks, etcetera, for the purpose of "learning the business" and gaining the opportunity of submitting their stories directly.

Obviously, only a small number of writers can avail themselves of either of these methods, and the most easily available and the best way for the beginner to get his stories to the attention of the studio executives is through an established agent favorably known to them. To be sure, the agent will get a percentage of the proceeds, but the services he offers are well worth his fee and few beginners can reach the studios without his help. He will see that the writer does not part with rights in his story that he should retain, and that his compensation is adequate and that it is paid according to contract.

(p. 187)

Still, she is not sanguine about the chances. "I receive hundreds of letters every year from would-be scenario writers. They come from society women, farmers' wives, schoolteachers, business men, lawyers, doctors, preachers! The motion-picture companies receive hundreds of thousands of scenarios from these amateur writers. And the figures show that only about *one* in *ten thousand* is worth taking." ("A Girl Who Has Won Fame and Fortune Writing Scenarios," in *The American Magazine.*)

She did say, however, in an essay "Scenario Writing" collected in *Behind the Screen*, edited by Stephen Watts,

When I began writing scenarios for motion picture companies in Hollywood nearly twenty years ago, directors frequently started a picture with only the slightest idea of what its plot was to be, and made up the story as they proceeded with the making of the picture.... Today, however, the studios have learned that nothing connected with motion-picture making, except money, is more important than the story, and the scenario writer's prestige and his remuneration have risen accordingly.... The scenario writer's work therefore is to produce a script that will approximate as closely as possible the scenes, dialogue, and background of the finished motion picture.

(p. 4)

Other very early women writers moved into the film business with acting as the point of entry. Bess Meredyth was an actress and vaudeville player from the east coast who was visiting Los Angeles and while there in 1915 decided to try acting and scriptwriting. At one point in the teens she tried directing, and she codirected, with Wilfred Lucas, *The Romance of Tarzan* in 1918. Eventually Meredyth became a studio writer in the 1930s. Later in her career she and her

Bess Meredyth between Maud Fulton and Michael Curtiz

husband set up an independent production company in the hopes of having Frances Marion work for them as a writer, but that didn't work out. Still, it was another effort in the direction of early female partnerships.

Born Helen MacGlashan in 1890 in Buffalo, she worked in films as an extra for D. W. Griffith at the Biograph Studios. This is how she summarized in *Motion Picture* magazine (January 1915) her transition from acting to writing:

> A chance meeting with Wilfred Lucas at the Biograph Studios in Los Angeles was the cause of my entering Motion Pictures. I had completed a long vaudeville tour in a pianologue act and was tired out, and so decided to go to the Pacific Coast for a change. Whilst there I arranged by wire for another engagement, when I paid that momentous visit to the Biograph. I was introduced to Mr. Lucas. "I am from New York," said I. "So am I," said he. And I felt I had found a friend, for I had not yet arrived at the stage where I wanted to stay in Los Angeles. He advised me to try the pictures, and after some hesitation, I canceled my engagement and allied myself with pictures. I enjoy it and keep busy for, besides acting, I write a number of scenarios, and I also keep up my music, in case I ever want to go on the stage again.

Some scripts that Meredyth was responsible for throughout her three-decade career include *The Grim Comedian* (1921); *The Dangerous Age, One Clear Call, Rose o' the Sea, The Woman He Married,* and *The Song of Life* (all 1922); *Strangers of the Night* (1923); *The Red Lily* and *Thy Name Is Woman* (both 1924); *A Slave of Fashion* and *The Love Hour* (both 1925); *Don Juan* (1926); *When a Man Loves, The Magic Flame,* and *Rose of the Golden West* (all 1927); *The Little Shepherd of Kingdom Come, The Yellow Lily, The Scarlet Lady,* and *A Woman of Affairs* (all 1928); *Wonder of Women* (1929); *Chasing Rainbows, In Gay Madrid, The Sea Bat, Our Blushing Brides,* and *Romance* (all 1930); *The Prodigal/The Southerner, West of Broadway, The Cuban Love Song, Laughing Sinners,* and *The Phantom of Paris* (all 1931); *Strange Interlude* (1932); *Looking Forward* (1933); *The Affairs of Cellini* and *The Mighty Barnum* (both 1934); *Folies Bergere* and *Metropolitan* (both 1935);

Half Angel, Under Two Flags, and the story for *Charlie Chan at the Opera* (all 1936); *The Great Hospital Mystery* (1937); the co-adaptation for *The Mark of Zorro* (1940); *That Night in Rio* (1941); and *The Unsuspected* (1947).

The beginning of *Sea Beast*, the 1926 adaptation of *Moby Dick* by Meredyth, starts this way, as she gives these specific visual instructions:

Showing the surging, restless water—nothing else. This is the first and last scene in the picture and is symbolical of the fact that while great loves and tragedies occur—lives are lost—hearts are broken—the sea remains unchanged, leaving no record of what has gone before.

This is very much in accord with the tone of the novel—the eternal, unchanging nature of the sea; and it is also in the vein of the classical way of beginning and ending works of art, particularly films, with the same shot or feeling. Meredyth has also captured the pristine feeling of New England in her initial description:

FADE IN
CORNER ANGLE SHOT—CLOSE-UP HOUSEWIFE IN KITCHEN

New Bedford housewife, tall, gaunt, raw-boned type wearing the dress of the period—about 1840. Several lamps stand on the table before her which she has just filled with sperm oil. She carefully adjusts the thick, hand-made wick, and as she lights it there is a light effect showing the flame which—

DISSOLVES TO

Miniature or profile shot of the town at dusk. Little houses nestling along the water and running up in terrace fashion to the hill tops. Lights come up in various windows until the entire town is lighted and finally the great light in the light-house comes on and swings about blindingly.

TITLE 1   *All the tapers, lamps and candles that burned around the globe, burned as before so many*

*shrines to the glory of the whale hunters. It was
the whale that lighted the world!*

DISSOLVE TO

TITLE 2 *It was the whale ship that ferreted out the
remotest parts of the world. American and
European men-of-war now peacefully riding in
once savage harbors should fire salutes to the
honor and the glory of the whale ship, which
originally showed them the way and interpreted
between them and the savages.*

DISSOLVE TO

TITLE 3 *The whalemen of America—those fearless, cool-
blooded Yankees, were first in this great and
noble profession. Scores of anonymous captains
sailing from Nantucket and New Bedford were as
great as Cook and Columbus.*

But Meredyth has humanized and romanticized Ahab in Hollywood fashion. It makes him a more appealing character, and his shy,
eventually thwarted love justifies his anger and blaspheming later in
the movie. Ahab (John Barrymore) is shown to be in love with Esther
(Dolores Costello) but afraid she won't like him because of his peg
leg.

CLOSE-UP AHAB SEATED IN CHAIR IN ANTEROOM

*As he sits there. He has arranged the leg of the one trouser
over his other leg, to hide it. The blood is pounding in his
temples as sits there—his eyes riveted on the door—
waiting for Esther. And then he sees her (out of scene)*

CLOSE-UP ESTHER IN DOORWAY

*As she comes breathlessly in. Her hand goes to her throat
as she pauses on the threshold. All her love is in her eyes.*

INT.   ANTE ROOM SEMI-CLOSE-UP TWO

*Of the two, motionless—looking at each other. Just hold
this—and then, slowly, Ahab gets to his feet. And as he*

*does, her eyes drop for the first time to his feet. His eyes
are on her face, trying to read her soul. For the moment
she stands motionless—horrified—lets out an involuntary
cry. His agony as he watches—Build scene very slowly.
And then her eyes come slowly up to his as she sees the
quivering face. Tears well into her eyes, and then with a
sudden rush of tenderness and love she comes to him—
arms outstretched—and throws them around him. It is the
mother with her child. They hold this. Instantly Ahab is
soothed—all his fears are forgotten.*

But without meaning to, Esther falls in love with Derek (George
O'Hara), and so the eternal triangle:

CLOSE-UP DEREK AND ESTHER IN ANTE ROOM

*As they are looking into each other's eyes—the realization
of their love—and then Esther drops her head on his chest
and clings to him, and his arms go about her. Then they
look up, and both remember Ahab and Esther says:
"Ahab!" They both look horrified, and Derek indicates the
door with a gesture—they must go to him and tell him the
truth, but Esther says quickly:*

TITLE 77: *"I cannot face him yet—I cannot hurt him—"*

BACK: *As she finishes speaking a couple come into the
room, look at them curiously, and Esther, desperate, points
off to the ballroom—they will go in there first—anywhere
to get away and not face Ahab. Derek nods his head and
they start for the ballroom.*

DISSOLVE TO

CLOSE-UP DEREK AND AHAB

*Derek finishes speaking. Ahab, white and stricken, sits
there unable to move. He is numb. Derek looks at him
with seeming sympathy and love as he finishes:*

TITLE 78 *"If you still want to marry her—she will go
through with it—I will go away."*

BACK: *Just the faintest gleam of hope in Ahab's eyes. His thought is: "Perhaps after all there might be a chance of her forgetting." Derek sees this and says quickly:*

TITLE 79   *"If you are willing to risk unhappiness in the knowledge that a woman has married you out of sheer pity—then go to Esther; if not—your ship sails in the morning."*

ANOTHER ANGLE CLOSE-UP DEREK AND AHAB

Ahab sits there. It is as though he had not heard, and Derek, who has played his last trump, sits waiting tensely. The hope has died out of Ahab's eyes. Derek puts his hand on Ahab's shoulder, but Ahab winces under the touch.

So there is an effective use of the close-up shot for facial reactions, for the touch on the shoulder and the wince. And—in Hollywood terms—there is an emotionally understandable reason for Ahab's alienation:

Scene 451   CLOSE-UP AHAB

As he sees this, terrible anger on his face—glances off toward direction of Moby Dick, ahead of him—realizes they are putting [sic] off the path—stumps out.

Scene 475   CLOSE-UP WHEEL

As Ahab grasps the wheel, sets his face defiantly to the storm and holds his course. He is cursing and blaspheming God. A huge wave washes over him but he clings to the wheel—the wild gleam to do or die...

Though the year is only 1926, and though indeed this is still a silent film, the script has a contemporary feeling and form. And— given the fact that the romantic angle obviously had to be thrown in—the character motivations are well-defined, and some of the spirit of the novel has been retained. Also, the writing is nicely descriptive.

Even more "modern" in theme is Alice D. G. Miller's *Two Lovers* (1928), a Fred Niblo direction of Baroness Orczy's historical novel *Leatherface* about an arranged marriage between Dona Lenora, a Spanish girl of nobility, to Mark, the son of a leader of Ghent. The marriage is supposed to cement relations between the conquered and the conqueror, but in fact is being used to find out the secrets of William of Orange, the hidden leader of the Flemish trying to get out from under Spanish rule. *Two Lovers*, which teamed Vilma Banky and Ronald Colman, has action scenes with a lot of the action—even the final plot turning—being conducted by a woman, the heroine Lenora. This is a fine irony when we are constantly on the lookout today for strong women's parts, particularly women's action roles. In this scene, Lenora has decided to help the Flemish take a fortress guarding Ghent. This is toward the end of the film, in Part 10:

4 CU *Lenora's hands bleeding from the strain she is using on the chains to open the drawbridge.*

5 CU *Lenora hanging on the chain*

6 SCU *Drawbridge opens and closes again.*

7 SLS *Troops outside of the castle waiting for the drawbridge to go down.*

8 SCU *Lenora hanging on the chain.*

[*More of this*]

19 SLS *Troops get on the drawbridge*

20 SCU *Lenora falls to the floor exerted [sic]*

21 SCU *Troops get on the drawbridge*

22 SCU *Troops enter the castle*

23 CU *Men passing Lenora who is lying on floor*

Miller can be comic too. About the forced political marriage, earlier in the film:

70 CU *Mark in bed—eating his breakfast—looks up and speaks*

71 *"Some men die for their country—I'll marry for mine!"*

And dramatic. When Mark meets Lenora and she takes off her veil, the line is "Were it not for your eyes, I could believe you were fashioned of marble." And romantic. On their wedding night, Mark says, "I don't want rights—I want your love!" There is a close-up of Lenora, looking up toward Mark. She answers, "Can one turn on love at will—like wine from a tap?"

A native of Milwaukee, Miller entered the film business in 1919 doing reading and editorial work for D. W. Griffith. (That must have been a banner year, as it is the year when Lenore Coffee, Adele Buffington, Jane Murfin, and Sonya Levien all also started working in film.) Miller, who was born in 1894 and died in 1985, is sometimes confused in film references and even *Variety* obituaries with the playwright, poet, and scriptwriter Alice Duer Miller, a wealthy East Coast writer who wrote the poem "The White Cliffs of Dover" and seems to be remembered mostly for that. In fact there is a funny short in a newspaper at the time describing how the two Millers finally met at the studio after many years of receiving each other's mail.

In 1977, Alice D. G. Miller gave her own list of films she worked on—a rarity to get it from the pen of the writer, as it were—and the list has the following annotation at the top of the page: "I give all the information I have." ADGM Feb. 22, 1977.

Here it is, as memory served Miller: *The Fourteenth Lover*, story only (1920–21); *So This Is Marriage, Cheaper to Marry*, and *Lady of the Night*, last listed from a story by Adela Rogers St. Johns (1924); *The Masked Bride* and *Pretty Ladies* (both 1925); *The Exquisite Sinner, Monte Carlo, The Boy Friend, Altars of Desire*, and *Valencia* (all 1926); *The Last Waltz* and *The Devil Dancer* (both 1927); *Four Walls, Man Made Woman*, and *Two Lovers* (all 1928); *The Bridge of San Luis Rey* (1929); *Disgraced* and *The Keyhole*, story only (both 1933); *Orchids to You* (1935); *The Girl on the Front Page*, coscriptwriter with Albert R. Perkins (1936); *On Borrowed Time*, script by Miller, Claudine West, and Frank O'Neill (1939); *Tangier* (1945).

For today's viewers, perhaps the best known of Miller's work is her adaptation of Thornton Wilder's *Bridge of San Luis Rey*, with Lily Damita. The script, which stresses an overwhelmingly mean Marquessa jealous of her daughter Camila, also has a triangle of two twin brothers, Manuel and Esteban, both of whom love Camila. The bridge has collapsed in the film, which takes its tone from the following speech by Father Juniper: "In all ages and all places—this question has risen: Do we live by accident and die by accident—or do we live by plan and die by plan?" Though *Bridge* may be the more familiar script, in fact *Two Lovers* seems superior.

One name that keeps cropping up in this overview—either as friend, confidante, story source, or writer of the stories on which some these films were based—is that of Adela Rogers St. Johns. In some sense she helped create the open, raucous, but hard-working atmosphere of the early Hollywood (or at least recorded and commented on it) though the primary occupation of this extremely colorful woman was not screenwriting. Adela Rogers (St. Johns was her married name) was a journalist and fiction writer who later went on to write scripts and also serve as a story consultant at MGM. But like every good journalist, she seemed to have the knack of being in the right place at the right time when events were taking shape.

Born in Los Angeles in 1894 and the daughter of criminal attorney Earl Rogers, the feisty and outspoken young woman joined the *San Francisco Examiner* in 1913 (pay—$7 a week) when she was sixteen, then went to the *Los Angeles Herald Examiner*. In 1919 she joined the staff of *Photoplay*, writing profiles of figures such as Valentino, Gloria Swanson, and Tom Mix. Three of her magazine serials published as books were the basis for movies: *The Skyrocket* in 1923, *The Single Standard* in 1925, *A Free Soul* in 1931. Her short stories were made into films as well: *Hollywood* in 1924, *Scandal* in 1925, and *Singed* in 1927. She also wrote some screenplays: early Westerns for Tom Mix, and *Wicked* starring Elissa Landi in 1931.

Rogers St. Johns was the role model for Norma Shearer's part in *A Free Soul*, and for Rosalind Russell's quick-witted reporter in *His Girl Friday* in 1940. About her it was said, "She was a kind of wild, uninhibited woman before feminism came in. She was a tough, hard newspaper woman, one of the guys...a figure from the old roaring days of Hearst journalism, which no longer lives." (Mel Durslag, *Los Angeles Herald Examiner* sports columnist quoted in the *Daily News*, August 11, 1988, in Rogers St. Johns's obituary. She died at the age of ninety-four.)

Rogers St. Johns was a strong influence on Frances Marion, and seemed to be the only one to know the scoop on June Mathis's love life (or lack thereof) and of the real, platonic, but very devoted relationship between Mathis and Valentino. And it was Alice D. G.

Miller working from a story by Adela Rogers St. Johns who created a memorable part for Norma Shearer in the 1925 film *Lady of the Night.* Shearer is in the dual role of finishing school graduate and also a young woman who has just gotten out of reform school in this melodrama about bankers and crime. Miller also wrote the lead role for ZaSu Pitts in *Pretty Follies* in 1925, a film based on a Rogers St. Johns short story. Pitts plays a prankster comedienne in the *Follies.* The interconnections become influences.

Other early screenwriters include, of course, Anita Loos, that phenomenal writing machine about whom little can be said that she hasn't already said herself in her autobiographical books *A Girl Like I* (1966), *Kiss Hollywood Good-Bye* (1974), and *Cast of Thousands* (1977), as well as numerous interviews. Novelist (known mostly for *Gentlemen Prefer Blondes*), short story writer, and playwright, Loos acted briefly on stage with a company managed by her father before turning professional writer (at thirteen, Loos started selling articles to the *New York Morning Telegraph*).

One unsolicited script she mailed from home to the story department of D. W. Griffith's Biograph Studio was *The New York Hat,* which sold in 1912. Griffith directed it, with text performed by Mary Pickford, Lionel Barrymore, and Lillian and Dorothy Gish. Loos landed a job writing subtitles for Griffith, including titles for *Intolerance.* She worked for Biograph from 1912 to 1916, writing over 100 scenarios, and in the year 1913 alone sold nearly forty (note, of course, at one page or so each) at $25 apiece.

By 1916, Loos's price had gone up to $500 a picture. In that year, she was given her first movie credit for *Macbeth,* by William Shakespeare and Anita Loos. In typically cheeky fashion, she is reported to have said "If I had asked, [they] would have given me top billing." In 1916 and 1917, Loos wrote a number of satirical scripts and wisecracking titles for Douglas Fairbanks in a series of films directed by John Emerson, and her reputation as a satirist began to build. Loos and Emerson married in 1919, and they later collaborated on numerous screen and stage plays, and on the books *How to Write Photoplays* (1919) and *Breaking Into the Movies* (1921).

In an interview she gave to *Women's Wear Daily* later in her life, Loos said, "I had more energy than most people. Writing came so easily that I paid no attention to it. I did it with my left hand while I was doing something else with my right. I was able to turn out so many scripts because there were so many different people to write for. I always wrote a script with a star in mind. And there were a great many different stars so I skipped around and wrote everything I could." Curiously, in the same interview, she said, "I never went to the movies even when I was in the movies. I wasn't interested."

Though this tone is very much in the offhanded spirit of the early practitioners of film, Loos's case was still not one of near automatic writing, as she would have you believe: Just a cursory look at the boxes of scripts (mainly play scripts in this case) in the Billy Rose Theater Collection at Lincoln Center in Manhattan shows version upon version, all perfectly organized and labeled. Author Nancy Lynn Schwartz has this to say about Loos in *The Hollywood Writers' Wars*: "Professional and reliable...she was known to go to bed at ten o'clock, rarely went to parties, belonged to no organizations, and had little frame of reference outside of the professional world. She was considered by studio executives to be the perfect screenwriter" (p. 19).

But by any standards, her output is astounding, including *The Telephone Girl and the Lady*, *The Power of the Camera*, *The Hicksville Epicure*, *Highbrow Love*, *A Narrow Escape*, *The Widow's Kids*, *The Lady in Black*, and *The Wedding Gown* (all 1913); *His Awful Vengeance*, *Gentleman or Thief*, *A Bunch of Flowers*, *When a Woman Guides*, *The Road to Plaindale*, *The Wall Flower*, *The Saving Presence*, *The Fatal Dress Suit*, *The Girl in the Shack*, *For Her Father's Sins*, *The Million-Dollar Bride*, and *A Flurry in Art* (all 1914); *Mixed Values*, *Symphony Sal*, *The Deacon's Whiskers*, and *Pennington's Choice* (all 1915); *His Picture in the Papers*, *A Corner in Cotton*, *Macbeth* (titles only), *Wild Girl of the Sierras*, *The Little Liar*, *The Half-Breed*, *Intolerance* (titles only), *The Social Secretary*, *Manhattan Madness*, *American Aristocracy*, *The Matrimaniac*, and *The Americano* (all 1916); *In Again Out Again*, *Wild and Woolly*, and *Reaching for the Moon* (all 1917); *Let's Get a Divorce*, *Hit-the-Trail Holiday*, and *Come On In* (all 1918); *Getting Mary Married* (co-writer), *Oh You Women!*, *A Temperamental Wife*, *The Isle of Conquest*, and *Virtuous Vamp* (all 1919); *Two Weeks*, *In Search of a Sinner*, *The Love Expert*, *The Perfect Woman*, *The Branded Woman*, and *Dangerous Business* (all 1920); *Mama's Affair* and *Woman's Place* (both 1921); *Red Hot Romance* and *Polly of the Follies* (both

1922); *Dulcy* (1923); *Three Miles Out* (1924); *Learning to Love* (1925); *Gentlemen Prefer Blondes* (1928); *The Struggle* (1931); *Red-Headed Woman* and *Blondie of the Follies* (dialogue only) (both 1932); *Hold Your Man* and *The Barbarian* (both 1933); *The Girl From Missouri* (1934); *Biography of a Bachelor Girl* (1935); *Riffraff* and *San Francisco* (both 1936); *Mama Steps Out* and *Saratoga* (both 1937); *The Women* (with Jane Murfin) (1939); *Susan and God* (1940); *Blossoms in the Dust, They Met in Bombay* and *When Ladies Meet* (all 1941); *I Married an Angel* (1942). Some of the above scripts were coproduced by Loos too. And—continuing the female partnerships—some of her plays were written with Frances Marion, including *Shotgun Wedding* and *Mother Was a Lady*. Loos also tried her hand at directing, with *Mama's Affair*, in 1920.

Though Loos is known primarily as a comedy writer today (H. L. Mencken said to her, "Young woman, do you realize you are the first American writer ever to make fun of sex?"), some of her films are not comedies, such as *White Collar Girl*, a melodrama about an insurance company. And even a comedy such as *Biography of a Bachelor Girl,* with Ann Harding and Robert Montgomery, seems to have its emphasis as much on character development as on wittiness: In Reel 4, bohemian artist Marion Forsythe (Harding) says, "I've thought I was in love more than once before, but it always turned out to be propinquity or a romantic mood or just vanity perhaps. Almost everything except the real thing." Later, when Marion asks why he disapproves of her, editor Richard Kurt (Montgomery) replies, "Because you're superficial and casual and irresponsible. You treat life, which is a tragic thing, as if it were a trivial bedroom farce. You're a second rate artist who has acquired a reputation by vamping celebrated nitwits to sit for their portraits."

Loos's adaptation, with playwright-turned-scriptwriter Jane Murfin, of Clare Boothe Luce's *The Women* remains a classic of stage to screen adaptation, in the way it opened up the film and broadened the humor to include a wider audience. The play begins in the middle of a bridge game, but the film has a clever and unique beginning that still captures the competitive spirit among these women:

As the view fades in we look down toward two female dogs being led along the sidewalk on leashes. One (a small breed such as a Peke) is coming from the north—the other from the south. Each is led by a woman who is only seen from the knees down. As the two dogs approach each other they begin to snarl. Their leashes tighten. As they pass, both strain to get at each other, their snarls rising in pitch. The hands of one of the women reach down and pick up the snarling little Peke.

Following this we see the woman who has picked up the Peke: She is a tall, Junoesque matron, etc.

The dog scene is returned to throughout the film as a kind of humorous emblem:

Close view of the dog, Sheba, fade in. As the dog is whining, the scene draws back to a view of Mary's boudoir, etc.

Loos and Murfin have also opened up the play to include a scene in Bermuda for the most obvious of that kind of play-to-film change, and—while many of the witty lines of the play have been retained—the adaptors have added a few of their own. For instance, Nancy, the unmarried novelist of the play/film, says of herself in the movie that she is "what nature abhors. I'm an old maid—a frozen asset!"

The play's more subtle nail polish color "Mauevre" [sic] has become the film's "Jungle Red" throughout, picking up on the play's observation that one of the women's husbands said the brighter color made it look as if she had "been at somebody's throat." And the movie has a number of broad comic scenes which are additions, such as the scene in which Crystal (Joan Crawford) is in the bathtub and being harassed by Sylvia (Rosalind Russell) in her gossipy, pseudo-friendly way. Or the film's revelation of Crystal's hokey "Western cowboy" boyfriend, a beau mentioned in the play but never identified.

Another extremely important early figure, though not quite as early in getting the worm as Loos, was Clara Beranger. The author of over sixty scripts, and a functioning screenwriter in the movie business for more than thirty years, Beranger wrote scripts primarily for Paramount and MGM. Originally from Baltimore, Beranger was first a successful playwright on Broadway before coming to Holly-

Clara Beranger

wood in the early twenties. In the first part of her career, in the silent era, she free-lanced for various companies, including Famous Players.

Some of Beranger's scripts include an adaptation of a George Broadhurst play, *Bought and Paid For* in 1922; an adaptation of *The Marriage Maker* in 1923; original scripts for *The Bedroom Window* and *Locked Doors* in 1924; an adaptation of the play *Men and Women* by Henry C. De Mille and David Belasco in 1925; and shared credit on *Buried Alive* in 1933, among other films. She is credited in a number of articles with writing *The Great Adventure* for Lillian Gish, though the copyright office has Dorothy Farnham listed as the scriptwriter.

In a second marriage, Beranger in 1928 wed William De Mille, producer-director brother of Cecil B. De Mille, and throughout her life gave numerous interviews and wrote articles on screenwriting. She also lectured on screenwriting at the University of Southern California after retirement and authored the classic *Writing for the Screen* in 1950. And—as with other early filmmakers who "discovered" the art of screenwriting by making it up as they went along—most of Beranger's advice stands today. This is especially true of her list in *Writing for the Screen*, "Don'ts for the Writer of Motion-Picture Dialogue":

1. Don't try to be literary or flowery. Verbal flourishes sound pompous and stilted on the screen.
2. Don't over-write, as there is neither the space nor the time in a film for too much talk.
3. Don't have your characters make long speeches without providing something interesting for the eye to follow; otherwise the attention of the audience will wander.
4. Don't have your characters speak your thoughts instead of their own.
5. Don't use incomplete sentences, except for a special dramatic effect. Letting the audience finish a thought for you is a lazy man's trick.
6. Don't attempt a dialect without first familiarizing yourself with it.
7. Don't repeat lines except for emphasis.

8. Don't put your emotional meaning in stage directions instead of in lines.
9. Don't use meaningless or unrevealing words.
10. Don't use a proper name at the end of a speech. This is a common fault of amateurs. It weakens the entire speech.
11. Don't rely on profanity to strengthen a line. It will almost inevitably be cut out by the censors. [This is the one rule which seems obsolete.]
12. Don't use soliloquy unless absolutely necessary. In modern drama, with the exception of the psychiatric play, a character talking to himself becomes unreal and ridiculous. This also applies to the "aside." If a character must talk when no one else is on a scene, he could express his thoughts to an animal, or to some inanimate object, such as the dictaphone in *Double Indemnity*. A person talking to his image in the mirror gives the effect of two people, thus avoiding the artificiality of the soliloquy.

(pp. 126–27)

These rules seem to be born out in Beranger's own scripts. In *The Bedroom Window* (although a silent film) the lead's niece, Ruth, says (through title cards), "Please help me clear Bob, Aunt Matilda, you're so wonderful in working out mysteries," a natural enough sounding speech spoken by a young girl with—note—the name of the person addressed mixed in during the middle of the speech, not at the end.

Beranger's descriptions also show a well-developed visual sense and ability to block out action for her characters. Here is a typical scene from *Bought and Paid For*:

Fanny and Jimmy, as Fanny closes door behind him. He puts his arm about her and kisses her affectionately. She rests for a moment in his arms, as though glad to be there, and gives a happy but tired little sigh. Then she remembers she has work to do and comes out of his arms. She takes Jimmy's hat and starts to take the bag. He stops her with a gesture of "Now wait a minute" and opening the bag himself, he proudly holds up a long string of frankfurters.

*Fanny frowns, shows she doesn't like them. Jimmy looks
from her to the frankfurters and says:*

SPOKEN TITLE:

"When you're long on appetite and short on cash, you
can't do better."

*Jimmy waves the frankfurters, and Fanny, with a resigned
air, indicates, "All right," and takes them.*

And Scene 148:

*Virginia in doorway. As Stafford comes over towards her,
she looks up at him, her face glowing with the look of love.
Stafford looks at her questioningly. She is beautifully
embarrassed as she takes the full-blown rose from her
bosom and holds it out to him. He takes it and as he gazes
at it, realizes what she is offering him. He looks from the
rose to her.*

Men and Women, a silent film written in 1925, has a distinctly easy
style, and a worldly tone that could pass for today's. After the opening
credits, the movie declares:

*There is no hero, no heroine, no villain in this story—the
characters are just men and women.*

*But they live in New York, the city which makes all
incomes seem too small to live on.*

And *The Bedroom Window*, starring May McAvoy, is like an early
action thriller with an arresting beginning: the hook. "Robert" is
found over a dead body with a gun in hand.

Even more important, there is an extraordinarily strong, professional, and proud female lead: a successful mystery writer. Though
Beranger's heroine writes under a pseudonym, her Matilda Jones is
as full of chutzpah as Angela Lansbury's Jessica Fletcher in television's hardy perennial "Murder, She Wrote." Is Matilda indeed a
prototype for this part? A tempting idea, though there have been

women mystery solvers (although they may not have been writers, too) from Dorothy Sayers novels to Nancy Drew to V. I. Warshowski.

Matilda (played by Ethel Wales) first appears after the bit with Robert standing over the dead body with a smoking gun. Her success as a writer is made evident by the large check she has just received from her publisher, with a letter pleading for her next work: effective cinematic shorthand to be seen in the work of all these professionals.

And she is motivated to take on the mystery not because of loyalty to her niece (whose boyfriend is Robert) but out of professional pride and a sense of competition with a colleague. Matilda (the lead character in the film, despite May McAvoy's billing) is also an active mystery writer who risks her personal safety while trying to solve the murder: by going out on a ledge and eventually—much later in the screenplay—being held at gunpoint by the murder suspect. Here is how Beranger describes Matilda, whom we first see in her Greenwich Village apartment. She is presented as a bit of an androgyne throughout—a type perhaps more familiar to the flapper era of the 1920s:

> *Matilda (dressed in a dainty, filmy blouse, but with a tailored skirt) is putting the finishing touches to her morning toilet. She has an electric iron attached to the light and is just finishing the last curl of her white, mannish-bobbed hair, watching herself carefully in the mirror as she does so. Then she disconnects the iron and begins carefully to powder her face, selecting the powder from a mass of bottles and boxes of cosmetics that litter up her dressing-table. She is wearing a dressing gown which is cut in "straight, masculine lines."*

We are also told that "the alcove...is essentially feminine and has all the dainty things that Matilda likes but doesn't dare show as John Paris." (Paris is her pseudonym, changed in the final version of the film to Rufus Rome.)

Constantly smoking through her long-stemmed cigarette holder, and just as constantly taking her horn-rimmed glasses off and putting them on, Matilda solves the mystery of the film, trouncing a lawyer and saving the day. But her main excitement comes at the end of the movie when she realizes she can use the solved mystery as a way of resolving the plot difficulties she is having in the novel she's writing, declaring, "And I've got the title, too!"

She is aggressive, independent, financially successful, adventurous, and consistently professional. Matilda is more interested in her work than anything, or anyone, else. In short, she is in many respects a more ideal female heroine than any of the women on screen today. At first glance, it seems most extraordinary that this figure, and script, could have been conceived of in 1924. Still, it fits the pattern of both the gutsy pioneers of the early film years, and of some of the more independent role models of the first part of this century.

Here is Beranger's own assessment of the beginning years of the film industry:

> Finally, when the producers realized that there had to be stories written for the screen, they did not use writers trained in screen technique, but brought out a perfect avalanche of writers from New York—novelists, playwrights, short story writers. When the producers said, "Go West, young man," the writers went—in special trains and deluxe compartments. The companies treated them well on the way out; the return trip was less deluxe. Among that group were Mary Roberts Rinehardt, Rupert Hughes, Sir Gilbert Parker, Gouvernor Morris, Rex Beach, Elinor Glyn, Clayton Hamilton, and many others. The only one who really made good was Elinor Glyn.
>
> (Lecture "Introduction to the Photoplay,"
> at University of Southern California, 1930)

Though Elinor Glyn was actually born in backwoods Canada in 1864, she was educated in all the social graces and was a smash in the Belle Epoque society of London and Paris, writing romantic and "scandalous" novels, including the influential *Three Weeks* featuring a Balkan queen who greets her lover, vamplike, from a reclining position on a tiger skin. In 1920, Jesse Lasky of Famous Players-Lasky offered Glyn $10,000 and traveling expenses to come to Hollywood to study filmmaking, write an original scenario, and supervise its production (a combo deal for which a lot of contemporary writers would give their eye teeth). This script was called *The Great Moment*, and Glyn was clever enough to write a novel adapted from the film script. The first spin-off?

Glyn stayed on in Hollywood to do nine more scripts and become a kind of Hollywood consultant on the manners of the British aristocracy. And though her term "It" was first used in an article in *Cosmopolitan* magazine, originally meaning "strange magnetism" (what we would probably today call charisma), in the popular mind "It" came to stand for sex appeal. And Clara Bow became the "It" Girl, starring in the 1927 film *It* from a story and script by Glyn.

Another writer who was a hit in England first before being beckoned by the movies was the elegant Gladys Unger. Born in San Francisco in the late nineteenth century, Unger was educated in London and studied art in Paris. In 1902 she successfully mounted a play, *Edmund Kean*, in London and continued to have plays produced there. In 1926 she started writing for motion pictures, with the scripts *Music Is Magic, The Mystery of Edwin Drood*, and *Rendezvous at Midnight* (all 1935, and all shared credits), *Daughter of Shanghai* (shared credit, 1937). She is perhaps best known for *Sylvia Scarlett* (shared credit, 1935).

Unger, who at one point married and then separated from a Persian prince, was a vocal advocate of women's rights. An article in the *New York American* (February 26, 1913) has the quaint headline GLADYS UNGER WANTS THE GIRLS RECOGNIZED and discusses her public protest against the law of primogeniture in England.

Miss Unger resents the favoritism for boys over girls in English families as decidedly unjust. She says, rather bitterly, that even when an estate is not entailed, the tendency is to leave most of it to the first-born son.... "Why do not English parents recognize that it is practically impossible for all their daughters to marry?" asks Miss Unger. "Why do not they face the future awaiting their girls?"

Perhaps it was Unger's strong feelings about feminist issues that gave the liberated, and liberating, tone to her 1935 film *Sylvia Scarlett*, which stars Katharine Hepburn and shows her as an androgynous figure cavorting around the nighttime countryside (with a young Cary Grant). A number of contemporary critics have declared sections of the film to be "Shakespearean" in its use of a

Gladys Unger

transsexual heroine in a magical woodsy setting, and some feminist critics have singled out Hepburn's performance as an early example of an unusually emancipated heroine. But reviewers at the time gave *Sylvia Scarlett* a decidedly mixed reception, and until the feminist revisionist "discovery" of this film, it was considered in the category of interesting failure by director George Cukor.

After contemplating all these rarefied and high-flying creatures, it's a pleasure to discover Adele Buffington, a young woman who got into the movie business as a writer after having been a cashier in a glass cage at a movie theater. After working there for three years, she sold her first script, "La Petite" for $300 to a film company.

"It was easy," Buffington told the *Fort Wayne Journal Gazette* in 1919.

> For three years I watched motion pictures—the kind of stories they flashed on the screen and how these stories were constructed and told. At the same time I watched the stream of folks who came to see themselves in these movie charac- ters—the villain, the old mother, the bride, the business man, soldier, society lady, and scrub woman.
>
> All I had to do was to sit down and write. The characters were there for me, in the life. When I put them on paper, they just unreeled themselves. Always there was action—and it's action, mostly, that makes the movies move. I had always wanted to write, but never had the nerve to try before. But there came the hour when I simply had to do it—and I did. Every night when my work in the cage was done, I went to the library and read, getting details and atmosphere for the scenes I had in mind—for the background against which I wanted those dear people I knew to move and make drama.
>
> Then when everyone else was asleep, I would write and write.

Buffington started with Thomas Ince in 1919, and she had more than 150 credits by the time of her death at seventy-three in 1973. Most of her movies were Westerns, and she wrote for Tom Mix, Buck Jones, and Col. Tim McCoy. In 1941, under the pseudonym Jess Bowers, Buffington wrote *Arizona Bound*, which featured three retired U.S. marshals on special assignment, coming into a small town to search out a gang of stagecoach robbers. This was the first of eight films in the popular "Rough Riders" series which teamed Buck Jones, Tim McCoy, and Raymond Hatton.

Other Western credits of Buffington's include *Dawn on the Great Divide, Below the Border,* and *Down Texas Way* (all 1942, the last two credited to Jess Bowers); *Flame of the West* with Johnny Mack Brown and *Bad Men of the Border* with Kirby Grant (both 1945); *Drifting Along* with Johnny Mack Brown (1946); *Crashing Thru* with Whip Wilson (1949); *Arizona Territory* with Whip Wilson (1950); *Overland Telegraph* with Tim Holt (1951); *Cow Country* and *Born to the Saddle* (both 1953); and *Bullwhip* with Guy Madison (1956). She was an original member of the Screen Writers Guild.

Luci Ward also wrote mainly Westerns, including the 1940 *Beyond the Sacramento* starring Bill Elliott, but she wrote other original stories for film, too, such as *Murder by an Aristocrat* in 1936. Ward was active from 1936 to 1967 and was also an activist in the newly formed Writers Guild. She testified to the National Labor Relations Board that Jack Warner tried to get her to resign from the Guild: "If you writers are smart you'll string along with us—there won't be any blacklist; it will be done over the phone and you won't know what hit you."

The Westerns of Buffington and Ward make it a bit of a joke that in our time a writer like Eleanor Perry was fired from the set of *The Man Who Loved Cat Dancing* because she was told she could not write Western dialogue that was macho enough. (See the chapter on "The Contemporaries.")

Another writer who came up through the ranks in the movie business is Claudine West. Born in England, West came to Hollywood and joined Metro's research department in 1918. (West, obviously a very bright woman, had been a code expert in the British Admiralty during World War I.) She made the transition to screenwriting, and her first credited film seems to be *The Last of Mrs. Cheney* in 1929. She also shared credits on such significant films as *Private Lives* (1931); *The Barretts of Wimpole Street* (1934); *The Good Earth* (with Tess Slesinger and Talbot Jennings in 1937); *Marie Antoinette* (1938); *Good-bye Mr. Chips* (1939); *The Mortal Storm* (1940); *Mrs. Miniver* and *Random Harvest* (both 1942); and *Forever and a Day* (1943), and was working on the 1944 movie *The White Cliffs of Dover*, based on Alice Duer Miller's poem, when she died.

It looks like the movie industry used West for a number of projects with a British theme, but she also worked on several films with coscreenwriter Ernest Vadja, including *The Guardsman* and *Son of India* (both 1931), and *Smilin' Through* and *Payment Deferred* (both 1932). Vajda also worked with her on *The Barretts of Wimpole Street*. And it's clear that West is one of those women who—like Marion, Meredyth, Loos, Coffee and others—owes her longevity in the screenwriting business to having established a toehold early on.

Yet one more example of the relative ease of movement to power for women at the outset of the movie business is the stunning case of Jeannie Macpherson. Born in Boston in 1884, she was originally a dancer and stage performer and appeared in many films from 1908 on, including some for D. W. Griffith. Later Macpherson had her own unit (!) at Universal, where she wrote, directed, and acted in many two-reelers. Turning exclusively to screenwriting after 1915, she collaborated on the scripts of most of C. B. De Mille's silent movies.

She described her career moves to *Photoplay* in October 1916. In New York, and appearing on stage,

> All I knew was that I wanted to act. Then someone told me about motion pictures, how drama was filmed. I was fascinated. I like mechanics anyway. I hunted all over New York for a studio—and couldn't find one. At last a super told me a man named Griffith was doing pictures for the Biograph company. Mr. Griffith wasn't in. His assistant was. I told him my stage experience. He ignored it, scorned it. "We want to know what you can do before a camera," he said.

Macpherson worked for Griffith for a year, playing emotive, ethnic parts. As she told the *New York Telegraph* on October 21, 1917,

> I have watched the scenario work from the beginning, from the time when the main object of the script was to keep some prominent object moving before the eyes of an astonished and delighted audience.... My first glimmer of the possibilities in the new industry came from David Wark Griffith.... From

Jeanie McPherson

those days on I have seen a variety of attitudes toward the script writers. But I now feel that the scenario work is shifting into its proper relation to the screen world.... The problem then is to find a theme so universal that personal and local prejudices are lost in it.

She mentioned her *Joan the Woman* as an example of an attempt to do just this, a late 1916 film which she seems to have been promoting at the time.

Another woman writer who wrote for women, Macpherson scripted *The Captive* (1915) for Blanche Sweet and *The Dream Girl* (1916) for Mae Murray. For Geraldine Farrar, the opera star, she wrote *Maria Rosa, Temptation*, and *Joan the Woman* (all 1916). At the Universal Film Studio she attracted the attention of De Mille and she started writing for him and continued to do so in a very influential capacity for over twenty-five years.*

In the ethnic typecasting typical of the early part of this century, Macpherson, because she had dark hair, was often cast in gypsy or Spanish roles, though she was of Scotch and French origin. As an actress, she was in *Mr. Jones at the Ball* (1908); *Mrs. Jones Entertains* and *A Corner in Wheat* (both 1909); *Winning Back His Love* (1910); *Fisher Folks* and *Enoch Arden* (both 1911); *The Ghost Breaker* (1914); and *Carmen* (1915). And as a scriptwriter, Macpherson wrote (in addition to those mentioned above) *Chimmie Fadden Out West* and *The Golden Chance* (both 1915); *The Heart of Nora Flynn* (1916); *Romance of the Redwoods, The Little American, The Woman God Forgot*, and *The Devil Stone* (all 1917); *Old Wives for New* and *The Whispering Chorus* (both 1918); *Don't Change Your Husband, For Better for Worse*, and *Male and Female* (all 1919); *Forbidden Fruit* and *The Affairs of Anatol* (both 1921); *Saturday Night* and *Manslaughter* (both 1922); *Adam's Rib* and *The Ten Commandments* (both 1923); *Triumph* (1924); *The Golden Bed* and *The Road to Yesterday* (both 1925); *Red Dice* and *Young April* (both 1926); *The King of Kings* (1927); *The Godless Girl* and *Dynamite* (both 1929); *Madam Satan* (1930); *Fra Diavolo* (1933); *The Crusades* (1935); *The*

---

*The only longer-lasting relationship of writer-director that comes to mind is the continuing partnership of writer Ruth Prawer Jhabvala, who started writing for the Merchant-Ivory producing-directing team in 1963 with the adaptation of her book *The Householder* and is still a part of the team as of this writing in 1994. (See the chapter "The Contemporaries.")

Plainsman (1937); *The Buccaneer* (1938); *Land of Liberty* and *Union Pacific* (both 1939); *North West Mounted Police* (1940).

Most of these scripts were written for De Mille in a partnership which depended, observers said, on his attraction to her high spirited courage, and Macpherson to his perfectionism and force of will. They both despised weakness which they defined as men being taken advantage of and degraded, and women who were shallow and money-hungry creatures looking for a man to take care of them. Both also believed, though, in the ameliorability of man, and many of the scripts showed that people could change their ways. De Mille provided the crowd shots and the epic sense; Macpherson's special contribution was to humanize the heroine. Thus her insistence on the title for Joan: *The Woman*. Joan is seen in this film as a scared young woman nevertheless impelled by her beliefs.

A similar tactic was used in *The King of Kings* (1927). Mary Magdalene (played by Jacqueline Logan) is portrayed as a woman who was not at all evil, just misguided, and Jesus (H. B. Warner) as a strong, virile man. Compare this humanization to the ruckus caused by Martin Scorsese's *The Last Temptation of Christ* in 1988 when church and fundamentalist groups picketed the movie; in fact it was a film no more lascivious, if a bit more graphic, than *The King of Kings*.

With *Male and Female* (1919) Macpherson as a writer started using a blend of past and present stories—often episodes from history or the Bible—to illustrate moral lessons about the excesses of the 1920s. (Griffith first used this technique—though more along the line of parallel editing—in movies such as *Intolerance*.)

An important early writer who doesn't readily present a discernable style, though she worked on many significant films is Sonya Levien. A Russian emigré, Levien earned a law degree, practiced briefly and then turned to writing for some New York magazines, the *Woman's Journal,* the official publication of the suffragette movement,and *Metropolitan*. Her first script story was *Who Will Marry Me?* in 1919 (that year again!) and the first full adaptation she did, from one of her own stories, was *Cheated Love,* in 1921. Most of her subsequent scripts were written in partnership or collaboration, such as *The Power of the Press* and *The Younger Generation* (both Frank Capra films in 1928); *Trial Marriage* (also 1928); *Song o' My Heart* (1930); *She Wanted a Millionaire* (1932); *Kidnapped* and *In Old*

Chicago (both 1938); *Drums Along the Mohawk* and *The Hunchback of Notre Dame* (both 1939); *Ziegfeld Girl* (1941); *Rhapsody in Blue* and *State Fair* (both 1945); *The Green Years* (1946); *Cass Timberlane* (1947); *The Great Caruso* (1951); *The Merry Widow* (1952); *The Student Prince* (1954); *Hit the Deck* and *Oklahoma!* (both 1955).

With her frequent partner S. N. Behrman, Levien wrote *Lightnin'* (1930); *Delicious* and *Daddy Long Legs* (1931 version); *Rebecca of Sunnybrook Farm* and *Tess of the Storm Country* (both 1932); *Cavalcade* (1933); *As Husbands Go* (1934); *Anna Karenina* (1935); *The Cowboy and the Lady* (1938); and *Quo Vadis?* (1951).

Levien seems to have been called in especially to create female characters, and most of her women parts are intelligent, independent, and noble, and often on a kind of quest. For instance, the role of Lana, played by Claudette Colbert in *Drums Along the Mohawk*, has her as an attractive but strong pioneer wife who can handle the hazards of the frontier. Levien also created strong roles for Greer Garson in *The Valley of Decision* (1946) and Eleanor Parker in the Oscar-winning *Interrupted Melody* (1955) and found a new dimension for actresses formerly cast as sex objects: *Cass Timberlane* (1947) for Lana Turner, *Bhowani Junction* (1956) for Ava Gardner, and *Jeanne Eagels* (1957) for Kim Novak.

Intelligent and hard-working, Levien often wrote as many as five films a year, ultimately writing seventy scripts. When the issue of unionization of writers came up in the 1930s, Levien first joined the counterrevolutionary group, the Screen Playwrights, then the Screen Writers Guild, but apparently with little interest in either.

William Ludwig (a SWG steward at MGM) said of Sonya Levien:

She was the least political person I had ever met. She joined both the SP and the SWG, but she wasn't active in either. She was completely work-dominated and not political on industry matters. She had old and dear friends in every echelon. When the SWG conflict came, it probably moved her toward the Guild. She had many good friends on the extreme left, and her daughter and *her* friends were radicals. When the SP set up shop, it was done by a bunch of old boys at Metro, her friends, the Thalberg-echelon group. It seemed like a good career-move to join, but she had no philosophical position. I'd say to her, "You know what this means?" and then I'd tell her and she'd say, "Does it? I didn't know." But she was the hardest worker I've ever known. She had a writing obsession.

(The Hollywood Writers' Wars, p. 73)

Yet another influential woman of the early years and beyond is the playwright/short-story writer/screenwriter Zoë Akins, a Pulitzer Prize playwright (Edith Wharton's *The Old Maid* in 1935) whose popular play *The Greeks Had a Word for It* was filmed as *The Greeks Had a Word for Them* in 1932: "It" being changed to the more decorous "Them." As a playwright, Akins's first hit was *Declassé* for Ethel Barrymore in the teens and it became a film in 1929, as did *Her Private Life* in 1929, reflecting Cecil B. De Mille's comment in a December 1919 *Photoplay* about the post World War I years that "The ruined woman is as out of style as the Victorian who used to faint."

Zoë Akins

Women Love Once and *Girls About Town* were both made in 1931. Much later her play *The Old Maid* was scripted for Bette Davis in 1939, as was her *Morning Glory* for Katherine Hepburn in 1933; *Stage Struck*, the remake of *Morning Glory* in 1958; and *How to Marry a Millionaire* in 1953. Her scripts include *Sarah and Son* (Ruth Chatterton) in 1930, *Christopher Strong* (Hepburn) in 1933, *Accused* (Dolores Del Rio) in 1936, *Camille* (Garbo) in 1937, *The Toy Wife* (Luise Rainer) in 1938, and *Desire Me* (Greer Garson) in 1947. As just her titles show, Akins's concerns were to create strong and interesting female roles, writing for a specific actress at times, and with women in mind.

2

The Two Thirties

*Frivolity and Flighty Escapes/
Social Realism and Social
Conscience*

It's almost as if there are two 1930s in the cinematic world of Hollywood: the escapist life of gold-grabbing chorines and madcap heiresses who dash around a post-1929 Crash America as though nothing had ever happened, and the darker movies of the era which touched in one way or another on the plight of the country, or at least reflected its dark mood.

"The movies proved to be the Depression's major antidote," says historian Carole Klein. "During the thirties, some eighty-five million people a week went to the movies, where, for twenty-five cents (ten cents for children) one could watch a lavish musical extravaganza with Fred Astaire and Ginger Rogers dancing to choreography by Busby Berkeley, or grow flush with romantic sentiment as heiress Bette Davis gave up 'everything' to run off with the man she loved." *(An American Bloomsbury,* pp. 283–84)

Serious writers responded in a different way, however, and writers such as Lillian Hellman, Dorothy Parker, and Tess Slesinger went West during an era of economic upheaval and social revolution in the country. In some ways screenwriting was a natural—a form more acceptable to a liberal or socialist temperament because it reached the masses rather than the narrower world of theatergoers. Also, the money had dried up in the East. Though most of the writers that the studio executives imported from the East were men, there were a few important females who were also beckoned out, including playwright Alice Duer Miller. And in the "Golden Age" of studio moviemaking producers were willing to import writers with ideas because the plain truth is that they were out of them.

But for writers like Anita Loos or Viña Delmar, the cinematic format provided a venue for audiences who did not want to hear about any more troubles, and particularly wanted to be taken to a place where they could forget their own. Costume designer Edith Head said, "In the 1930s, costumes didn't have anything to do with real life. The poor working girl was smothered in furs, and Mae West wore a simple black velvet festooned with rhinestones and ruffles when she met Cary Grant in the park." (*Mae West* by George Eells and Stanley Musgrove; New York: 1982, p. 113.)

While many critics make the most of Anita Loos's script for *Gentlemen Prefer Blondes*, for this fan it is the 1932 *Red-Headed Woman* that most captures the zeitgeist of an age, while still presenting us with a heroine who takes charge, gets it all, and never ever lets her glamorous image slip even by so much as a droopy negligee strap.

Jean Harlow plays Lil Andrews, an office worker from the wrong side of the tracks, who uses men to get money and status, but unlike her sisters in sin, she always maintains total control. It's the men who are invariably undone. When *Red-Headed Woman* begins, Lil has set her sights on Bill (Chester Morris), the wealthy son of the business owner (Lewis Stone). He's married, but that presents no real obstacle to Lil. This is how Loos has Lil describe her very specific plan of action to her friend Sally (Una Merkel). It is one of those bedroom scenes when girls talk heart to heart with each other, and Lil is describing having been caught in near flagrante delicto by her boyfriend's wife:

LIL

And there we were, like an uncensored movie—when in waltzes Mrs. William Legendre, Junior, and catches us— right in the old family parlor!

Anita Loos with Jean Harlow, going over script of *Red-Headed Woman.*

SALLY

Oh, you dirty little homewrecker. Well what do you think that's going to get you?

MCU—*Lil seated looking o.s. [offscreen] to left—throws stocking down o.s.*

LIL

Listen, Sally, I made up my mind a long time ago that I'm not going to spend my whole life on the wrong side of the railroad track.

MCS—*Sally and Lil seated on bed—*

SALLY

Well, I hope you don't get hit by a train while you're crossing over.

LIL

A girl's a fool that doesn't get ahead. Say, it's just as easy to hook a rich man as it is to get hooked by a poor one.

SALLY

Oh—so that's what you're going to do.

LIL

That's it. I'm going to amount to something, in this town.

Lil, as the spunky Harlow plays her, is not stupid enough to be bought off by the boss: she's going to hold out for the real thing— marriage to Bill. "Well I don't want your money! I wouldn't touch a penny of it! Not a penny!" Mr. Legendre asks, "Just what is your game?" and Lil responds, "I've worked hard in this office and I've been a decent self-respecting girl! And now just because I happen to love your son and you're rich and powerful, you think you could pay me off! You think you can make me do whatever you want! Well, you can't! Do you understand? You can't"... "if he [Bill] wants me to go, why doesn't he ask me?"

The confrontation, of course, gets her what she wants, which is to be further entangled in Bill's emotions. Ultimately she does trick him into a divorce, and a marriage with her, Lil. Her enemies find out about her affair with the butler (a very early screen appearance by actor Charles Boyer) and she has a temporary setback, but the last scenes of the film find her triumphant in Paris with another rich fool finagled into paying her bills, with her butler by her side.

Naturally some of the effectiveness of the dialogue depends on the delivery that Harlow gives it, which is slinkily seductive and makes some of the blond bombshells of the 1950s look coarse by comparison. The scene when Harlow is on the divan trying to seduce Bill is a classic:

CS—*Lil lying back on divan—looking o.s. to right—gestures with finger.*

LIL

Aw, Bill, come here.

MCU—*Bill—looks o.s. to left—*

CS—*Lil lying back on divan—looking o.s. to right—gestures with finger.*

MS—*Bill—he walks to Lil on divan at left—*CAMERA PANS *with him—Lil pulls him down beside her—he rubs his head—*CAMERA MOVES UP *to a CS of the two—Bill covers his face with his hands.*

LIL

Come here. Gee Bill, I'm crazy about you.

As Harlow plays it of course, and as the lighting picks her up, she's luminescent. Lying flat, and crooking her finger, she says "Be-a-ll" in an irresistible way: Bill is a goner.

Some of the tone of thirties worldly cynicism can be seen too: Aunt Jane (May Robson) advises her niece (Leila Hyams), Bill's wife: "You know, I surprised your Uncle once, and it gave me enough material to blackmail him for ten years." And there is the requisite gold-digger patter too; Sally: "You dropped your fur." Lil: "Oh, it's only a silver fox." Sally: "Haven't you got a gold one?" Lil: "No. Well, I might have this one plated."

Another writer who perfectly picks up on the lighthearted tone of the screwball and lightweight films of the thirties is Viña Delmar, a writer responsible for the slick but poetic interchange of Irene Dunne and Cary Grant at the end of *The Awful Truth* in 1937. And though there were plenty of contemporaneous newspaper articles which credited Delmar with the script, oddly enough Leslie Halliwell's *The Filmgoer's Companion* (fourth edition, 1974) lists Leo McCarey as the writer as well as the director. The American Film Institute Catalog of 1993 does credit Delmar with the script.

Viña Delmar with Joan Crawford

The Awful Truth, however, is a sole credit, as is *Make Way for Tomorrow* (also 1937). Other Delmar credits include the stories for both *King of Burlesque* and *Sadie McKee* with Joan Crawford; *Hands Across the Table* with Carole Lombard (1935); *The Great Man's Lady* with Barbara Stanwyck (1942); and *Cynthia* with Elizabeth Taylor (1947).

Delmar was from New York and tried in 1921 with her new husband to get jobs acting in the theater. When this didn't work out, the couple started writing fiction. Though initially many of the stories were written as a team, Delmar has said that only her name went on them because "there was a convention then that female names on a magazine cover were more inviting." (Unmarked, undated clip in the Billy Rose Theater Collection at Lincoln Center)

But on her own Delmar wrote the bestselling novel *Bad Girl* which became a Literary Guild Selection in 1930, a successful 1930 Broadway play, 1931 film, and eventually the inspiration for a 1933 sequel, *Sailor's Luck*, the script for which was eventually written by Marguerite Roberts. And a number of her serials for magazines, such as "The Portrait of Sadie McKee" were the basis for films (*Sadie McKee* in 1934), as was a 1932 short story, *A Chance at Heaven*, purchased by Paramount as a vehicle and story for Frances Dee. (It ultimately became an RKO film starring Ginger Rogers and Joel McCrea, Frances Dee's husband!) Her script (sole credit) for *Make Way for Tomorrow* (1937) is the sensitive story of an elderly couple in financial difficulty.

The Awful Truth is based on a 1922 play by Arthur Richman, and some of the arch dialogue, as well as the plot, is reminiscent of Restoration drama. Dunne is caught by husband Grant coming home in the middle of the day in an evening gown, accompanied by her male music teacher, also in evening clothes. She gives a story about a car breaking down which is clearly not believed by Grant, and a drop-in guest departs, saying with tongue-in-cheek, "They always say, four's a crowd."

Dunne's defense is a sophisticated one:

I've been unlucky, that's all. You've come home and caught me in a truth and it seems there's nothing less logical than the truth.

There are a number of witticisms, such as "His car's very old. So's his story." Or Grant's comment to the mother of his rival for Dunne's hand, (a bit later in the film after a divorce, posited on his suspicions, has been decided on): "Excuse me, you're sitting on my prospectus." When Grant picks up another (hidden) beau's hat by mistake and puts it on his head and it settles around his ears, Dunne helpfully whitewashes, "Did you have a haircut?"

Delmar's real tour de force comes at the end of the film, however. It is an extraordinary piece of writing—at first appearing simple, perhaps, but in actuality very complicated, with layers and layers of ambiguity sandwiched into these simple-seeming words. The couple is attempting to spend their last night together (in separate bedrooms) as a married couple in the half hour before their divorce decree becomes final.

Their bedrooms are separated by a jiggly door which keeps them from sleeping; the door also serves as an excuse for their continuing dialogue as their chatting inches toward reconciliation.

SHE

It's funny that everything's the way it is on account of the way you feel.

HE

Huh?

SHE

I mean if you didn't feel the way you do things wouldn't be the way they are, would they?...I mean, things would be the same if things were different.

HE

But...uh...things are the way you made them.

SHE

Oh, no. No. Things are the way you think I made them. I didn't make them that way at all [Dunne says it with an upper class "a'toll"]. Things are just the same as they always were, only you're the same as you were too, so I guess things will never be the same again. Good night.

No more disturbing door rattling, and Grant is found on his hands and knees on the floor trying to figure out why the door isn't making noises any more: his excuse for coming into her room.

SHE

You're all confused, aren't you?

HE

Aren't you?

SHE

No.

HE

Well, you should be because you're wrong about things being different because they're not the same. Things are different except in a different way.... You're still the same, only I've been a fool.... But I'm not now. So long as I'm different, don't you think that, well, maybe things could be the same again? Only a little different.

SHE

You mean that?

Happy end of scene, and there is a close-up of a cuckoo clock which has appeared throughout the scene. This time the Tyrolian male figure does not go into his slot, but follows the dirndled girl into hers.

The superb plays on the words "simple" and "different" are myriad. And the fact is that something so apparently easy can only be accomplished by a really skilled writer. Though the tone is different, the language is used as cleverly as Beckett uses it.

Probably the best-known writer to work in the escapist comic mode in the 1930s is Mae West, a woman who arrived in Hollywood at the age of forty and wrote and starred in her own movies: a cinematic feat that hasn't been matched by even contemporary actresses, though Barbra Streisand tried it once, with *Yentl*. West's scripts throughout the thirties include *I'm No Angel* (1933), *Belle of the Nineties* (1934), *Goin' to Town* (1935), *Klondike Annie* and *Go West Young Man* (both 1936); *Every Day's a Holiday* (1938) and—in 1940—*My Little Chickadee*.

In *I'm No Angel*, for instance, West managed to create an exceptionally strong and witty heroine in Tira the lion-tamer. Tira is no fool, takes more from men than she gives them, and even argues her own case in court and wins. "I'm writin' the story and I'm the star," West told director Ernst Lubitsch when he complained that she took all the good lines for herself. Perhaps West was easily able to deal with the Hollywood powers in place because she, as a writer, had successfully mounted plays on Broadway: *Sex*, *Catharine Was Great*, and *The Pleasure Man* were among the twelve she performed in on the Great White Way.

Hardly the Hollywood supplicant or hopeful, West wisecracked at her first West Coast press conference, "So this is the place a leaf falls up in some canyon and they tell you it's winter." And she also told the newspaper people present at her arrival in California from New York, "I'm not a little girl from a little town here to make good in a big town. I'm a big girl from a big town who's come to make good in a little town."

True to her habits of taking over a project and making it her own, once on her first film *Night After Night* in 1932 with George Raft, West rewrote dialogue on the set. And she also converted director Archie Mayo and the producers at Paramount to her method of line delivery: fast dialogue, accompanied by (very) slow physical movement. This required screenings for those in charge to prove to them that audiences laughed *through* the next line if it were delivered too quickly, right away. (Critic Alexander Walker would later observe in his book, *The Celluloid Sacrifice,* by the way, that Mae West's "memoirs show her continually dissatisfied with any story or dialogue she did not write herself or at least improve on," (New York, 1967, p. 6) and in a separate but somewhat related point that West's brand of languorous physical movement makes for the most effective cinematic sexuality, too.

By 1936 West was earning $300,000 a role with an additional

Mae West

$100,000 thrown in if she did the scenario. With the exception of William Randolph Hearst's, income tax returns show that West had the highest declared salary in the country. (Always a smart businesswoman, West invested heavily in California real estate, and by the time of her death she was a multimillionaire.)

Censorship run-ins are generally thought of as having a deleterious effect on West's movie work, and of course it is true that the Hays office—a center for industry self-regulation which was responding to an outcry for government censorship and preferred to handle its own problems—did "take on" West to a great extent. But if you really look at the film scripts it becomes clear that only a few lines were altered in the major screenplays; most frequently it was gestures or blocking which was changed or deleted.

This is in part due to a clever strategy of West's; she said that she would deliberately put in an obviously risqué line for the censors to focus on. And what she *really* wanted in the script would therefore remain. A typical alteration would be like the one from *I'm No Angel*. Directions and deletions from the censorship files of the New York State Archives in Albany order: "In scene in tent where Tira is bending over basin washing hands, eliminate views where Slick presses his body against her posterior. REASON: Indecent."

"I use my voice, my eyes and the movements of my body, instead of physical contact," said West to a magazine in the early thirties, and she went on:

> The worst thing about the whole business of sex is the hypocrisy. If only people would treat it a little more casually! In Europe, at least, sex is treated as a matter of fact, but here we are ashamed of it, though it is the most beautiful thing Nature has given us. We can no more eliminate the primary emotion of sex-hunger (the biological urge) from our birthright than we can remove our hearts.

And—true, to the anarchic spirit of comedies in the 1930s, and any time really—West said, "If I ever become conventional, in any language, I'm through."

Another magazine interviewer quotes West as saying:

> The very best thing that I have done for the public during this

Depression has been the humorous manner—even ribald sometimes—in which I have treated sex. My fight has been against depression, repression and suppression. You know *A Farewell to Arms*, a great picture, was a story of sex, but it was tragic and awfully depressing. Men saw it and were afraid ever to fall in love again. They didn't even want to take a pretty girl around the corner and give her a kiss. I don't want to leave that sort of a feeling with them. I want to treat sex and love lightly—enough to make both men and women feel that life is worth living; that it still holds heaps of fun, no matter what the conditions. I fight always to keep people from feeling depressed by sex. It's not right that they should be. It makes them feel cheated when love is presented tragically.

West also seemed to intuitively understand the difference between acting for the screen and for vaudeville and the stage, both of which she had done before trying her luck on the West Coast. She told the *Los Angeles Times* upon her arrival in 1932 that "the screen doesn't require as much acting of a certain type. The camera catches the slightest twitch of the eye. What you must make emphatic on the stage you can suggest in a less obvious manner on the screen."

The story idea for *I'm No Angel* came from writer-publisher Lowell Brentano, who wrote a brief treatment about a woman lion-tamer, and West had Paramount buy the property. But it is pretty obvious that the lines of dialogue in the film have the familiar Westian ring. West plays Tira, a small-time carnival lion-tamer who suckers chumps into hotels and into giving her money. The wealthy gentleman Clayton (Cary Grant) falls in love with her and she decides to leave the carnival life. There is a complication where the lovers are driven apart, but there is a happy ending when Tira, ripping up his check she has won by arguing her own case in court for breach of promise, says, "I get better as I go along." And referring to the million she sued for, "You've got a lot of other things to make a girl happy." And when Clayton asks her what she is thinking about, Tira says, "The same thing you are."

Other dialogue is extremely witty: "You just tell me about my future," Tira instructs a fortuneteller. "You see, I know all about my past." When asked how she acquired so many beautiful things, she replies, "It's a gift, honey, it's a gift! Take all you can get and give as little as possible." And "Find 'em, fool 'em, and forget 'em." When asked if she believes in marriage, she says, "Only as a last resort." When Clayton asks if he can trust her, Tira answers, "You can. Hundreds have."

Lighthearted comedies as an antidote to the Depression are to be found in the works, too, of other writers who broke in during the teens and twenties. This includes *Girls About Town* (1931) with a script by Zoë Akins; *What Price Hollywood?* (1932) based on an Adela Rogers St. Johns story with a script by Murfin; *Dinner at Eight* (1933), on which Francis Marion is credited; *Our Betters* coscripted by Murfin; and other Anita Loos comedies.

There was a pocket, however, of more serious films, reflective of the mood of the times, if not directly of social conscience—and consciousness—of the era. These were written by Lillian Hellman, Tess Slesinger, and—to a much lesser extent—Dorothy Parker. Most of the writers came from New York, and many had a hand in the formation of the Screen Writers Guild.

The playwright Hellman's commitment to social causes is directly reflected in her film work—though necessarily, because of the assignments—in varying degrees. But, unlike Slesinger and Parker, Hellman didn't stay in Hollywood for very long and even when there went back and forth between coasts a great deal. She collaborated on the film *Dark Angel* in 1935; did a screen version of her play *The Children's Hour* called *These Three* in 1936, which, in order to pass the censors, had to leave out much of the lesbian theme; and wrote the script—a sole credit—for Sidney Kingsley's *Dead End*. She did the script for *The Little Foxes*, the film version of her 1939 play with dialogue additions by Dorothy Parker. In a more overt left-wing statement she helped write Joris Ivens's great documentary *The Spanish Earth* in 1937.

Hellman's 1943 script about Russia, *The North Star*, was heavily rewritten and cut to accommodate anti-Russian feeling after World War II. She eventually disowned the film, which in the fifties was retitled *Armored Attack*, but the original script for *The North Star* demonstrates Hellman's strong pacifist feelings, and her feelings for the Russian people.

The beginning description is of the 1941 German invasion of the Soviet Union. Here are Hellman's instructions in the typescript:

I would like to hear music over the titles and over a very slow FADE IN. *These are the last hours of peace, and it would be fine if the opening music could be remembered as suggesting those last, normal days. It should be gay music and healthy music. It is just beginning to be morning.*

And Hellman's description of the village collective store is lively and loving—her proletarian sympathies are apparent:

It is like most village stores, but it has certain items which less general stores do not carry: there are furs, racks of Soviet champagne, accordions and mandolins, leather jackets, two bicycles, bad perfumes, a barrel of herrings, carefully wrapped sausages, hams and cheeses, and boxes of dried fruits and smoked fish. Back of the counter is a large, elderly man who is glaring at a fat lady. The fat lady is pinching a roll of sausage. As he stares at her, the fat lady moves off, pinches a plum. Sophie watches the above proceedings with amusement. (original typescript at MoMA Film Studies)

Later the tone changes to a more serious one, and we know these are very much Hellman's private thoughts, for she puts them in parenthesis:

(I do not know how to describe the effect I would like to see here, but I would like the audience to feel as if they were in on the bombing—somewhat the way audiences used to feel in shots where the trains were coming head on. I would like to see the dirt and dust obscure the scene so that we only suggest the death and devastation. Later, when we come back down the road, we will see what has been done. Now I think the most we should see is a woman's market bag hurling through the air; one of Karp's pigs, a lunch box, a horse, the wheel of a wagon.

I know from the air raids in Spain—it has never been photographed correctly—that the chief impression in an air raid is of smoke, dirt, noise, and of strange things flying through the air. One really only sees and realizes what has been done after everything is over and the dirt has settled.)

In *An Unfinished Woman,* her autobiographical book, Hellman has said, "During the war in Spain, Hitler and Mussolini could have been stopped, [but] the bumblers and the villains led us into this (I had tried to write some of that in *Watch on the Rhine*)." *Rhine* is Hellman's 1941 play which was made into a 1943 film with a script by her friend/lover Dashiell Hammett.

Here is that same sensibility as both Rodion (Dean Jagger in the film) and a group of guerrillas in *The North Star* take oaths:

RODION

I who am about to become a guerrilla fighter of the Soviet Union: I take this solemn oath:

[*Group of guerrillas repeat*]

RODION

I will not lay down these arms until the last Fascist is driven from our land.

[*Group of guerrillas repeat*]

RODION

I am willing to give my life, to die in battle, to keep my people from Fascist slavery.

[*Group of guerrillas repeat*]

The Little Foxes (1940) is a protest against the grasping, turn-of-the-century bourgeois businessmen (and women, as in the person of Regina, played by Bette Davis) and the way they are stripping the poor folks—farmers, blacks, sharecroppers and the like—of their land and money. As a Southerner herself, from New Orleans, Hellman is also sympathetic to the plight of the remaining preyed-upon old-line aristocrat, here in the person of the delicate Birdie. But all Hellman's hatred is reserved for the money changers and their viperous ethics.

Hellman's famous speech about not being able to cut her conscience to fit the political cloth of the times came much later, of course, in her appearance for the House Committee on Un-American Activities in the 1950s, and her refusal to name names left her blacklisted. Contributing factors were her helping to form the Screen Writers Guild, which contained many well-known leftists and Communists. "The first thing that happened to me [when I went to Hollywood] was that Lillian Hellman came into my converted broom-closet office and asked me to join the guild. It was most extraordinary," says Maurice Rapf, now a professor at Dartmouth College. And Hellman held many Guild meetings in her home. Retrospectively, during the 1950s, *The North Star*, along with other forties films like *Mission to Moscow*, written by Howard Koch, and *Song of Russia*, by Richard Collins, were deemed Communist party propaganda.

In 1963, Hellman wrote her last film, an adaptation of her play *Toys in the Attic*, which was directed by George Roy Hill. The film *Julia*, which she did not script, is the story of women's friendship during the harrowing days of World War II based on Hellman's remembrances of smuggling information across the German border in *Pentimento*. Jane Fonda played Hellman in the 1978 film: a person and story inspiration reminiscent of the use of Adela Rogers St. Johns as a persona, though with much different theme and tone.

Another East Coast "rabble-rouser," Tess Slesinger, was originally from New York and attended the Ethical Culture School, Swarthmore College, and Columbia School of Journalism. She was assistant fashion editor at the *New York Herald Tribune* and assistant literary critic at the *New York Evening Post*, and was a social activist in New York City, occasionally arrested for political protests. Her short stories were published in the prestigious *American Mercury* and *Vanity Fair*, among other periodicals, and she was invited to come to Hollywood after the publication of two successful books: *The Unpossessed*, about intellectuals attempting to found a revolutionary magazine, and *Time: The Present.* Her Hollywood work includes the screenplay for Dorothy Arzner's *Dance Girl Dance, The Good Earth, Remember the Day,* and *A Tree Grows in Brooklyn.*

The script for *The Good Earth* in 1937 was a group effort, with Slesinger sharing credit with Talbot Jennings and Claudine West. Finding the individual writer's voice is of course impossible in this situation, though the literary sensibility seems closest to Slesinger's. It's a serious adaptation of the 1931 Pearl Buck novel about greed ruining the lives of a simple Chinese farming couple.

Wang, the main character, is described as "tall and self-important, and there is a mole on his cheek, from which three long hairs hang down." He "feels that intimate reflections, though engaging, are dignified." And a scene description goes like this, "The thunder rolls, at first distantly, ominously, then with staccato violence, as though an angry god were hurling a succession of thunderbolts across the heavens." The rhythm of the writing in *The Good Earth* is very much Slesinger, particularly in the description of the female characters, and close to the feeling in the other scripts:

> *A close-up of O-lan shows her face, wet with rain, clear-cut in the candlelight. Her eyes are lowered in humility, but she lifts them and in this moment achieves so great a beauty of expression that she seems physically beautiful. The view then draws back, showing Wang looking down on her, seeming to see in her this same beauty that until this moment has been hidden from his unseeing eyes. He raises her chin to his face, and laughs. O-Lan looks up at him, then as Wang laughs again, she moves away a little. Wang puts out his hand, draws her toward him, and blows out the candle. The room is in darkness and rain is heard beating on the roof as the scene fades out.*

In style this is similar to the writing in *Remember the Day,* which Slesinger scripted in 1941: "[Mr. Roberts] is a sweet, vague, frustrated little man with damped dreams," who later "seems to have thrown off his mood and returned to the blind, jolly shell he lives in." A little girl, Kate, "looks up and grins ice-creamily at Nora."

Slesinger's script for *A Tree Grows in Brooklyn,* which she wrote with her husband, Frank Davis, in 1945, has the same subtle observations and quiet tone of her other scripts. A public library is to be depicted as "a rather small library, but it has dignity" according to directions in the script. And the young girl in the script is described this way: "Francie, her daughter, is about thirteen. She is a rather quiet child. She has inherited from Johnny, her father, a sensitiveness and an imagination that make her by far the more difficult problem in parenthood for the Nolans." *A Tree Grows in Brooklyn* was adapted from Betty Smith's novel.

The mother in the film, played by Dorothy McGuire in a nice combination of harshness and vulnerability, is worried that her children will turn out like their daydreaming father: "I won't have the kids taking after him and those dreamy ways of his I used to think were so fine. Not if I gotta cut it out of their hearts." Though eventually she gets to make the most touching speech of the film, at the end, after her husband has died and she tells the coroner (in a cadence which is similar to Maureen O'Hara's big final soliloquy at the end of *Dance Girl Dance*). "I got two nice kids who are going to grow up to be something. They said he wasn't drunk. He was out looking for work. Why'nt you put that down? Why do you have to say he died of the drink when that's only a part of the truth?"

James Dunn won an Oscar for his portrayal of the charming ne'er-do-well of a dad who can reassure his daughter (played by young Peggy Ann Garner), "God invented time, and when he invented something there's always plenty of it," just as he can weave a spell for his family, especially his daughter—which he later admits was partly made up—about a wedding at which he was a singing waiter: the blarney really flows as he tells of the beautiful bride decked out in diamonds (not so young, really, is an aside) and the smell of the champagne, the flowers, and the ladies' face powder all mixed in with a "new perfume they made up."

But the crown jewel of Slesinger's writing with Davis is to be found in the perfect union of director, writer, and subject matter in the film *Dance Girl Dance*. As directed by Dorothy Arzner, it's a film that—with its sympathy for the "poor working stiff" as well as its commitment to a woman's right to fulfillment through work—blends the heritage of the socially aware 1930s with the more clearly articulated demands of women in the early 1940s.

The film was made on the exact fulcrum of 1940, and the twin themes are delineated in the Slesinger–Davis script right off as a nightclub is being raided, but the spunky chorus girl Bubbles, played by Lucille Ball, says, "We won't go till we get paid." This is seconded by Judy O'Brien (Maureen O'Hara) saying, "We're just trying to earn our living like you, Officer."

They do get paid, through contributions from the crowd solicited by a wealthy playboy, but the movie moves quickly out of the gold-digger mode as O'Hara arrives in New York, telling her Russian coach (the indomitable Maria Ouspenskaya) that she has hitched all the way back to New York from Ohio. And the first third or so of the film is devoted to finding work, or not. His secretary says to Ralph Bellamy, the head of a prestigious dance troupe, "You will condemn a girl just because she has to make a living?" And we see immediately the more serious career yearnings of poor but proud Judy who wants to be more than a dance hall girl.

The dialogue is crackling in the snappy thirties way: the Russian coach, bemoaning her fate as toppled from the ballet world, says, "A flesh peddler I must be! A jellyfish salesman," in hustling her girls. And the sharpest lines of all go to Bubbles: "Can you dance, Bubbles?" "Well, it's been called that." "Give it all you got, baby," a stage manager tells her before she goes on. "They couldn't take it," replies Bubbles. (Curiously, the reviewer in the *New York Times* called the film confused in its intent and said it had "some of the season's more inane lines.")

Naturally the knockout speech is reserved for the near end of the film, as the anger of the underclass merges with the resentments of women when Judy really lets the burlesque audience have it in one of the most powerful soliloquies written for a woman in film:

> Go ahead and stare. I'm not ashamed. Go on, laugh. Get your money's worth. Nobody's going to hurt you. I know you want me to tear my clothes off so's you can look your fifty cents worth. Fifty cents for the privilege of staring at a girl the way your wives won't let you. What do you suppose we think of you up here with your silly smiles your mothers would be ashamed of? We know it's a thing of the moment for the dress suits to come and laugh at us too. We'd laugh right back at the lot of you only we're paid to let you sit there and roll your eyes and make your screamingly clever remarks. What's it for? So you can go home when the show's over and strut before your wives and sweethearts and play at being the

stronger sex for a minute. I'm sure they see through you just like we do.

The script—and Arzner's direction of it—has triumphed even over the classic female rivalry over a man between Bubbles and Judy, letting their female friendship remain intact after all: a neat trick that. And in this the gold-digging chorine type, Bubbles, is elevated to something more than just a hustler.

The concern with dignity about work has begun out of the escapist, frivolous, and terribly deprived thirties: an initially schizophrenic time for women's voices in film.

3

The Forties

The Woman's Film and the War Years

Another more than enterprising woman who entered the film business in the teens was Lenore Coffee—someone who, like Clara Beranger and Frances Marion, had a career which lasted throughout her life. And like many a writer who entered the film business when it was still wide open, she hung on and hit an apex of sorts in the forties with *The Way of All Flesh* (1940); *The Great Lie* (1941); *The Gay Sisters* (1942); *Old Acquaintance* (1943); and *Beyond the Forest* (1949), highlights of a decade filled with other Coffee films. According to *Backstory: Interviews With Screenwriters of Hollywood's Golden Age:*

> In the sound era she flourished as an adaptor of popular women's fiction written by authors such as Lloyd C. Douglas, Fannie Hurst, Stephen Longstreet, Gwen Bristow, and Margaret Echard. She prospered as one of the favored writers of Joan Crawford and Bette Davis vehicles. And she reigned as a maharani over her Mandeville Canyon estate in the days when lady screenwriters were the toast of Hollywood.
>
> (p. 133)

Lenore Coffee

Coffee gives her own reasons for her success, and longevity, in the same interview:

I flourished [when talking pictures arrived]. I'm not sure why, but I'll tell you something interesting. A silent film was like writing a novel, and a script was like writing a play. That's why women dropped out. Women had been good novelists, but in the talking pictures women were not predominant. You can't tell me the name of one good dramatist. [Lillian Hellman] was the only one.

(p. 143)

Coffee, who died in 1984 at age eighty-seven, was originally very much an outsider. In 1919 Coffee, who was working as a copywriter in her native San Francisco, read in the *Motion Picture Exhibitor Herald* that a studio was looking for a story idea for Clara Kimball Young. This is how she describes the episode in her 1973 book, *Storyline: Recollections of a Hollywood Screenwriter:*

One day when I walked home by an unfamiliar way I was about to pass a cigar-stand when something on a magazine rack caught my eye. It was a large, thick magazine with a shiny orange-red cover and, lettered in black, were the words THE MOTION PICTURE EXHIBITORS' HERALD, January 1919.

I had no idea what an "exhibitor" was (it meant a cinema-owner), but I did know a trade paper when I saw one; so I bought it and it opened up a new world to me—an inside look into the fabulous realm of the "movies." I went through it, page by page, gleaning bits of information, news and gossip. Then, almost at the back, was the announcement that Clara Kimball Young was in desperate need of a story.

My heart really leapt and I felt I must find an idea to turn into a story for Clara Kimball Young! She was a most beautiful woman with dark hair coiled low on her neck, great lustrous dark eyes and a very emotional yet sweet personality; not lacking in strength, either. I thought back over the films I had seen her in and tried to think of a new role—something she had not done before—and I couldn't remember ever seeing her in a picture with a child. But I didn't want her married, for I wanted a love story. So my next idea was that she should meet a man who had no wife, but did have a child. From that small seed the story grew; and that is precisely the way I work today. Find just one small idea, or the germ of an idea, then build a story round it.

I still have the carbon copy of that original story. It was called *The Better Wife*. On 8 January I sent it to the Garson Studio and on 22 January I had a letter saying they would buy the story for one hundred dollars. I was tremendously excited, even though it was an absurd sum which I didn't know then.

At least I had the wit to telegraph my acceptance (for I knew telegrams were a matter of record) saying, "Offer accepted provided I am given proper screen recognition." I got the cheque, and I got the screen recognition, and my career began.

Coffee then goes on to say that she had read that Harry Garson, the studio head, was in San Francisco, and that she went to his hotel:

The clerk looked at a box which was full of long envelopes and said, "His key is here so he's not in the hotel." I made up my mind that I would sit with my eyes riveted on that box for I knew that the man he gave those envelopes to would be Harry Garson. Three hours later, in walked a large, handsome man with almost white hair, olive skin and golden-brown eyes; as I had anticipated, the clerk handed him all the large envelopes. I was up from my chair in a matter of seconds and practically skidded across the large lobby to say, "Are you Mr. Garson? I'm Lenore Coffee." He gave me a startled look. "Are you the girl who wrote that story for Miss Young?"

When I said "Yes," he asked, "Where did you learn how to write for the movies? Do you realize that something you wrote could be photographed? Of course, the story wasn't long enough and we had to add incidents, but everything you wrote was a fine scene. How did you learn to write in this form?"

I told him how much I liked pictures and how often I went to them, and that I supposed I had absorbed the form unconsciously.

(pp. 11–12)

According to Coffee, Garson told her that movies were about to become a "mammoth industry, and it's going to be bigger than anybody ever imagined," and that she should leave San Francisco and come to Hollywood. He offered her a contract of fifty dollars a week for a year. Coffee's job turned out to be—at first—mail opener, assistant director, continuity girl, title and scene writer. The directing gig came about, according to her book, because she was assisting at a scene when the director and his assistant were having an argument. As an object lesson Garson told Coffee to go ahead and do the scene, that's how easy it was to do it. When things went smoothly, but there was still an altercation between the two, the director fired the original assistant and Coffee got the job. It's impossible to think of something happening so painlessly in the movie business these days.

Coffee also did titles for *Wandering Daughters* and *The Age of Desire* (both 1923). Her first feature was *The Volga Boatman* for Cecil B. De Mille in 1926. In the early years she also wrote *For Alimony Only* (1926), *Chicago, The Night of Love,* and *Angel of Broadway* (directed by Lois Weber) in 1927, *Thirst, The Bishop Murder Case,* and *Mother's Cry* (all 1930). At the Louis B. Mayer Mission Road Studio, she wrote some of the first titles to be prominently used for advertising purposes: in 1922 for *The Dangerous Age,* with Lewis Stone and Florence Vidor. One of which appeared on billboards and has since been quoted widely: "When a man of forty falls in love with a girl of twenty, it isn't her youth he's seeking, but his own." Another scene much used in ads showed a train, with a group of laughing men surrounding the lead: "Away from home where all his old jokes are new."

In the early twenties, too, Coffee made a reputation as someone who could "rescue" sick scripts and get them off the shelf at the studio, thereby making up the losses some of these scripts had entailed. She charged $1,000 for such doctoring. During this period she also wrote the story for the 1923 script *Daytime Wives.* Selling just the story seems to have been a bit more of a convention in the early days, like Coffee's selling the story for *The Glittering God* to

Harry Cohen at Waldorf Pictures. (It is not clear from *Storyline* if this is Harry Cohen with an E, a general manager and treasurer of Popular Plays and Players Company in New York, a company absorbed by Metro in 1917, or the Harry Cohn without an E who later became the tyrannical head of Columbia Pictures. Since the year Coffee sold the story is 1923 it seems most likely that this would be the infamous Harry Cohn, as he arrived in California at this time.) *Storyline* also says that Coffee wrote the first draft script of the film of the best-selling novel by Harold Bell Wright *The Winning of Barbara Worth* (with which Frances Marion is credited).

During the spring of 1924 Coffee says that she had been working for Metro under Thalberg when the Metro-Goldwyn-Mayer merger took place. This is how Coffee describes the atmosphere:

> Everything was very exciting during that time. I think we all lived in a state of euphoria....
>
> The first thing Irving [Thalberg] did after the merger was to inaugurate Saturday morning meetings. All the offices were small and shabby but no energy was wasted on that sort of thing. Talent, stories, ideas were what counted. Irving said at our very first meeting, "Anyone can buy equipment—but you can't photograph it."
>
> So we held our meetings in a poky little ground floor room. We were a small group—only a handful of us; there was only one other producer besides Thalberg, Harry Rapf, and quite a bit later on, Hunt Stromberg. Besides our group of writers and a director or two, there was Paul Bern, still Thalberg's assistant.
>
> There were discussions of what films we had seen during the week; which ones were doing good business and why? Which films were not doing good business and why? It was really like someone holding a seminar. Everyone spoke very freely—there was no trying to create personal impressions. Much good came out of these informal meetings—as informal as Thalberg could ever be. Once the studio got rolling we were expected to see every MGM preview no matter what director or star or writer was associated with it. Between these previews and other openings one hadn't much free time. But Thalberg felt that our sole aim in life was to find out why some

films could "tune into" the audience and why others could not....

Between 1924 and 1936 he put together a stable of stars which has never been equalled: Greta Garbo, Joan Crawford, Norma Shearer, Jean Harlow, Myrna Loy, William Powell, Wallace Beery, Marie Dressler, the Barrymores, Clark Gable, Robert Taylor—the list could go on and on.

An interesting and revealing side of Thalberg was that he created only women stars. He developed male stars, but he didn't create them. Perhaps his not particularly liking women enabled him to be impersonal in assessing their possibilities and their box-office value.

He built up a stable of writers, as well. People asked him why he had to have one hundred and eight writers under contract when the studio only turned out some fifty films a year, if that. He had two reasons for this: the first was that when he wanted a writer he didn't want to have to borrow one from another studio. The result was many of us sat idle for weeks at a time, but always available. The second was an extremely astute one: he had half a dozen stars who were enormously popular with audiences and he always had four or five scripts in preparation for each one, so he could never be caught without a picture. A junior writer could say quite truthfully that he was writing a Clark Gable story, for he would be; but at the same time three or four more important writers were doing precisely the same thing. There never was that hysteria of "What are we going to do, we haven't got a story for Garbo! We haven't got a story for Clark Gable! We haven't got a story for Norma Shearer!"

(p. 97)

She also says that in the early studio days—before the Writers Guild—contracts were something writers had to be extremely careful about. Most required that a writer could not be sick for more than an aggregate of two weeks per contract year or the contract would be canceled; and that a writer could not work on any other project, including a project of his or her own. She recounts a funny story about producer-director John Stahl who directed, among other films,

Magnificent Obsession in 1935 and *Leave Her to Heaven* in 1945. Stahl started in the movie business in the silent era.

The story is about the making of *Parnell*, the 1937 film about the Irish leader:

> ...I think there were five, maybe six, of us on *Parnell* when it was being prepared for Clark Gable—a triumph of miscasting—all of us supposedly thinking we were the sole writer. I'd sidle out the back door of Stahl's office as Johnny van Druten nipped in at the front.
>
> When Stahl had all our scripts, his secretary would type each writer's contribution on a different color paper. Then this rainbow script would be given to Stahl and the writer who had the largest quantity of one color got the credit! All this sort of thing was before the Screen Writers Guild became a really militant organization and writers had to inform each other of these tactics.
>
> (*Storyline*, p. 126)

While this may have changed some over the years, Coffee's description probably hasn't.

> The sad part is, from the writer's point of view, that by the time he (the producer) has engaged his two top players, his director, his cameraman, and has rented studio space, the budget has been blown clean out of the window. But, alas, too late to do the writer any good.
>
> (p. 123)

Coffee worked primarily for MGM and Paramount, and wrote mainly romantic dramas and suspense films, including, as well as the earlier mentioned films, *Evelyn Prentice* (1934); *Vanessa—Her Love Story (1935); Suzy* (1936); *Four Daughters* (nominated for an Oscar for best screenplay in 1938); *Night Court* and *The Way of All Flesh* (1940); *The Great Lie* (1941); *The Gay Sisters* (1942); *Till We Meet Again* (1944); *Tomorrow Is Forever* (1946); *Lightning Strikes Twice* (1951); *Sudden Fear* (1952); *Footsteps in the Fog, Young at Heart,* and *The End of the Affair* (all 1955). Her last film was *Cash McCall* in 1959.

Though *Four Daughters* was a collaborative effort with coscreenwriter Julius Epstein (and his first breakthrough success for the eventual scriptor of *Casablanca*), Coffee has said, "I never met Mr. Epstein." Possibly more to the point about a "woman's film" is that the film was an adaptation of women's fiction by Fannie Hurst in the magazine *Cosmopolitan*. Early in the script, four young women represent and present the various positions on men, love, marriage, and motherhood. Though it may seem a bit corny today, the movie still devotes itself to the resolution of these themes.

In the bedroom, once more the place for girl talk while dressing and hair brushing, one sister says that she is going to marry for money and place—"Love's overrated, it's old-fashioned, it's the last generation"; the second sister declares that she wants all the old-fashioned stuff—storybook-style love and a wedding with all the trimmings; the third sister expresses the passive position that women have been taught for centuries, trusting in fate—"if you've got anything coming to you it'll come." But the fourth, the youngest sister, says she wants to live, have fun, and is leery of marriage as being "short of fun." Still, she would like to take care of something, a kitten or a baby, but not necessarily with a husband. *Four Daughters* works on all these themes throughout the film, with the last one—the need to nurture—expressed in a socially acceptable way. The fourth daughter marries the "wrong" man because she has misplaced just those care-taking feelings.

Writing for women became one of Coffee's specialties, and she has said:

> The two stars for whom I wrote most were Joan Crawford and Bette Davis, so completely different and yet, in a strange way, so alike. Bette came from New England, with a good conservative background and education, which gave that special "bite" to her words. She was theater-trained. She was not, according to the rules, especially photogenic.
>
> Joan's background was varied. She had almost no education, and her speech, originally, was not cultivated. She had no theater training except in the chorus of a New York show. She was startlingly photogenic.
>
> Bette was much more of a technical actress, first by temperament and second by her theater training. She

thought herself into a part. Joan felt herself into one. Bette's talent was basically intellectual, Joan's emotional. Here are two amusing anecdotes about these women, so heavily endowed with talent: whenever Bette Davis found nine or ten pages during which she did nothing, she would say, "And what am I supposed to do? Stand here with egg on my face?"

And Joan, when really aroused, would kick off her shoes, walk about in her stockinged feet and shout. One producer had the temerity to say, "Please Joan... don't shout!"

The reply came back to him as if from a slingshot, "Why not? I got where I am by shouting. Why should I stop now?" [In the interview with *Backstory* Coffee added, "Bette spits out her words, Joan doesn't. I gave Bette short sentences, short speeches.... I think Joan could be more susceptible. I think Bette could be pretty tough." p. 148]

I had the pleasure of writing again for Claudette Colbert in the film *Tomorrow Is Forever,* and she gave a faultless performance, tender in the right moments, yet revealing the steel which lay beneath what strength was needed.

Another happy experience, my only one with Deborah Kerr, was in *The End of the Affair.* It should have been a much better picture than it was, due in large part to considerable cheese-paring by the company which financed it.

(p. 106)

Coffee's insights into these actresses surely enhanced her scripts for them, and reinforces the points made by the contemporary screenwriters that perhaps the reason we have had so few great parts for women is because there have been so few women screenwriters in the past twenty years or so. Coffee said that specializing in women's stories came very early for her.

Irving Thalberg called me in one day and said, "I'm going to give you a very tough assignment but I think you can do it. Joan Crawford has done all these flapper stories, and she's getting on to twenty-five. I've got to get a new personality for her."... Now in this movie, which was called *Possessed* [1931], Gable played the leading man; and I gave Joan Crawford a whole new personality. It was a very successful picture. Thalberg said to me once, "The only trouble is, she's been playing it [the same character] ever since."

(*Backstory*, p. 144)

Coffee was quite clever at "handling" stars as well as movie producers, and gives a telling anecdote about her soft-soaping of Cary Grant for the 1936 film *Suzy*, a movie he did not initially want to do. Coffee told him, "Speaking bluntly, Mr. Grant, you realize that I'm under contract to this studio, and it is my job to rewrite your part so successfully that you will sign the contract. However, in truth, I am very much on your side for you are at a critical stage in your career, moving into leading-man parts, and then on to being a star....So, being on your side, I want to make this part a stepping-stone, for it would be a fine thing if your first part of this sort was with Jean Harlow [the already predetermined star of *Suzy*] which guarantees you an audience. That puts me on both sides. Now let's get to work." And according to Coffee, this did the trick. (*Storyline*, pp. 116–17)

My Son, My Son was written in 1940. It's about two men and their feelings about paternity, and shows very well that a craftsmanlike woman writer can "handle" the male point of view also. One of the men is McDermot, described thus: "A tousle-headed, young Irishman comes out and hangs over the banister railing with a half-lathered face. He is red-headed with fly-away eyebrows, sensitive hands with long fingers. Hot-headed, warm-hearted." He encourages his friend, a writer, "Look Will—a spider spins its web out of its own insides. You've got to dig down and pull it out of your heart and body...the things you know." His friend is Essex, a writer who is exceptionally happy to find out he's going to be a father:

ESSEX

A man sees bits of knitting about the house...socks and things that look as if they might fit a canary...and then one day he's kicked out like a homeless cat and, after a century or two, somebody shows him a bundle that might be Mrs. Flannigan's wash. He takes it, fearfully and gingerly...but something happens to him at the first touch. His heart melts and his bones turn to water! And he's a slave to it for the rest of his life!

[*He breaks off and turns away a little and sees Oliver's hand fluttering over the edge of the pram. He reaches over and takes it very gently and lays it on his so it is like a tiny starfish in his palm.*]

In his *New York Times* (May 10, 1940) review of the film, Bosley Crowther singled out the writing:

The necessity of being selective while maintaining the essential idea constitutes a considerable strain, and it is notable that Lenore Coffee has cut straight to the principal theme of this story and brought forth a screenplay which, in every respect, preserves the emotional content of the original.

It's not so much that this praise is lavish (it's not extraordinarily so) but that it matter-of-factly mentions the screenwriter, and the writer happens to be a woman. While increasingly today scripts are mentioned in reviews, it would be somewhat singular to have a female writer so offhandedly kudoed in the past couple of decades.

One possible explanation for this notice of the female screenwriter in a woman's film is given in the book *Hollywood in the Forties* by Charles Higham and Joel Greenberg:

The thirties had seen the establishment of an extraordinary number of gifted women stars: Claudette Colbert, Carole Lombard, Rosalind Russell, Katharine Hepburn, Ginger Rogers, Bette Davis, and Joan Crawford, to name only some of the most outstanding. Most were cast in comedy or broad melodrama, and the idea of constructing a full-scale dramatic vehicle around a specific performer had largely been restricted to Garbo, and, on a more minor scale late in the period, Crawford and Davis. With the advent of *Gone With the Wind,* and its more modest black-and-white rival, *Jezebel,* studio heads began to see how a lavish production built around a female character could ensure box-office returns. In the forties, with the vast audience of lonely women left behind by their soldier husbands, lovers, and sons, the need for escapist vehicles of this kind became clearly pressing.

MGM decided to meet the need by mounting a succession of films that reflected the shrewdly sentimental mind of Louis B. Mayer, starring the radiantly genteel Greer Garson and Walter Pidgeon. Theirs were the "nice," safe, films in which middle-aged women could find solace, a sense that, amid restrictions and shopping queues and the long wait for letters from the fronts, Life after all could be Beautiful....

At Warners, formerly a stronghold of the male starring vehicle, the mood was different. The brothers evidently decided that as well as an escape into a world of beauty almost untouched by any reference to war, the female fans also required emotional catharsis. They were to achieve it through Bette Davis, Joan Crawford (after her period at MGM), Ann Sheridan and Barbara Stanwyck, the studio's chief stars playing the roles of women mixed up in mayhem, battling against mishaps to build decent lives for themselves in a world run by men. All-American—sometimes wicked, sometimes good—they typified the emancipated woman fighting for love and security. And usually in settings so grand, so Home Beautiful, photographed with such elegance, so cosily shut off from reality, that wish-fulfillment could be indulged along with emotional empathy.

(pp. 156–57)

Unfortunately Higham and Greenberg do not bother to mention the writers of most of those pictures.

Coffee's script for *The Great Lie* is the 1941 movie about two very different types of women (Bette Davis and Mary Astor), and their love for the same man, George Brent. It is in many ways the ultimate woman's film, as the two women end up alone in a cabin awaiting the birth of Brent's child. All the issues of the forties woman's film are there: the two types of women, the rivalry for one man, and the complicated, ambiguous friendship between the women which involves both bonding and envy, and in this case the birth of a child and the question of motherhood.

Here is some of the very marvelous opening description in the script:

> *Pete Van Allen is about forty-two or three, good-looking in*
> *a rather hard-bitten way and wears extremely good clothes*
> *very casually. He is the sort of man who would be at home*

in a mining camp or a London club....Maggie is in the
traditional beagling costume which consists of a short,
knee-length, flared white skirt, a green gabardine coat, long
green woolen stockings with brogues and a black velvet
hunting cap. It is extremely smart and becoming.

MAGGIE

Why, Pete—

[*But Pete ignores her greeting and outstretched hand and*
goes straight to one of the beagles and shakes its paw.]

PETE

Ah, Ponsoby, old chap—been looking for you everywhere!
Great news! Take a look at this!

And then there is the biting repartee between Maggie (Davis) and
Sandra (Astor), like the following discussion about their shared love
object.

MAGGIE

I let him lie to me.

SANDRA

You're smarter than I thought you were.

MAGGIE

All women are smarter than other women think they are.

We can also observe Coffee's high irony in her treatment of the self-
image of what she clearly perceives as the two types of women
prevalent in the forties society. Here is a speech by the self-styled
bohemian "artiste" Sandra as she discusses her coming out-of-
wedlock pregnancy:

SANDRA

This experience is the tone color which will bring my life

and my art to its full flower of perfection. [*with growing emotion*] Ah, you conventional women—you're afraid to live freely! But *me*—I'm an artist [*with a sort of luxurious stretch of her arm she continues*]

A bit later, turning the tables on her, the Southerner Maggie has this to say about her own iron butterfly qualities:

MAGGIE

No hard New York veneer about me! It goes a lot deeper than that. I can be tough!

Even a reviewer who was lukewarm about the film, Bosley Crowther, admits that "women will probably love it, since fibs are so provocative of fun." He also briefly identifies the two types of women the film so cleverly delineates, as the film "gives Miss Davis an opportunity to display her fine talent for distress, to be maternal and noble," and Astor's character is a "resplendent concert pianist [who] provides a beautiful contrast of cold and poisonous" (April 12, 1941).

A fuller examination of the forties "bad" girl is to be found in *Beyond the Forest,* which Coffee adapted from a Stuart Engstrand novel and which was directed by King Vidor in 1949. Of course Rosa Moline, as Bette Davis plays her, doesn't look so terrible from the contemporary point of view, even though she does reprehensible things (adultery, murder, and a self-inflicted miscarriage are just a few). A more modern reading of the film might see her as trapped in her circumstances, and at the very least attractive due to her restless energy.

Certainly some of the lines of Coffee's script—particularly as Bette Davis delivers them—pick up on Rosa's own understanding of her character. And of the situation she is stuck in (married to a small-town doctor and wanting desperately to escape to the big city in the film). Rosa has reconciled with her husband after an unsuccessful attempt to run away to Chicago and her millionaire lover who has rejected her. She and Lewis, played by Joseph Cotten, are having a quiet picnic together in the woods.

ROSA

Funny, isn't it? All these trees standing here feeling so

strong. Then someone comes along and says, "It's your turn." And they get the mark of death on them. I wonder if they know.

LEWIS

People don't. It's not always death though. Sometimes it's a disability or an ordeal.

ROSA

See any mark on me?

LEWIS

Of course not.

ROSA

Don't you see it, Lewis?

LEWIS

No, what?

ROSA

I always thought you were a rotten doctor. I'm going to have a baby.

LEWIS

Aren't you glad?

ROSA

Not glad and not not glad.

LEWIS

I should think a baby would make you happy.

ROSA

Will it, Lewis?

DOCTOR

Ought to. Why should you be different from any other woman?

ROSA

I always thought I was. Now I'm like all the rest.

Delivered ruefully by Davis.

Particularly insightful from the female point of view, is the ambivalence Rosa expresses at her pregnancy; a specific emotional mix perhaps only a female can know.

Coffee gives the script some snappy lines, too, like the narrative voice-over during the scenes describing the sleepy small town of Loyalton, Wisconsin, in which a horse is shown peacefully waiting: "Horses don't mind waiting—people do." Or when Rosa says, early in the movie, "Life in Loyalton is like sitting in a funeral parlor and waiting for the funeral to begin." More clever, too, than the famous "What a dump!" which has been picked up by the camp subculture, is Rosa's rejoinder to her married lover when he tells her he's in love with a young girl.

NEIL

She's like a book with all the pages untouched.

ROSA

And nothing on them.

As someone who survived and thrived in all the decades of moviemaking, Coffee appears to have very well learned the art of compromise necessary to a group project like the making of a film. Here is her advice to the writer of film scripts:

...first, that you must never leave out one essential ingredient; it is like baking a cake. No matter how delicate and costly the ingredients may be, if you have left out an essential one, you will not have a cake—you will have a disaster. But if you use cheap and inferior ingredients, but use them *all*, you will have a cake. Not a good one, but indisputably, a cake. The other thing I learned is that a second-rate idea can be better than a first-rate one, if it permits you to "ring all the changes." [By this she seems to mean cover a range of emotions.]

(*Storyline,* p. 196)

Interestingly, the cooking analogy is also used by Nora Ephron in her thoughts on screenwriting, but it's for the group effort that is part of making movies:

Here is what I always say about screenwriting. When you write a script, it's like delivering a great big beautiful plain pizza, the one with only cheese and tomatoes. And then you give it to the director, and the director says, "I love this pizza. I am willing to commit to this pizza. But I really think this pizza should have mushrooms on it." And you say, "Mushrooms! Of course! I meant to put mushrooms on the pizza! Why didn't I think of that? Let's put some on immediately." And then someone else comes along and says, "I love this pizza too, but it really needs green peppers." "Great," you say. "Green peppers. Just the thing." And then someone else says, "Anchovies." There's always a fight over the anchovies. And when you get done, what you have is a pizza with everything. Sometimes it's wonderful. And sometimes you look at it and you think, I knew we shouldn't have put the green peppers onto it. Why didn't I say so at the time? Why didn't I lie down in traffic to prevent anyone's putting green peppers onto the pizza?

(Introduction to *When Harry Met Sally,*
New York: 1991, pp. xiii–xiv)

Coffee's method of writing was to work at home, block out in longhand, and then dictate to a secretary. One of the funnier stories she tells in *Storyline* about the brush wars of being a working screenwriter is that once Thalberg called her at home to say that a scene for the star Irene Rich wasn't working and requested that Coffee write one on the spot. She did so in a half hour, she reports, and dictated the speech over the telephone to her secretary at the studio. All Coffee knew was that it was a war film and Rich was addressing women members of a wartime association to stir them to greater efforts.

She says she decided to use simple phrases in Rich's speech: "When we entertain these boys let us not wave flags and use big words. They get enough of that. Let us talk of their families, the people they hope to come home to. The people they love...the people who love them. And now I should like to end this gathering with one moment of silence for those boys and men who, *tonight*, will give their lives." Coffee reports that she never did know what film she had written the speech for. (*Storyline*, p. 124)

According to her book, Coffee got on well with most of the directors she worked for, with the possible exception of Louis B. Mayer, but her favorite working relationship was with Cecil B. De Mille. Her influence was such that she, like other writers, was able to give advice to directors on star-making. Coffee spotted Clark Gable and, according to her book, tried to convince De Mille of his worth but he delayed. Irving Thalberg got there first, and had bought the Adela Rogers St. Johns novel *A Free Soul*, the film version of which Gable was cast in to sensational effect.

Coffee's flexibility allowed her to move into the fifties and the "modern" age with apparent ease, as her mastery of the thriller mode in *Sudden Fear* with Joan Crawford in 1952 shows. Much like today's thriller genre, the setting is glamorous with a touch of foreboding:

INT.   MYRA'S DRAWING ROOM (NIGHT)

Beautifully dressed women and faultlessly tailored men fill the room, many of them silver-haired with that "Old San-Francisco-family-look."

And a bit earlier, during a scene when Myra, the female protagonist, is running:

LESTER

Don't you ever do it again!

MYRA

Why not? You know what Nietzsche said—"Live dangerously!"

LESTER.

You know what happened to Nietzsche?

MYRA

No.

LESTER

He's dead.

Eventually the heiress Myra discovers the plot against her life by her husband and his girlfriend by accidentally listening to a dictating machine. Here are the very effective action directions:

Myra moves toward dictating machine as though it were a venomous serpent. She must preserve the recording, but it costs her every ounce of will she has to bring herself to touch it. She puts her hands out to remove the record, and going to the bookshelf, stands on a chair and removes two or three books to make a hiding place for the record. Just as she is about to place the record behind the books, the recording falls from her hands to shatter on the floor. Myra almost falls from chair, runs out of room.

There is also a quite clever scene where Myra is lying in bed, and Coffee has her imagining in a "semi-impressionistic manner" the possible scenes of her murder by Lester. They almost seem prophetic of contemporary thrillers, excepting possibly letter A.

A. Poison for sleeping tablets
B. Falling from a height
C. Drowning in tub
D. Lester fooling with steering wheel
E. Car going out of control
F. Lester holding pillow over her head

But perhaps the most impressive thing about Coffee is her salesmanship, the fact that she could pitch a story extremely well, in spite of the fact that she had a stammer, nearsightedness, and a kind of nervous disorder. She says:

I sold many stories just by telling them. I was a good actress and would have become an actress if my parents were not opposed to it when I was young. For example: when I was young, contraceptives were unheard of. Birth control was something you did after, not before. In those days there was a very popular item advertised called a "whirling spray," a form of douche. I was so good at selling stories that one day, when I was telling a story to a producer, a man walked by and said, "Don't listen. You'll find yourself buying it. She could sell a whirling spray to a nun."

I had a lot of things to overcome—a dreadful speech impediment, bad eyesight before I had my cataract operation. And I woke up stone deaf in one ear one morning after being thrown from a horse Christmas Eve day and have never heard in it since. Also, I suffered from a nervous disease. I used to excuse myself from meetings at the studio, slip out to the bathroom, and shoot myself in the arm with a hypodermic of medicine. I was very good with a needle, as they say.

(*Backstory*, p. 143)

Following the pattern of the rest of the country in its sudden opening of the doors to jobs formerly held by men, the movie industry was exceptionally open to women writers in the forties. Some of the women who broke in in the early years, like Clara Beranger or Lenore Coffee, really hit their stride during the 1940s. Some, like Salley Benson, came in from other pastures in the 1940s; others, like Marguerite Roberts, worked their way into screenwriting by starting in the secretarial pool at the studios. Still others, like Mary McCall Jr., made inroads during the Depression years, when economic uncertainties forced many writers to the West Coast, and then peaked during the war years.

One of the most flamboyant women writers in all of Hollywood history was Mary McCall Jr., someone who defined herself as a working writer throughout her entire life, whether she was working as a copywriter, film critic, or fiction writer (her early, New York years), or as a movie industry writer and finally television writer during the fifties. Outspoken and full of chutzpah in every arena, McCall was an organizer of the Writers Guild and served as its president three times. A list of the movies she wrote includes *Babbitt* (1934), *Secret Bride,*

Mary McCall

Woman in Red, Dr. Socrates, and *A Midsummer Night's Dream* (all 1935), *Craig's Wife* (1936), *Women of Glamour* and *I Promise to Pay* (both 1937), *It's All Yours, Breaking the Ice,* and *Dramatic School* (all 1938); *Maisie* (1939); *Congo Maisie* and *Gold Rush Maisie (1940); Maisie Was a Lady, Ringside Maisie,* and *Kathleen* (all 1941); *Maisie Gets Her Man (1942); Swing Shift Maisie* (1943); *The Sullivans* and *Maisie Goes to Reno* (both 1944); *Keep Your Powder Dry* (1945); *Mr. Belvedere Goes to College* and *Dancing in the Dark* (both 1949); *Thunderbirds* (1953).

According to one of her daughters, Mary-David Sheiner, "If she were alive today she'd be at a pitch meeting."

And since there's no substitute for getting it from the horse's mouth, perhaps it would be good to let McCall summarize her own career, as she did at a tribute to her at the Writers Guild of America West in 1978:

I was in my junior year at college [Vassar] 'way back when motion pictures were silent. A friend, who'd been graduated three years before, was working as a film reviewer for the Hays office in New York. She had a chance to go to Europe for two months in the summer, if she could get someone capable of filling in for her. I quickly suggested me. She asked if I knew anything about movies. I told her I'd learned to read by spelling out subtitles. She gave me a glowing reference at the office, and they agreed to hire me: $25 each five and a half day week....I saw a great many Tom Mix pictures, so grainy they looked as if they'd been photographed through rye bread, and six or eight segments of a serial starring Jack Dempsey. When my boss went on his vacation, I moved up to somewhat classier reviews: Norma Shearer...and Enid Bennett...

Graduated from Vassar and home from a year at Trinity College, Dublin, I interviewed directors for a dreary magazine called *Cinema Art*—King Vidor who was shooting *The Crowd* in New York, Herbert Brenon en route home after making *Sorrel and Son* in England. My editor at *Cinema Art* lost his job to the new owner's nephew, and I got a job in an advertising agency, still at $25 a week. I left then to be married, did free-lance advertising...

I began to write short stories, and was both pleased and surprised when editors bought them. One novel, *The Gold-fish Bowl,* written at the height of [and about] the frenzied hero-worship of Lindbergh and Admiral Byrd, was bought by Warner Brothers. My wistful suggestion that I write the screenplay was turned down. "We never employ writers on their own material. They haven't the proper perspective." Then they offered me an eight-week contract to write a picture based on someone else's book. I'd never been west of Trenton, N.J. I'd never had a chance to write for the screen. I left my year-old daughter Sheila and her nurse with my parents in Scottsdale, Arizona, and came to Hollywood.

The picture I worked on was, to be blunt, a dog. But the screenplay based on my book was written by Robert Lord, and I was delighted with it.... The picture was made and previewed. The cards were good. Two weeks later the Lindbergh baby was kidnapped. The book died a mediocre death. The picture could not be exploited.

Knowing I wanted to be a screenwriter, I went back to New York and the magazines. In 1934, I got my chance. My husband [Dwight Franklin] was working as a production designer and technical adviser on *Treasure Island* at MGM, with another picture to follow. Those were Depression days—and the Hollywood fields seemed green and pleasant. I went to see Hal Wallis, who'd been my "supervisor" two years before, and was now head of the studio. He was looking for a vehicle for a girl named Jean Muir. I had an unpublished novelette which I sold the studio. The picture was called *Desirable.* It was produced by Edward Chodorov, who rewrote my mistakes, kept me on the track, and with whom I enjoyed working. The picture cost relatively little, and I think it was good. He left the studio for Columbia and I was sorry to see him go.

When a $50 a week raise was dangled before me, I signed a contract with the studio. I write fairly facile dialogue and was used primarily as a corpse rouger—"Brightening the dialog" in other people's scripts. With the late Charles Kenyon, I worked on *A Midsummer Night's Dream* [the Max Reinhardt version with Mickey Rooney]. Shakespeare was dead. Charles Kenyon was deaf, but too proud to wear a hearing aid. Everyone else connected with the project was German. We were given copies of the text with German on one side and English on the other. I was pregnant, very pregnant, so when someone said, for the fifth or sixth time, "It sounds better in German," I had to keep my outraged voice within reasonable limits.

My twin sons, Gerald and Alan McCall Franklin, were born twenty-four hours after my last conference. With the twins launched, I went back to work. I began to work actively in the Guild. The average pay of screen writers equaled that of the body makeup men. Employees were bullied by The High Brass—told, not urged, to donate to campaign funds—given a list of films, players, directors to vote for in the Academy's balloting. . . . I collected signatures to a letter protesting the studio's action. All the men who had signed it were summoned to Jack Warner's office. He demanded to know what individual had written this. They all said, "We wrote it." But J.L., through native shrewdness and information from a fink, knew I was the culprit. I was not Mrs. Popularity on the Warner lot.

And then came a call from my rescuer—Eddie Chodorov. How would I like to come to Columbia and write the screenplay of George Kelly's Pulitzer Prize winning *Craig's Wife?* Ohhhh, would I not. I completed a first-draft screenplay. Then Dorothy Arzner and I went over it, line by line. She said that she would like me to be on the set during the shooting of the picture. I was there for a day or two, when I was recalled to Warners—and laid off. I came in every day, until I got orders from Harry Cohn to stay away, because he was trying to persuade Jack Warner to let him take over the balance of my Warner contract. This he succeeded in doing.

That Eddie Chodorov had confidence enough in me to give me a fine, interesting assignment; that Dorothy Arzner saw in me at least the makings of a good screen writer, gave me determination and self-confidence. . . . My fourth child, Mary-David Sheiner, a full-fledged member of the Guild, was born while I was at MGM. And at MGM, I had the great good luck to write, alone or with others, a series of pictures about a

girl named Maisie. Ann Sothern was Maisie—a perfect
Maisie. Her comedy timing was what any writer would pray
for in a star. I love her. I've even forgiven her for what a New
York critic said about one of the Maisies I wrote all by myself.
He said, "Miss Sothern's unceasing flow of bright sayings
redeems a dull script."

Howard Hughes made me unemployable at most of the
studios and the TV companies in Hollywood. [Particularly
angry about her backing of left-wing writer Paul Jarrico,
Hughes made certain that McCall's blacklisting stuck.] Financially, I never recovered. But Howard Hughes met with a
lingering death. I'm alive. I have a husband who loves me
and whom I love. I have two daughters, two sons, six
grandchildren, all of whom are intelligent, affectionate and
good company. When I heard the plans for tonite, I was
afraid that the younger members of the Guild would read the
name Mary McCall, and say: "Who?" Or worse still: "Why?"
But you came tonight, and this seventy-four year old...says
from her heart: "Thank you!"

(Writers Guild of America West News,
June 1978)

Even given McCall's great drive and style, and the fact that she
was already a well-known, much published author, one fact stands
out: her break came because the studio was looking for a vehicle for a
female star (Jean Muir). And another leap ahead was made when a
woman director, Arzner, extended herself to McCall and let her affect
the making of their film together as well. She was therefore in place to
write most of the popular Maisie films. And just try to imagine a
whole series of films being made today about a comic female
character.

In an interview with McCall's daughters, Sheila Benson, the
former film critic of the *Los Angeles Times,* and Mary-David Sheiner,
a free-lance television writer, in the spring of 1992 in Los Angeles,
both spoke with admiration of McCall's utter fearlessness and her
irrepressible spirit. (McCall died in 1981.)

"Nobody intimidated her," said Benson. "One day Harry Cohn
yelled at her, 'Where are you going?' She said, 'I'm going to lunch.'
He said, 'Nobody goes off the lot to lunch.' Well, *she* did." Benson

said that McCall liked Cohn. "She thought he was a scoundrel, but he was a scoundrel through and through. An honest scoundrel. Louis B. Mayer was another matter. She thought him a scoundrel, but sanctimonious."

Benson also said that her father, designer Dwight Franklin, was very supportive of McCall's work, and introduced her to the Algonquin Circle of writers and pundits in New York. "But," said Benson, "if she hadn't been a writer, she would have been a lawyer. Because that's the way her mind worked. She could look through a proposal and find its weak points." Benson also said that she was of Irish extraction and had the storytelling gift, as did McCall's own mother. "My grandmother could make even a trip to the market sound interesting," said Benson. "'Went I down to the store,' she would start and everyone would be transfixed." Undoubtedly the "gift for gab" was useful to McCall in pitching story ideas in the movie business.

McCall, who appended the Jr. to her name early in life as an interestingly unisexual way of saying that she had the same name as her mother, seems to have had a unique and exciting personality far in advance of her time. Benson said that she never bothered much with makeup since she was too busy for it, and would just dip a finger into a pot of rouge for lipstick (as was the fashion then) and dash off to work. "She never wore a bra," said Benson, "and I'm not sure if she wore underpants either." "When other mothers were preaching chastity to their daughters, our mother was telling us, 'Don't buy the shoe until you've tried it on first,'" added Sheiner.

Her first marriage had an "open" side to it ("I'm not so sure it was open on my father's side," said Benson, and she mentioned a few interesting Hollywood men with whom McCall had liaisons). The couple had an arrangement that each partner could do whatever he or she wanted so long as it did not embarrass the other spouse. And it was very much to McCall's surprise that she fell—"head over heels"—according to Benson, in love with Sheiner's father, a World War II officer McCall met while doing volunteer work at a canteen. "She told my father, 'Look, I'm sure this thing will blow over,'" said Benson. "But it didn't."

Yet each daughter had a very different view of her mother, perhaps because of the fact that Benson was McCall's first child, born when McCall was in her twenties, and Sheiner her last, born when McCall was forty. For Benson, McCall was not around much during her formative years and went to the studio nearly all the time. "I thought the [Writers] Guild was where your mother went when she came home from the studio," said Benson.

For Sheiner, McCall was working at home on television shows, because of declining status due to being blacklisted during the fifties, and so was more available to her. "It was erratic, but she still got the work out one way or another, such as a pilot for 'The Millionaire' and various episodes of 'Leave It to Beaver.' She told me once if I could come up with an idea for an episode of 'Beaver' I could get a bike, and I did," said Sheiner, still proud.

Each daughter said that McCall was always the breadwinner in domestic situations (McCall married twice) and that at the height of her career she was earning more than men writers, making $3,000 a week. "Mary McCall didn't need the Guild to do negotiating for her—she did her own negotiating," said Sheiner. "At Vassar they told her she was too commercial and she thought that was just grand," remembered Sheiner. "Still," said Benson, "she always said, 'Careers for women are the shits.'" Both said that McCall's commitment to the Writers Guild did not include the idea of a women's division, or wing, of the Guild; she felt that this would just segregate women more.

One of the principles that McCall stood for in her work for the Guild was to discourage television producers from taking advantage of writers who might be tempted to write a script on speculation, in all probability wasting their time. The essay, "The Bespoke Script," which she wrote for a collection published by the Writers Guild, cleverly presents the viewpoint (though in fact the practice does still go on):

> The bespoke script, like the bespoke suit of clothes, is ordered in advance to fit the needs of an individual customer. These needs are usually so specialized that the script custom-tailored for one buyer and rejected by him cannot be altered to fit another....
>
> The first frail, green shoots of a reputation in any writing field will attract an agent. Established agency representation will enable the writer to receive a personal briefing in the needs of various television series or to learn of them by correspondence. He is then in a position to submit the basic outline of a story, either orally or in skeletonized written form. If the producer is favorably impressed by this indication of the story's essential elements, but wishes to read it in more fully

developed form or with changes made in it in accordance with suggestions from him, the writer, without violating the Guild's rule against speculative writing, may furnish him with a two-page outline. For this outline, the producer must pay the writer one hundred dollars, deductible from the writer's first payment if his story is later accepted, but retained by the writer if it is rejected.

> (undated collection of essays in the McCall file at the Margaret Herrick Library at the Academy of Motion Picture Arts and Sciences)

Benson said that, no matter what the project, McCall saw herself mainly as a writer, a craftsperson. "'Do your level best,' she taught us, 'Whatever you do, whether it's a jingle or the great American novel.' We also learned, stand up for your beliefs, but also don't expect to be applauded for them." (In this latter vein, Benson pointed out that though McCall worked hard to organize the Guild, her pension only came to $26 a month when she retired.) And she defended the left-wing writer Paul Jarrico, which particularly brought down the wrath of the powerful Howard Hughes.

McCall was called before the Tenney Committee (the California Senate Committee on Un-American Activities) and an undated article from the *New York Times* in the Billy Rose Theater Collection at Lincoln Center has a picture of an angry-looking McCall declaring to the Committee, "I'd rather be dead" [than be a Communist]. In testimony characterized by the *Times* as eloquent, she told the Committee that such references to her had damaged her economically and "adversely affected her reputation as a private citizen and mother of four children." As an example, she testified that an advertising agency refused to accept a teleplay she had written on grounds that she was "a Communist." She defended her work in the Guild as three-time president, and explained, "the laziness of the middle-of-the-roaders—like me—enabled a small Communist minority to take over."*

As a writer, McCall never forgot her audience. We can see in both

---

*McCall died of Alzheimer's disease at the age of eighty-one, and her daughter Sheiner remembers being with her at various moments of lucidity. "One time I said to her, 'Do you know Ronnie Reagan [a longtime enemy of the Guild] is President?' And she looked at me and said, 'Oh, shit,' and went back to sleep."

Craig's Wife and the Maisie scripts—though extremely different in tone and content—that they are both very much written for the female viewer.

In *Craig's Wife*, Mrs. Craig (Rosalind Russell in the movie) is a woman whose home is more important to her than anything else, including her husband. McCall's set directions for the living room, which she has added to the play, read like this, in a specific gearing to the female segment: "This room must be so beautiful that this first sight of it will bring a gasp from every woman in the audience. There is no litter of casual living—no magazines, books, pipes, spectacles, packs of cigarettes." It cuts right to the chase, emotionally speaking.

The opening set directions in George Kelly's play are more formal, and not so obviously geared to women: "This room, like all the other rooms in the house, reflects the very excellent taste and fanatical orderliness of its mistress. It is a kind of frozen grandeur, in dark, highly polished wood—strewn with gorgeous, gold-colored rugs and draped in rich brocades."

And McCall shortens somewhat, but keeps the significant character of, a speech of Mrs. Craig's from the play which in part explains if not excuses her not very likable character:

MRS. CRAIG

I saw to it that my marriage should be a way toward emancipation for me. I had no private fortune, no special training, so the only road to independence for me was through the man I married. I married to be *independent.*
[emphasis in text]

The play reads like this:

I saw to it that my marriage should be a way toward emancipation for *me.* I had no private fortune like you, Ethel; no special equipment—outside of a few more or less inapplicable college theories. So the only road to independence for *me,* that I could see, was through the man I married.

The language has been smoothed out and simplified in the film version; and the emphasis is on independence, Harriet Craig's inability to make a living on her own, not on the egocentric *me.*

And in the film:

ETHEL
[*puzzled*]

You don't mean independent of your husband, too?

MRS. CRAIG
[*decisive*]

Independent of *everybody*.

And later:

My dear, young, romantic Ethel—if a woman is the right
kind of woman, it's better that the destiny of her home
should be in her hands, than in any man's.

In the play Ethel (her niece) accuses "Aunt Harriet" of being "not
quite honest," though this is not in the film. The change is perhaps a
small Hollywood type concession to making her more appealing than
she might otherwise have been. Also, McCall gives a kind of
psychoanalytic angle—something not in the play—to explain away a
bit of Mrs. Craig's behavior:

MRS. CRAIG

I saw what happened to my own mother, and I made up
my mind it'd never happen to me.

[*She turns and comes forward again*]

She was one of those "I will follow thee, my husband"
women—that believed everything my father told her—and
all the time he was mortgaging her home over her head for
another woman. And when she found it out, she did the
only thing that women like her *can* do, and that was to die
of a broken heart.

In the play, Mrs. Craig doesn't have such an acceptable "ra-
tionale" for her behavior:

MRS. CRAIG

...I lived with a stepmother, Ethel, for nearly twelve years, and with your mother after she was married for over five: I know what it is to be on some one else's floor. And I married to be on my own—in every sense of the word. I haven't entirely achieved the condition yet—but I know it can be done.

What was the reaction to such a figure? While naturally it is not possible to retrospectively interview a sample of the film's first-time viewers, while researching *Craig's Wife* this writer was overheard by a ladies-who-lunch type volunteer matron in the library who started to wax rhapsodic about the play, and the remembered impact of the "Mrs. Craig" character upon her. And all the popular press of the time took a position on the film, undoubtedly because the play had won a Pulitzer Prize. "Nobody wanted to play a cold-blooded female who inspired enduring hatred," observes *Newsweek* (September 28, 1936). "What if the drama did win the Pulitzer Prize...? Most of the stars wanted roles more in harmony with their own delightful characters." Still, *Newsweek* admits, *Craig's Wife* will probably be among the Ten Best films of the year.

A more thoughtful review is to be found in the December 1936 piece by *McCall's* reviewer, Pare Lorenz, a famous documentary filmmaker himself (*The River* is perhaps his masterpiece). "Dorothy Arzner, our only woman director, understood what she was about and pointed the movie craftily toward the great climax of the play when, servants, neighbors, niece, sister and husband, all having left, Mrs. Craig paces madly the polished floor of her home." Is McCall's presence on the set an influence here? Hard to say, but at least Arzner opened the door to this. And Lorenz characterizes Rosalind Russell's performance as a "fine portrait of a woman carved out of pre-historic ice."

Time magazine (October 12, 1936), with a female as well as male readership, has a most sophisticated response to *Craig's Wife:*

Consideration for the Hays office on one hand and the feelings of its own patrons on the other combine to make the cinema's view of matriarchy at most times a highly sympathetic one. Consequently the current cinema season may well be remembered for the way in which two first-class pictures have revealed two rich and respectable U.S. wives as altogether worthless characters.... [Mrs. Craig] loses her husband through psychopathic selfishness [and she has the] discovery that those who live to themselves are left to themselves.

Time also goes on to observe:

The work of Dorothy Arzner, Hollywood's only woman director, is equally distinguished for giving pace without apparent effort to a picture that might, with less expert treatment, have seemed pedestrian.

Within the structure and intent of the play, McCall has humanized Harriet Craig a bit, emphasized her independence, mentioned her lack of vocational training, and added a possible psychoanalytic motivation. We may not sympathize with Harriet Craig, but at least we understand her better.

McCall worked successfully in not just the mode of serious melodrama: in the humorous genre, there is her handling of *Swing Shift Maisie* (1943), a script that you might initially find easy to dismiss as a lightweight comedy about a misguided friendship between women. One character, Iris, is a silly sort who actually is selling out the lead, Maisie, played by Ann Sothern, for a man and every other advantage she can get.

Still, the Maisie script offers one very real cinematic equivalent we have for the Rosie the Riveter figure: the image of the female World War II worker happily working in a plant. McCall, with cowriter Robert Halff, has captured the romance of work in the following sequence—and in the film—in fleshing out a heroine who loves to work and who is sure of her right to do so. First there is the strong visual symbol:

Maisie with tool kit and cushion—CAMERA PANS *her left— she looks upward o.s. to right*—PANS *up to left with Maisie as she climbs on platform*—CAMERA PULLS *back as she starts to climb on plane*—

LS—*Maisie and workers in defense plant—Camera shooting down on them—Man helps Maisie into cockpit of plane—she speaks—sits down—*

And just a bit later in the scene she is seen writing and leaving a "good luck" note for the pilot of the plane, a bit that will prove important later for the plot of the film. It also tells us that she is good with equipment and not afraid of weaponry. From the very beginning of the film, Maisie's right to do work of this nature is an issue, and a roundly defended one.

BREEZY

And what does a dame like you know about defense work, anyhow?

CS [*must mean close-up shot*]—*Maisie looking to r.f.g.—*

MAISIE

Listen, brother, I've been doing defense work of one kind or another all my life. I'll make out.

CS—*Breezy smiles to f.g.—Curley at left—*

BREEZY

I don't doubt that. Eight hours a day, six days a week? Ha! Ha!

CS—*Maisie looking to r.f.g.—reacts*

MAISIE

Ha-ha! Well, what do you think show business is, pray tell?

CS—*Curley and Breezy—Breezy looks to left f.g.—*

BREEZY

Well, throwin' your hips around is no trainin' for factory work. Why, you'd let a hot rivet drop while you repaired your paint job, or regilded your hair.

MS—*Maisie, Curley and Breezy—Maisie at left—she reacts and sets suitcase down—*PAN *right as she backs Breezy to wall—*TRUCK *in slightly—*

MAISIE

Listen! I tell you my ha—

BREEZY

No, I know—it's natural. No, Goldilocks, in an aircraft factory you'd be just so much excess baggage. You're not the type.

MAISIE

Not the type, huh? Well, it's gonna take all types to win this war. From General MacArthur way on down to you!

MCU—*Breezy smiles—reacts—Maisie in l.f.g.—*

MAISIE

And I'll get in it, and I don't need no introduction from you, nor none of your ilk!

MCU—*Maisie—Breezy in r.f.g.—*

MAISIE

He's my Uncle Sam too, you know! And as for how I'm dressed, I wear what suits the job I'm doin', and make up in proportion. And I'll handle myself in the factory just as good as on the stage. If you can fly planes, then brother, I can build 'em.

It's a positive image, and one to be found in magazines of the time. An ad, for instance, for Pond's Cold Cream which is found running throughout a number of 1943 *McCall's* shows an attractive brunette named Susan Tucker holding a drill in a most craftsmanlike way. The caption is LEARNING TO DO A JOB THE U.S. NEEDS and the copy reads "At her bench at the Delehanty Institute, Susan drills precisely accurate holes in metal castings—a process she'll use often when she starts her war job. 'Warren would be surprised to see how mechanically exact I'm getting to be,' she says." A 1941 ad for Kellogg's Cereal features an "in-action" photo of a "U.S. Civilian Flying Instructress."

A cartoon in a 1943 *McCall's* also makes the point, showing a tall woman in a worker's uniform and a tiny nebbishy looking man standing next to her in front of a desk with the sign, AJAX AIRCRAFT EMPLOYMENT. "No!" says the female figure to the person behind the desk. "He's the stenographer. I'm a welder." The cartoon is on the same page with Eleanor Roosevelt's "If You Ask Me" column which answers the letter "I have heard girls say...women who put on uniforms are aping men" by this reply of Roosevelt's: "...[That's] ridiculous....They are wearing the kind of clothes which are suitable for the work they intend to do."

These social attitudes are not caused by Rosie the Riveter, of course, but there were other real-life versions of Rosie. *Time* magazine (January 5, 1942) has an article about a woman who shares corporate responsibility for the Beech Aircraft Corporation, the largest U.S. mass producer of heavy, twin-engined "bomber trainers." The article features a photograph of the woman, Olive Ann Beech, and the copy reads like this:

> Walter Beech is only half of Beech Aircraft. As secretary-treasurer, Olive Ann works 10–12 hours daily. When expansion plans were afoot last year, she was in a Wichita hospital having her second baby. But she had a direct hospital-plant telephone and the directors met at her bedside.

Did Olive Ann Beech model herself after a Maisie film? Of course not.

Still, there are very few such articles or role models popularized after 1945, and in fact immediately after the war ended, articles appeared like the one in the July 1945 *Ladies Home Journal* entitled "Why I Am Against the Equal Rights Amendment" by Alice Hamilton, M.D., president of the National Consumers League. Even more effective because written by a woman, the article declares, "No law can compel a man to employ a woman or to promote her, no law can compel a hospital to place women doctors on its staff or admit them as interns and residents, no law can prevent an employer from passing by a competent woman appointing a less competent man."

Immediately after the war ended, government pamphlets were issued which strongly encouraged if not demanded that women resign their jobs in favor of returning veterans, almost as a patriotic duty. According to New York attorney Carol Calhoun, Calhoun's aunt said the entire factory of female workers burst into tears when told they had to quit their jobs at the end of World War II.

But in the 1943 *Swing Shift Maisie,* the work sequences are done with sprightly humor, and so is the rest of the script. McCall's spin on Hitler might be seen as some kind of equivalent of the famous Chaplin sequence showing Hitler bouncing a world-shaped bouncing ball off his buttocks. (You could easily imagine Mel Brooks in this part or having written this dialogue.)

BRUNO

Say, the Kaiser and the Crown Prince was bad enough, but this Hitler.

WALDO

Oh, Brother!

CS—*Maisie and Otto—latter facing right—they speak—*

OTTO

To fall two times for such phonies. Deep down something is loess. [sic: should be lost?]

MAISIE

Yeah. For anybody who knows show business, that's an awful corny routine.

MCS—*Otto—Maisie—Bruno and Waldo—boys imitate Nazi salute—Otto combs hair Hitler style—puts comb under nose for mustache—boys repeat Nazi salute—all laugh—* PANS *left as they march around making fun of Nazi salute—*

WALDO

With all this shouting, "Heil!"

BRUNO

And screaming, yet.

OTTO

Like so. Heil!

WALDO AND BRUNO

Der Fuehrer!

OTTO

Actung! (Attention)

WALDO

Actung! (Attention)

OTTO

Marsh [sic]. (March)

WALDO

Marsh [sic]. (March)

And so on with an imitation of a Nazi goose-step.

It is obvious that McCall understood the demands of movies early on too, and that even in her first efforts, such as A *Midsummer Night's Dream*, she is cognizant of things that can be easily and humorously done in movies: both young heroes, Lysander and Demetrius, proclaim "Helena" at the same moment, and both blow their noses together. Many close-ups of the characters are broadly funny, often in the "double-take" vein.

Best of all, the adaptation keeps many of the wonderful speeches and leaves out some of the longer and more recondite explanations. "The course of true love never did run smooth" is a line used, though the one immediately following in the Shakespeare play is dropped: "But, either it was different in blood." It is quite hilarious when Lysander scorns Hermia as "You minimus, you bead, you acorn," shortening the original "You minimus, of hindering knot-grass made;/ You bead, you acorn." "Hindering knot-grass" might have slowed down the speech and lost some viewers. In other respects, the "cat-fight" between Helena and Hermia is much played up, with a lot of movement, and is faithful to Shakespeare, as well as to this time-honored cinematic convention.

McCall is not the only writer to declare that she was a writer first, and in the business to make a good living as a professional. Sally Benson, also imported from New York, always said she would do whatever work came along that was in the writer's vein. This kind of "pen for hire," tough-cookie attitude is perhaps typical of writers of the thirties and forties. In an interview Benson gave to the *New York Post* (February 7, 1944) and true to the mode of high irony that captures the tone of a certain class of very successful writers in that era, she said that it was only the need for money that inspired her to write.

True or not, Benson's daughter, Barbara Benson Golseth of Tucson, said that her mother's busiest years were in California during World War II. "She made a lot of money at that time," Golseth recalled and then laughed, "And she spent it. It was her money of course and she should have done what she pleased with it." Golseth, a former reporter and woman's page editor at the *Arizona Daily Star,* spoke about her mother over the telephone in the fall of 1993.

In the years that Benson was writing for the movies, she wrote *Conspirator* (1950), *Summer Magic* (1963), *Viva Las Vegas* (1964), *Signpost to Murder* (1965), *The Singing Nun* (1966), and collaborated on *Shadow of a Doubt* (1942, with Thornton Wilder and Alma Reville), *Meet Me in St. Louis* (1944 with Irving Brecher and Fred F. Finklehoffe), *Anna and the King of Siam* (1946 with Talbot Jennings), *Come to the Stable* (1949 with Oscar Millard), *No Man of Her Own* (1950 with Catherine Turney), *The Farmer Takes a Wife* (1953 with Walter Bullock and Ann Joseph Fields), and *Joy in the Morning* (1965, with Alfred Hayes and Norman Lessing).

It is interesting that Leslie Halliwell's *Filmgoer's Companion* doesn't even mention Benson, but credits Irving Brecher and Fred Finklehoffe as the scriptwriters for *Meet Me in St. Louis,* though Benson's daughter was specific about the amount of money her mother made while working on the dialogue for the film. And some newspaper clippings of the time list Benson as having worked on both *National Velvet* in 1944, usually ascribed to Helene Deutsch, and the

1949 remake of *Little Women,* though this is not corroborated in film history books. She also wrote several Disney films and contributed to television shows such as "Dr. Kildare" and the Chrysler Theater in the early years of television. In the fifties—not a prime time for women writers in movies—she was making over $100,000 a year.

It is certainly true that as a writer Benson was not only prolific, but agile at moving among forms. Her first formal job was interviewing celebrities for the *New York Morning Telegraph* (her sister had a column at that paper), and she became a film critic under the pen name Esther Evarts for *The New Yorker,* to which she also regularly contributed short stories. Benson also adapted fiction by Booth Tarkington and F. Scott Fitzgerald for the Broadway stage. Perhaps she was best known for her "Junior Miss" series in *The New Yorker* which eventually became a play and successful film. Her nostalgic stories of her St. Louis childhood first appeared in *The New Yorker,* under the title "5135 Kensington"; the film version was highly successful and starred Judy Garland.

Benson was the youngest of four sisters and one brother, and moved with her family to New York when she was eleven years old. She was educated at the Horace Mann School. Golseth said her aunts—Benson's sisters—were all witty and accomplished women and that dinner table conversations at their family home were wonderful to listen to, probably because their generation's sensibility was actually formed in an era when a number of women were in the professions and leaders of the community with very little fuss made about it. (Golseth said that Benson was born in 1896, though the *New York Times* obituary has her birthdate as 1900.) This suffragette movement is viewed by most social historians as the second great wave of feminist activity, with the first concurrent with the Abolitionist movement. And the third, of course, in our own time.

Golseth did draw this distinction, however: "My mother was totally apolitical. She was a feminist, though I don't think she ever really thought about it that much one way or another. But she would have died rather than stay at home and be a housewife. It was sort of just assumed that I would be a writer, or something." Golseth's father was a coach at Columbia University. (The couple eventually divorced amicably. He remarried, but Benson did not.) Golseth said that her father was very much in awe of Benson's talent, stepping aside, as it were, to let Benson's talent shine.

An article in Benson's journalistic alma mater, the *New York Morning Telegraph,* explains her break into writing in the following way, adopting Benson's attitude of carefree worldliness that seems to be common to the cosmopolitan writers of the late thirties and forties:

> Back in 1923, the idea of becoming a professional writer was as foreign to Miss Benson's scheme of things as a rocket journey to the moon. Her only source of income had been derived from a job in the foreign exchange department of the National City Bank.
>
> In the late fall of 1923, however, she attended a performance of *Queen Victoria,* presented by the Equity Players at the Forty-Eighth Street Theater. In the role of Prince Albert of Coburg was a handsome actor named Ulrich Haupt. Miss Benson determined to meet him. She went backstage after a performance, introduced herself as a staff writer for *The Morning Telegraph* and asked for an interview. Haupt, who had been completely ignored by the metropolitan press, was only too happy to comply. Miss Benson found him a fine fellow, began to have qualms over the deception she had practiced, and finally resolved her dilemma by deciding to write a story about the actor to submit to *The Morning Telegraph.*
>
> The editors accepted it readily—as editors have been wont to do with Miss Benson's copy ever since—and asked her to write special features for their Sunday editions. For approximately three years she interviewed such celebrities of the day as Sinclair Lewis, Roger Wolfe Kahn, Howard Carter (King Tut's digger-upper) and other notables of the mid-twenties.
>
> (unsigned and undated article in the *New York Morning Telegraph,* Billy Rose Theatre Collection, Lincoln Center)

This is clearly a valentine to one of the paper's former writers, but it is also and obviously the zippy version that Benson wanted to get out. (One of Benson's sisters, Agnes Smith, had been a columnist at the *Telegraph.* Benson also wrote for a number of movie fanzines, one of which, *Photoplay,* was edited by Smith's husband.)

The tone is similar to the chipper dialogue Benson uses in her movie dialogue: here it is from *Anna and the King of Siam:*

KING
[*turning to her*]

Why do you contradict me?

ANNA

But I'm only trying to help you.

KING

Is it help to say I am wrong? How can King be wrong and woman be right? I ask you that! How?

ANNA

I'm afraid, Your Majesty, that it does happen sometimes.

There's an ease and sprightliness here in even a "male-female" discussion that one would never find in our more self-conscious age. In a very flattering interview with Benson for the *New York Post* (February 7, 1944), this is the description of the next stage of Benson's professional career:

> Next came movie reviews for a magazine. For interviews or reviews, she never took a note nor kept a program. In 1930 she decided she needed some extra money, dashed off "The Apartment Hotel," sold it [a first try, to *The New Yorker*], and basked in the glory of it until she was broke again nine months later, when she wrote another.
>   And so it goes. She says she still never writes unless she needs the money—which is all the time.

This sounds a bit disingenuous from a woman who regularly contributed fiction to *The New Yorker*, *Scribners*, *Collier's*, and the *American Mercury*, wrote numerous film scripts, and even a Broadway play. One contemporaneous critic (Charles Poore of the *New York Times*) compared her short stories to those of Katherine Mansfield and Dorothy Parker. Flighty or unmotivated? It wouldn't seem so.

Sally Benson

Barbara Golseth did say,

She was a very finished writer. She never kept a copy of anything. I think she worked it all out in her head at night, and then just went in the next day and wrote it all down. In the New York years, she had an office at *The New Yorker.* And when they found out she never kept a copy of anything, they nearly died.

Next to John O'Hara, she was their most prolific writer. She would write twenty-four short stories at twenty cents a word. Of course she was paid a lot more when she went to Hollywood. I think Ross [Harold Ross, *The New Yorker*'s editor] was very bitter when she went to Hollywood.

Up through the early forties Benson had been doing a film review column for *The New Yorker,* sometimes as Esther Evarts, sometimes under her own name. Here is her carefree style in her review of *The Boys From Syracuse* in the August 10, 1940, issue:

The Rodgers-and-Hart musical comedy...has been revised, not very successfully, as summer-weight amusement for the films. It seems almost more than one can bear to have to put up with two Allan Joneses and two Joe Penners during the dog days. And what might seem sprightly and even gay in crisp football weather is somehow too much to stand in one of the hottest spurts of the year. When you are yearning to bundle off to the beach and relax under an umbrella, the sight of Martha Raye working like a beaver is oppressive.

Like other writers from New York—in a pattern that ranges all the way from Unger to Alice Duer Miller to Delmar to the Ephrons—Benson was a "name" and a best-selling author when she was called for by the studios. (In some sense though she had a strong female professional support base through her sisters and their connections.) MGM bought *Meet Me in St. Louis,* based on Benson's magazine pieces, for a film musical to star Judy Garland. Margaret O'Brien was cast as Tootie, the youngest sister and stand-in for Benson. Garland was Esther, Tootie's older sister. (According to Golseth, "When my Aunt Esther was dying she said, 'Don't forget Judy Garland played me.'" These deathbed stories always have an apocryphal ring to

Judy Garland with Tom Drake in *Meet Me In St. Louis*

them of course, such as Phoebe Ephron's telling her daughter Nora "Take notes. It's all copy," when she was dying of cancer, as described by Henry Ephron in *We Thought We Could Do Anything.*)

Golseth said that Benson was very pleased with *Meet Me in St. Louis,* which came out in 1944. She also said that Benson was considered a very good dialogue writer and was paid $5,000 to write dialogue for the film. But Benson is nowhere mentioned on the title page of the script except for the line indicating that *Meet Me in St. Louis* was based on her book. The screenplay credits are given to Irving Brecher and Fred F. Finklehoffe. But since we know Benson was the dialogue coach, and we also know that the part of Tootie is based on her, it might be safe to say that she had a strong influence on specifically this dialogue.

About St. Louis, Tootie says early in the film, "It isn't a town, Mr. Neely. It's a city. It's the only city that has a World's Fair. My favorite. Wasn't I lucky to be born in my favorite city?" And a bit later the spunky Tootie says, "Here comes the invalid. I have to have two kinds of ice-cream. I'm recooperating [sic]."

And though there are of course three screenwriters who worked on the psychologically intricate Hitchcock film *Shadow of a Doubt,* it is possible to pick up a bit or piece that might have come from Benson: the picturesque, nostalgic feeling in the beginning of the film is underscored as the family, which uncle and murderer Joseph Cotten is visiting, looks at old pictures. Cotten, or Uncle Charlie, says to his niece, who is named after him, "Everybody was sweet and pretty then, Charlie." Or the snippy little bluestocking-in-the-making who plays Teresa Wright's younger sister with some speeches which are tartly Bensonlike. When her older sister refuses a gift, her younger sibling says, "Just like girls in books. The ones who say they don't want anything get more in the end."

Golseth said that Benson very much liked California after she moved there. She did return east on demand, writing, for instance, the Broadway musical adaptation of the Booth Tarkington story "Seventeen." But she mainly settled in California, bridging the gap from films to television in the fifties, such as the musical movie *Hans Brinker* with Tab Hunter for TV.

Conspirator is a 1950 political thriller starring Elizabeth Taylor, sixteen at the time of the making of the film, and Robert Taylor (no relation). Although it was based on the novel by Humphrey Slater, Benson was the sole author of the film which picked up on the fear of Communism. Here is the facilely written scene in which the hero is found out by his wife, and he tries to explain his feelings to her:

INT. *Bedroom*—MS—*Melinda seated at left—Michael standing beside her*—CAMERA PANS *right, then left, as he paces forward, then back to her—he exits left—*

MICHAEL

If you only knew what it was like to be in Dublin in those days right in the thick of it. Secret meetings, shades drawn, lights turned low. Those great men all talking at once. The Party lost the battle in Ireland, but I learned. I used to sit on a footstool by the fire and listen. They didn't even notice me then. But they noticed me, I can tell you, when I drilled with them in the rain in the wild Wicklow Hills. Think of it, Linda. I was only fifteen then, and—and drilling with the best of them. That was summer. At the end of it, I had to go back to my father, who didn't even like me.

MCS—*Michael turns and looks to r.f.g.*—CAMERA TRUCKS *back to right as he steps forward, entering—Melinda seated at right—*

MICHAEL

But I'd learned to keep secrets, important secrets; and I used to laugh to myself because he didn't know what I was thinking. Have I made you understand, Linda? Have I made you understand any of it?

MELINDA

No, Michael. I can't understand you. I can't understand any of it. All I know is it's wrong and I hate it!

MICHAEL

And me? You hate me?

MCU—*Melinda looks up left and reacts—*

MELINDA

You must give it up! If you don't, I swear I'll find some way to stop you. I'll leave you…

MCS—*Michael standing at left—Melinda seated at right— Melinda puts her hands on his arms—she stands—*

MELINDA

…but I'll find some way to stop you, too.

MICHAEL

Turn me in? Is that what you're thinking?

MELINDA

Oh, give it up, Michael! Give it up! We'll never mention it again. We'll forget it ever happened—never think about it!

MICHAEL

So I must choose. My whole life up to now, or you. My whole life or you. Well, there can't be any doubt, Linda— no doubt which I choose. I love you, darling.

MELINDA

You give it up?

MICHAEL

I give it up.

(Reel 3, p. 18)

He doesn't of course, but that's later in the script.

It's odd to think of a former writer for *The New Yorker* doing a movie for Elvis, but Benson's 1964 script for *Viva Las Vegas* again shows her versatility. Or else you could say she's working with the kind of material offered to her at that time. Here's the central duet scene between Lucky (Elvis Presley) and Rusty (Ann-Margret):

EXT. *Dressing Room*—CS—*Lucky leans closer to door as he sings—people at pool at l.b.g.—*

LUCKY
[*sings*]

The lady loves me
But she doesn't know it yet...

INT. *Dressing Room*—MCS—*Rusty stands behind screen, her garments flung across top of screen—she sings, gesturing—*

RUSTY
[*sings*]

The gentleman has savoir faire
As much as an elephant or a bear...

EXT. *Dressing Room*—CS—*Lucky—people in l.b.g. moving about pool—others swimming—*

RUSTY
[*sings o.s.*]

I'd like to take him on a spin
Back to the zoo, to visit his kin...

INT. *Dressing Room—*MCS*—Rusty comes forward from behind screen, singing—*CAMERA TRUCKS *back to left as she moves toward entrance at left—leans against door—folds her arms in front of her—picks up garment and starts to exit left—*

RUSTY
[*sings*]

He's got about as much appeal
As a soggy cigarette
The lady loathes him
But he doesn't know it yet...

EXT. *Dressing Room—*MLS*—Rusty comes out of dressing room and faces Lucky who strums his guitar at left—*CAMERA TRUCKS *back to left as she moves toward l.f.g. and he follows her—*TRUCKS *in to left as she moves to pool and grabs onto pole, turning to face Lucky at right—*TRUCKS *in to left as she backs to another pole...*

LUCKY
[*sings*]

The lady's got a crush on me

RUSTY
[*sings*]

The gentleman's crazy, obviously

LUCKY
[*sings*]

The gentleman needs a psychiatrist
I'd rather kiss a rattlesnake
Or play Russian roulette

[*cont'd*]

(Reel 2, pp. 3, 4)

Benson could do the kind of low-life dialogue and atmosphere typical of a Vegas club, too:

MS—*Employee runs forward to casino manager at left, as latter mops his head with handkerchief and reacts— Camera shooting past Lucky and Mancini who move toward him from r.f.g.—employee exits right, in excited manner as Lucky and Mancini approach manager—gesture with him—he reacts in nervous manner, mopping his balding head again with his handkerchief—loud and indistinct ad libs heard from wild crowd—*CAMERA TRUCKS *in as Lucky gestures to manager again, then holds up his hand, moving toward crowd in b.g.—he takes a Western hat from head of Texan and grabs pistols from other Westerners—then he moves through crowd to distant b.g.—wild confusion seen—*

EMPLOYEE

Boss, I've done all I could, but—

MANAGER

I know—I know! Go get yourself a drink—or ten!

LUCKY

Do you have a girl working here, about so high?

MANCINI

With legs—incomparable!?

MANAGER

I don't know what kind of girls I got, but troubles I got plenty!

LUCKY

What time does the next show go on?

MANAGER

There isn't going to be any show until I get these crazy sons—until I get them out of here!

(Reel 1, p. 17)

Here's an action scene with Rusty that is quite forward-looking for 1964, Beatlemania notwithstanding; and for a writer who was either sixty-four or sixty-eight when she wrote the script.

EXT. *Racing Area*—MLS—*Rusty and Lucky come forward on motorcycles and Lucky rides without hands*—CAMERA TRUCKS *back ahead of them*—*Rusty rises up on her motorcycle and rides without hands, also*—

MCS—CAMERA TRUCKS *back ahead of Lucky, riding motorcycle*—*he jigs about*—

MLS—*Rusty stands up on her motorcycle as Lucky watches from behind on his*—*she gestures and moves with rhythm on moving motorcycle*—

(Reel 2, pp. 15–16)

And no less a reviewer than Howard Thomson in his May 21 *New York Times* review praised the "tunes" or interpolated songs as they were termed, as "nice, especially one poolside duet by the hero and heroine....All this, from the pen of no less a writer than Sally Benson, unfolds against the stunningly picturesque bckground of the famed resort, photographed in excellent color. Miss Benson's script snugly combs the entire area."

According to her daughter, Benson had very few complaints about the way the movie business treated her; she even liked Louis B. Mayer, which makes a telling contrast with McCall. "I don't think she ever felt she was prejudiced against in the movie business at all because of being a woman." Benson died with very little money, said Golseth, as she had no head for business. (Some newspaper accounts of Benson say she liked the racetrack, though she claimed to have bet very little on each individual horse.) "She was once offered a house on Rodeo Drive [today's chic high rent shopping district in Beverly Hills], but turned it down because it cost $55,000, too much she thought," Golseth chuckled. Benson died in California in 1972.

Benson's own tongue-in-cheek assessment of her Hollywood years appeared in the *Brooklyn Eagle* (July 8, 1952), "I'm a fast worker—they found that out when I was under contract in Hollywood, and you never saw more jobs shoved onto one author. I was darned well paid, of course, but I realized too late that they actually were saving money by letting Benson do it." She added, with characteristic bite, "I've been accused of violating the child labor laws by getting so much mileage out of teenagers in my writings, but that isn't quite the point."

Catherine Turney was an MGM woman writer in the late thirties and forties, and she was a working writer at the age of eighty-seven in summer 1993 when interviewed by telephone at her home in her native California. She said she now works every day at the Huntington Library at the University of California. Turney studied at the Pasadena School of the Theater in California before moving to New York and becoming a successful playwright. With Jerry Horwin, she wrote a well-received 1939 Broadway play, *My Dear Children,* which starred John Barrymore. She also wrote radio sketches and *Bitter Harvest,* a 1936 play about Byron. So once more it was a case of a name writer rather easily making inroads in the movie business.

"*They* came after me," said Turney. "I think it's still the same today. If you can get a name for yourself, they may take a chance with you. But I think it's even harder today. I don't know what I would advise people now. And television—that's one thing I really don't understand anymore."

But getting in was not the same as staying in, she observed. "It was really quite brutal. One day you would go in and they'd be packing up the things of a person working next to you at the studio. No notice. They'd just be putting his things in boxes when he came to work. He had no idea."

At MGM, Turney said she worked on the 1937 *The Bride Wore Red* ("a terrible film" she said). In 1942 she was hired at Warner Brothers, and while there wrote *My Reputation* for Barbara Stanwyck (1945), the second version of *Of Human Bondage* (1946) for Paul Henreid and Eleanor Parker, *Cry Wolf* (1947) for Stanwyck and Errol Flynn, and *Winter Meeting* (1948) for Bette Davis. She shared writing credit for *One More Tomorrow* in 1946. In 1950 she and Sally Benson cowrote *No Man of Her Own,* also a Stanwyck film. Additionally, she wrote the script for the 1947 film *The Man I Love,* directed by Raoul Walsh and starring Ida Lupino as a cafe chanteuse in love with a pianist who is in love with a society girl. The precise credits are "screen play by Catherine Turney; adapted by Jo Pagano and Miss Turney from a novel by Maritta Wolff." And she wrote *Japanese War Bride* in 1952 and *Back From the Dead* in 1958.

Turney also said that she worked on the script of *Mildred Pierce* in 1945, and added, "Joan Crawford didn't want to play the part at first. Nobody wanted the role of a mother to a teenage daughter."

Turney's name does not appear on the title page of *Mildred Pierce*, however, which credits—as do all film source books—Ranald MacDougall, adapting the James M. Cain novel. It is the same problem of uncredited writers—women and men alike—throughout film history, though it may be more acute with women writers. In any event, Turney knew enough details about the making of the movie that she must have worked on it. Her version of the script did not use flashbacks, she said, and retained Veda's—Crawford's cinematic daughter—interest in classical music.

She said that her personal favorite is *A Stolen Life*, the 1946 Bette Davis film about the popular forties female duality: twins with very different characters, generally representing the good and bad girl. Some feminist critics now see this forties phenomenon as film's way of dealing with the only two distinct possibilities for behavior that American society's double standard offered at the time. (Other forties twins movies, not written by Turney, are *Cobra Woman, Dark Mirror,* and *Here Come the Waves.*)

A Stolen Life, which was directed by Curtis Bernhardt, and based on the novel by Karel J. Benes, has Bette Davis playing identical twins: a sexy, "bad" Pat who temporarily gets the man—Glenn Ford, playing Bill, with whom both sisters are in love—because she dresses provocatively. The other twin, Kate, is plain, straightforward, and sporting: she says at one point to her sister, "I know my limitations. And I'm satisfied to stay within them."

Turney has written a scene which captures the difference in the appeal of the two women to a man. Bill has been confused and thinks there is only one woman for a while, and hasn't been attracted to the less adorned Kate. When he meets the more dolled up Pat, this is how Turney has the scene play out:

[*She (Patricia) is dressed all in white and is very chic.*]

BILL

You really are dressed up today.

PAT

I always dress up for a luncheon date.

A bit later in the scene:

BILL

Maybe I can explain it this way. It's like you were a cake—
a cake—er—without any frosting.

PAT

I guess most guys—they kind of like frosting.

PAT
[*smiling*]
Today, you think I'm well frosted.

PAT
[*giggling*]
You thought I wasn't frosted!

When the more earnest Kate opts for a career as an artist after
not getting the guy, a would-be suitor says to her, "All this art stuff.
That's been a substitute for something else. You're always running
away. You'll never land a guy, always closed up inside like this." And
when she rejects this suitor because she is still in love with Bill, the
other man, Karnok, says, "Now don't be so feminine. Try to
understand yourself." And finally he accuses her in disgust of being
like all women, and of wanting "the grand passion or nothing." "Yes.
We do," answers Kate.

A Stolen Life was enormously popular with audiences, and
Charles Higham and Joel Greenberg in *Hollywood in the Forties* call
it "the most enjoyable of Bette Davis's vehicles. . . . Once more, the
film has cultural overtones: the good twin is a painter, who has a
tormented love affair with another, more avant-garde artist, played
with unshaven chin and bad manners by Dane Clark ('Man needs
woman, that's basic'). The script is full of the usual Warners cultural
talk: attending an exhibition of the good girl's work, Sylvester Pringle,
New England's greatest art critic, says: 'Excellent. . . a touch of
Rousseau?'" (pp. 164–65) Still, no mention is made of Turney as
screenwriter.

As a dialogue writer, Turney can be witty. At one point, Bill says,
"Your sister is a dangerous woman. She could extract secrets out of a

Catherine Turney (a contemporary photograph)

sphinx," and Kate excuses her affairs during her eventual marriage to him: "Naïveté is hard to live with."

Turney's script for Stanwyck in *Cry Wolf* (1947) has also been praised. According to Higham and Greenberg:

Apart from her major classics of the period—*The Lady Eve, Double Indemnity,* and *Sorry, Wrong Number*—Stanwyck's best remains *Cry Wolf* (1947), beautifully directed by the neglected Peter Godfrey. She played Sandra Demarest, a geologist arriving at the mansion of her late husband, who is supposedly dead but is in fact incarcerated in a private lunatic asylum on the grounds. Convinced that evil things are afoot, Sandra suspects the chemist custodian of the house (Errol Flynn, equipped with pipe and spectacles) of murder. Enterprisingly—this was a part "made" for Stanwyck—she clambers over roofs in the middle of the night or even essays a journey by dumb-waiter, to spy on Flynn in his laboratory (he rudely orders her out the same way). Screams in the night, creaking stairs, two death-falls from balcony to patio, and sinister journeys through woods make up a rich melodramatic brew.

All of this is done with a great deal of sophisticated flair, and Franz Waxman's score is brilliantly menacing. Sandra Demarest's first arrival at the mansion is on a storm-swept afternoon, a mysterious girl on horseback galloping past her car, thunder gathering over brooding trees, is marvelously shot and cut. And even better is Sandra's long hunt through the woods for her lost husband, crickets ringing deafeningly in the underbrush, the camera tracking Rashomon-like through trees and scrub, birds flapping startled from beneath her feet.

(p. 169)

Everything else—director, score, acting—gets mentioned. Though the authors do note that the part was "made" for Stanwyck, they don't say by whom.

Turney said that she felt no financial discrimination against her as a woman writer in the era she was at her peak and that she was very well paid indeed. But her marriages, one to a director and one to an actor, suffered as a result of her success. "They were both nice guys. But it was very hard for their egos when I was making much more money than they were. It wasn't really their fault. They tried."

She said that she believes it was an obvious fit that what we've come to think of as the "woman's film" of the forties would have scripts by women writers, and—in a similar observation though cast in a different light by a number of different contemporary writers— Turney said, "It's a natural that certain topics are best treated by women." She pointed out that Stanwyck and Davis would both request that Turney be put on a picture for this very reason.

"Byron said it best. Love is a woman's whole existence, isn't it?" This seems to be some primitive, perhaps more reactionary, version of Nora Ephron's more witty observation, in the character of Dottie, in *This Is My Life* (1990) that "Men are never between women. They are between meals, or between games, or between appointments."

But feminist politics aside, the economic incentive was clear. Underscoring Hollywood's awareness that women writers being used for women's parts was a saleable commodity in the early 1940s, screenwriters' names were used to advertise films. Sonya Levien's name is mentioned in the 1945 ad for *The Valley of Decision,* a film starring Greer Garson, adapted from the novel by Marcia Davenport. "You'll remember a lot of the lines from the screen play by Sonya Levien and John Meehan," declares the ad, which promises an exciting story about Mary Rafferty, an Irish beauty who is quite a character.

Another "woman's specialist" was Joan Harrison, who wrote *Jamaica Inn* in 1939, *Rebecca* and *Foreign Correspondent* in 1940, *Suspicion* in 1941 for which Joan Fontaine won the Academy Award, *Saboteur* in 1942, and *Dark Waters* in 1944—all except the last for Alfred Hitchcock. She was his longtime assistant and you might say her work in the Gothic melodramatic mode returned the genre to its Brontë-esque, female origins.

However corny and melodramatic it might appear today, *Jamaica Inn* does at least feature a spirited, inquisitive heroine, as much a part of the Gothic mold for a female—"I've come all the way from Ireland alone," says Maureen O'Hara—as well as the additional "modern" fillip of her trying to get her aunt to leave her abusive husband. This

Hitchcock film has a script by Harrison and Sidney Gilliat, and continuity by Alma Reville, Hitchcock's wife.

Harrison was British, born in 1911, and educated at the Sorbonne. Though she came from a newspaper publishing family, she was not allowed to go into the "dirty" business of journalism. She first was a secretary to Hitchcock, eventually becoming an editor, a script reader, and then a scriptwriter.

Though there are the usual newspaper reports of her beating out the other two hundred applicants for the job of secretary, perhaps an added appeal was that her uncle was a keeper of the Old Bailey, which housed the law courts of London. Harrison developed an interest in and regularly visited Scotland Yard and—later—the daily police lineups.

In an interview given to the *Christian Science Monitor* in December of 1960, she had this advice for young women starting out in writing or television: "Don't be too proud to start at the bottom. Experience in all phases of the work—secretarial, cutting, story editor, scriptwriter—all this experience helps. But get in and don't expect to earn very much at first."

Eventually Harrison made the move to full-time producing— along with Virginia Van Upp and Harriet Parsons (Louella's daughter), one of the very few women producers in the late forties—and kept producing through the sixties, mainly in television, with a series of thirty-nine films for her friend Ella Raines, and—of course— "Alfred Hitchcock Presents." As a movie producer her work included *Phantom Lady* in 1944 and *The Strange Affair of Uncle Harry* in 1945 (both with Ella Raines), *Nocturne* in 1946, *They Won't Believe Me* and *Ride the Pink Horse* in 1947, *Once More My Darling* in 1949, and *Eye Witness* and *Circle of Danger* in 1950.

In a 1944 *Screen World,* Harrison is discussed in an article describing her departure from screenwriting for Hitchcock, and declaring her the only woman producer in Hollywood, taking up offices at Universal. "She's going to specialize in mystery films— 'from the woman's angle,' she adds. 'Women must have something to pull for, you know, whether it's a dog, a horse, an old beggar—or even another woman!'"

And following the pattern of the media making the most of women in positions of power in the early forties, an article by Myrtle Gebhart in the *Boston Sunday Post* (August 13, 1944) opens:

Are the motion picture companies beginning to realize that a woman may have something besides legs and a pretty face? Always the feminine sex has fought a losing battle in Hollywood in producing or directorial capacities, though Lois Weber and Dorothy Arzner, to name but two of several, gave us some of our best "woman's angle" films.

Now it seems that the higher-ups are giving women a chance at the helm. Virginia Van Upp, who has written countless scripts, produced *The Impatient Years* at Columbia. Harriet Parsons is assigned to produce *The Enchanted Cottage* for RKO. And Joan Harrison is associate producer of *Dark Waters,* now being reeled.

Alma Reville and Harrison were the coscriptors of *Suspicion,* a novel adaptation, which depended on a shy English girl (Joan Fontaine) married to a man she eventually comes to suspect (following the *Jane Eyre* pattern of course, as does *Rebecca*). Reville started as an editor, or cutter, in England, at the age of sixteen in 1915 on the first screen version of *The Prisoner of Zenda*. She met Hitchcock at the Famous Players-Lasky Studio in 1922, and became his assistant director on *The Pleasure Garden* (1925) and *The Lodger* (1926). Films as cowriter for Hitchcock include *Juno and the Paycock* (1929), *The 39 Steps* (1935), *The Lady Vanishes* (1938), *Jamaica Inn* (1939), *Suspicion* (1941), *Shadow of a Doubt* (1944), and *The Paradine Case* (1947). For other directors, she cowrote *The Passing of the Third Floor Back* in 1935 and *It's in the Bag,* a 1945 Fred Allen vehicle.

Film historians have generally assigned Reville a secondary role as a writer, particularly after her marriage to Hitchcock, observing that after the birth of their daughter she generally only worked on films which were in trouble, and often on films which reflected a betrayal of a woman by a man in a kind of art-imitates-life parallel: Hitchcock is reported to have lost interest in Reville after a time. Others give her the secondary role of "constructive critic" for the male director's work.

Still, the knockout speech in *Shadow of a Doubt* that Joseph Cotten delivers does not seem to have the Sally Benson peal, nor the tone of Thornton Wilder either, and it is this journalist's guess that it must have come from Reville, it is indeed so darkly, misogymistically

Hitchcockian:

> The cities are full of middle-aged women. Women whose husbands spent their lives making fortunes and died. And what do the wives do? These useless women. You see them in the best hotels, these silly women. Every day by the thousands. Eating their money, drinking their money. Playing bridge and losing their money. Playing all day and night. Proud of their jewelry but nothing else. Horrible. Faded, fat, greedy women.

Teresa Wright, playing his niece Charlie, cries out, "But they're alive! They're human beings." Extreme close-up on Cotten's eyes: "Are they, Charlie? Or are they fat wheezing animals? And what happens to animals when they get too fat and too old?"

Strong female parts can be found in the work of playwright and screenwriter Jane Murfin, who had joined the movie business in the teens, being lured from a successful career as a playwright on Broadway (though Murfin was originally from Michigan). Her first stage play, *The Right to Lie,* was produced in 1908 and later turned into her first motion picture, directed by Edwin Carewe in 1919. Other plays of hers written in collaboration with or for actress Jane Cowl were also made into movies: these include *Daybreak,* in 1917; and, specifically for women stars, *Lilac Time,* with actress Colleen Moore in 1928; their play was the basis for the film *Smilin' Through,* with Norma Talmadge in 1922; the same play-into-film with Norma Shearer in 1932; and again with Jeanette Macdonald in 1941. Murfin wrote for Constance Bennett in *What Price Hollywood?* and *Rockabye* (1932), Irene Dunne in *The Silver Cord* and *Roberta* (1935), and often for Katharine Hepburn.

In the thirties and forties she wrote films including *Crime Doctor, The Fountain, The Little Minister,* and *Spitfire* (all 1934); *Alice Adams* (1935); *The Shining Hour* (1938); *Stand Up and Fight* and *The Women* (co-authored with Anita Loos, both films 1939); *Pride and Prejudice* (1940, co-authored with Aldous Huxley); *Andy Hardy's Private Secretary* (1941); *Flight for Freedom* (1943); *Dragon Seed* (1944).

Murfin had already started writing scripts for Famous Players-

Lasky while still in New York; in Hollywood, she wrote more than sixty scripts, and directed and produced some of them, particularly in the twenties, in the same pattern of other writers who went after some powerful positions during this era. In one of her earliest projects, Murfin wrote a series of pictures for Strongheart—a German shepherd dog who had formerly served in a Red Cross unit in the Army. Beginning in 1922, five pictures were made for First National, and Strongheart—along with Rin-Tin-Tin—was a big canine movie star.

In 1934 Murfin was appointed the first woman supervisor of motion pictures at RKO and some of her first writing projects there included *The Little Minister* (1934) with Katharine Hepburn and John Beal and the Jerome Kern musical *Roberta* (1935) with Irene Dunne, Fred Astaire, and Ginger Rogers. In 1935 Murfin went to Samuel Goldwyn where she wrote *Come and Get It,* directed by William Wyler. For Katharine Hepburn, Murfin, who died in 1955, wrote five films, the last being *Dragon Seed.*

Dragon Seed is the adaptation by Jane Murfin and Marguerite Roberts of the Pearl Buck novel, with Hepburn playing the very strong, unusually independent Jade. The movie contains numerous discussions of a woman's place in society and within (and without) marriage. There's a thrashing out of what we might today call feminist issues, though the film is set in rural China, about to be attacked by Japan on the eve of World War II. The advertisements for the film told the prospective audience that it was "the glorious story of a girl with a fighting heart and the man who fought by her side."

Jade can read, while her husband can't, and the opening discussion in the film about a Chinese family concerns whether or not Jade should get a book she wants. She is referred to in the movie as "newfangled": ultimately Jade even fights with the men in the hills and—employing the best of both worlds—flirts with the Japanese army while poisoning their food. And unlike her sister-in-law, who sacrifices herself by diverting the enemy from her two babies by walking in front of the soldiers (and thereby getting raped and dying, though still for the honor of the family), Jade is a triumphant, self-reliant, and yet still loving to her husband figure throughout. The implication of this 1944 movie is that perhaps Chinese women should learn to become strong and independent: i.e., like American women.

Some of the writing in the script is extraordinarily lovely—when

Jade and her husband are on the road, traveling with the army, there is "mud so thick it held them back like evil hands. Rain so thick fish could live in it." And after a bomb has dropped on the farmland, the patriarch says, "How could men do this to other men? The sky is over us all."

The movie opens with an elegiac voiceover about the Chinese family: "They were both good and bad. Both wise and foolish. And sometimes all these things at the same moment. And therefore they were very much like such families in any other land." Jade is described by her young husband in the beginning of the film as "like the Western wind. When I reach for her she is gone. . . . She is mine and she is not mine. When I touch her, her spirit goes. Only her body remains. . . . I have not found Jade in the same place twice and never waiting for me."

And it can be funny too: Jade's mother-in-law complains that "these new-fashioned women are not so easily beaten," and that "nowadays women run around like goats."

Marguerite Roberts was cowriter of the screenplay for *Dragon Seed*. Roberts's rise in the film industry came through her own hard work, and not from any prior reputation. Born in Nebraska, she worked as a model, then a reporter in California before becoming a secretary for a number of studio executives at Fox in 1926. Bit by bit she worked her way up, first as a reader and then a screenwriter. Her first screenplay credit was on the 1933 film *Sailor's Luck*, directed by Raoul Walsh.

This in fact is how the *New York Sun*, on April 4, 1933, rather charmingly described her breakthrough in a brief "filler" article:

Those two young stenographers at Fox Movietone City, Marguerite Roberts and Charlotte Miller, who broke into scenario writing with *Sailor's Luck*, are now definitely on the writing staff. They are working on *The Tough Guy*, Mauri Grashin-James Seymour original which will star James Dunn. The two script writers are hunting story atmosphere at the Union Stock Yards in Los Angeles. This story, like David Karsner's *Red Meat*, in which Edward G. Robinson will appear, has a stock yard background.

Marguerite Roberts

In the thirties, Roberts wrote the Paramount pictures *Hollywood Boulevard, Florida Special,* and *Rose Bowl* (all 1936) and *Turn Off the Moon* and *Wild Money* (both 1937). At MGM she shared credit on *Escape* in 1940, wrote *Ziegfeld Girl* with Sonya Levien in 1941, shared credit on *Honky Tonk* in 1941, wrote *Somewhere I'll Find You* in 1942, shared credit on *Undercurrent* and *Sea of Grass* in 1946, shared credit on *If Winter Comes* in 1947, and wrote *Desire Me* in 1947 with Zoë Akins.

But in 1951 Roberts was described to the House Committee on Un-American Activities as a Communist by screenwriter Martin Berkeley. She took the First and Fifth Amendments in declining to tell the committee what she knew about Communist infiltration in Hollywood. She was blacklisted for nine years after refusing Dore Schary's demand that she change her testimony and name names. Since she was at the time about to begin a new five-year contract with the studio, she was able to negotiate a lucrative settlement that helped her and her husband, also a blacklisted writer, survive those years.

Columbia producer Jerry Bresler rehired Roberts to write *Diamond Head* in 1960, and she resumed an active career which included *Love Has Many Faces* (1965), *5 Card Stud* (1968), *Norwood* and *Red Sky at Morning* (both 1970), and *Shootout* (1971), as well as *True Grit* in 1969, adapted from Charles Portis's novel, which won John Wayne his only Oscar, and for which Roberts received a Writers Guild of America nomination. In 1988, Roberts appeared on a PBS Special, "John Wayne Standing Tall." There was irony in her working on the same project with Wayne, a blacklist supporter.

Marguerite Roberts died in 1989 at age eighty-four.

The heyday of women's pictures, and writers, was, however, drawing to a close. Film historians Higham and Greenberg, in *Hollywood in the Forties,* say that by the end of the decade,

women's pictures were on their way out as a genre. With the war's end, and the upsurge of neo-realist crime films, the beginning of a new need for true-life stories, soap-operas began to lose their appeal. By 1950, Bette Davis and Joan Crawford, Ann Sheridan and Ida Lupino, had left Warner

Brothers and Greer Garson was almost finished at Metro. They went their separate ways, to cheaper and cheaper vehicles, until they wound up in crude B quickies (Crawford), death or retirement (Sheridan and Garson), or a new and more modest career as director (Lupino). Only Bette Davis has managed to hang on, with increasing insecurity, as a star of, at least, minor-A productions.

(p. 173)

One important writer who made the transition from the forties was Isobel Lennart, a playwright who was in Hollywood from early in the decade and who received three Oscar nominations. Alone or in collaboration (basically at MGM) she wrote *Lost Angel* (1944); *Anchors Aweigh* (1945); *Holiday in Mexico* (1946); *It Happened in Brooklyn* (1947); *The Kissing Bandit* (1948); *Holiday Affair* and *East Side West Side* (both 1949); *A Life of Her Own* (1950); *My Wife's Best Friend, It's a Big Country,* and *Skirts Ahoy!* (all 1952); *Latin Lovers* (1953); *Love Me or Leave Me,* which won a joint Oscar with Daniel Fuchs (1955); *Meet Me in Las Vegas* (1956); *This Could Be the Night* (1957); *Merry Andrew* and *Inn of the Sixth Happiness* (both 1958); *Please Don't Eat the Daisies* and *The Sundowners,* for which she was nominated for an Academy Award (both 1960); *Period of Adjustment* and *Two for the Seesaw* (both 1962); *Fitzwilly* (1967); and *Funny Girl,* from her own play, in 1968. She also won a number of Writers Guild awards.

Born in Brooklyn in 1916, Lennart worked as a stenographer and script girl and then enrolled in the junior writer course at Metro, where she became a reader and eventually one of the studio's most prolific writers. Lennart was killed in a car crash in 1971 at age fifty-five.

Lennart seems to have been a writer first and studio worker second. According to MGM colleague Dorothy Kingsley, a writer who often wrote uncredited on lightweight films (though she eventually shared credit with *Seven Brides for Seven Brothers* with Frances Goodrich and Albert Hackett), Lennart took her work very seriously. In answer to the question if there was camaraderie among the women writers in the forties, Kingsley said:

> Oh yes. Isobel and I were very close. She used to run into my office [to talk] all the time. She was a "real writer." I never

think of myself as a "real writer." I only wrote because I needed the money. I had no desire to express myself or anything like that.

When I got home [at night], I never thought about my work or mentioned it. I mean, I wanted to do a good job, but I certainly wasn't going to pace the floor at night. Isobel lived for her work. She would get up in the middle of the night and write down a line. If someone didn't like her script, she'd throw up. I just didn't care. Just give me the money. I needed the money.

Kingsley also mentioned other women writers working for MGM in the forties: "Helen Deutsch was in and out; Dorothy Cooper who started as a junior writer; and Marguerite Roberts." (Interview with Dorothy Kingsley, *Backstory 2: Interviews With Screenwriters of the 1940s and 1950s,* Berkeley: 1991, p. 120).

A former radio writer for Edgar Bergen, Kingsley said that the star Constance Bennett was helpful to her in getting her started in the writing business, another example of the informal female connections system intact up through the forties. In addition to *Seven Brides for Seven Brothers,* Kingsley's films include *Girl Crazy* (uncredited, 1943); *Bathing Beauty* and *Broadway Rhythm* (coscriptor, 1944); *Easy to Wed* (adaption of *Libeled Lady,* 1946); *A Date With Judy* (1948); *Neptune's Daughter* (script, 1949). And in the fifties: *Two Weeks With Love* (1950); *Texas Carnival* (1951); *When in Rome* (coscriptor, 1952); *Kiss Me Kate* (coscriptor, 1953); *Jupiter's Darling* (Kingsley's seventh and last Esther Williams movie, 1955); *Pal Joey* (1957); and *Green Mansions* (1959). In the sixties: *Can-Can* (coscriptor, 1960); *Pepe* (1960); and *Valley of the Dolls* (coscriptor, 1967).

And perhaps Kinglsey should be in the forefront of women who deserve reevaluation. Her 1951 script *Angels in the Outfield,* written with George Wells and directed by Clarence Brown, was called "charming" and "convincing" by the *New York Herald Tribune. Vareity* pointed out the film features Janet Leigh as a newspaperwoman reporting on baseball "from the woman's angle," and the Kingsley-Wells script is indeed the basis for the 1994 Disney film of the same title. Happily, the original script is mentioned in many of the ads for the remake.

4

Writing Teams

It may seem odd to have a chapter about husband-and-wife teams in a book about women screenwriters. And indeed it is.

But the fact is that six important women writers—Sarah Y. Mason, Ruth Gordon, Fay Kanin, Frances Hackett, Dorothy Parker, and Phoebe Ephron all wrote with their husbands as their partners. Of course it's difficult to tell who wrote what in such a collaboration. But it is possible in some cases to see the persona of some of these women shine through some of the female parts they helped create. And if nothing else, many of the films they worked on are simply too important not to mention.

Duo-sexed writing teams were in vogue during the late thirties and forties: "Why, we all had a woman," says Albert Hackett, now in his nineties, quite cheerfully. Hackett was married to Frances Goodrich. Other married screenwriting teams included Mason and Victor Heerman, Ruth Gordon and Garson Kanin, Phoebe and Henry Ephron, Fay and Michael Kanin, Tess Slesinger and Frank Davis, Dorothy Parker and Alan Campbell.

Mason wrote with writer-director husband Victor Heerman, and their work together includes *The Age of Innocence* and *The Little Minister* (both 1934); *Break of Hearts* and *Magnificent Obsession* (both 1935); *Stella Dallas* (1937); *Golden Boy* (1939); and *Little Women* (both 1933 and 1949 versions). But Mason entered the film business on her own, in the early days, and made her inroads in much the same way we have seen other women writers take a shot. In the pattern of other long-timers like Frances Marion and Jane Murfin, Mason managed to make her career last after establishing a strong base early on.

Originally from Tucson, Arizona, Mason entered the movie business in 1918 with the Douglas Fairbanks Company, and then she went to the Thomas Ince Studio as a scriptwriter. An original story, and script, *The Heart of Twenty*, was produced by Robertson Cole, and she wrote original stories and scripts for Metro, Famous-Players, and Selznick, including *Broadway Melody* and *Alias Jimmy Valentine* (both 1929); *They Learned About Women, Love in the Rough*, and *The Girl Said No* (all 1930); *The Man in Possession* (1931); and *Shopworn* (1932). At RKO she wrote with Heerman (who gave up his directing career in 1930 to work exclusively as a writer with Mason) and did *Chance of Heaven* and *Imitation of Life* on her own in 1935, though William Hurlbut is also credited with *Imitation of Life*. Mason was a writer early on, and Heerman followed her lead.

For *Little Women*—the 1933 version, directed by George Cukor—Mason and Heerman won Oscars for Best Screenplay. (They also did the 1949 remake, with the addition of writer Andrew Solt.) And indeed it is a very faithful adaptation, with important passages and episodes retained. Very early in the film, after a reading of a letter from their chaplain father away during the Civil War—nearly exact to the one in the novel—the four girls give their dollar (a Christmas gift from Aunt March) to buy presents for their mother, Marmee (played by Spring Byington). As in the novel, she opens the gifts, and all eagerly await their breakfast. Then Marmee "stops everything with a gesture":

MARMEE

Wait a minute, girls [*from her tone all stop short, realizing something is wrong*]. I want to say one word before we begin. I've just come from a poor woman with a newborn baby and six children huddled into one bed to keep from freezing, for they have no fire. They are suffering from cold and hunger. My girls, will you give them your breakfast as a Christmas present? [*This is a bombshell—but only for a moment.*]

JO
[*breaking the silence, impetuously*]

I'm so glad you came back before we started.

MARMEE
[*joyously*]

I knew you would!

BETH
[*eagerly*]

May I help carry the things, Marmee?

MED. SHOT

MARMEE

We shall all go. Take the coffee, Hannah.

JO

I'll get some firewood.

[*Hannah and Jo go toward the kitchen while the girls pick up the food from the table.*]

MEG

I'll take the cream.

BETH

I'll take the bread.

AMY
[*looking at pop-overs longingly*]

I'll take the pop-overs.

[They start to exit with the dishes of food. LAP DISSOLVE]

INT. ROOM OF HOVEL—MED. SHOT

A desolate picture—broken windows, no fire, ragged bedclothes where the mother is with her wailing baby. The

*other children, half-frozen and hungry, are huddled
together in one corner on a mattress with a thin old quilt,
trying to keep warm. Marmee comes in, followed by the
girls carrying baskets, which they put on the table and
prepare to feed the children.*

MARMEE

Here we are, Mrs. Hummell.

MRS. HUMMELL

Oh, Gott im I Ilimmel! Goot angels come to us.

JO

Funny angels with food and mittens.

[*Everyone, laughing, pitches in. They put wood on the fire.
Jo lights it, then goes to help take care of one of the
younger children.* LAP DISSOLVE *Beth is seated holding the
tiny baby, looking down at it lovingly, while we hear the
girls busy about the room, clearing away the dishes and
putting the place in order.*]

The dialogue and the character of each girl—though shortened a
bit—adheres closely to the novel. Jo is always first: impulsive and
impetuous; and Amy's personal demon is her vanity and love of nice
things. Beth's holding the baby foreshadows her death from nursing
it, but the scene is cheerfully active and noisy, giving the audience
something to look at and hear. The description of the poor woman
and her family's plight has been successfully borrowed: it too has
significant visual impact. (In the film, as in the novel, Mr. Lawrence—
or Laurie—finds out about their act of charity and sends his breakfast
instead.)

Other key visual sequences which reveal the girls' characters are
used, as when Jo and Meg each wear one good glove to a ball and
hold a stained and crumpled one in the other hand. As in the novel,
Jo emerges as the strongest, most interesting character (Katharine
Hepburn in the film) though she mourns the loss of her sister Meg
(Frances Dee), who is falling in love; Jo says to Meg, as in the novel,

"Why can't we stay as we are? You're getting so far away from me."

Another strong and unforgettable female role is to be seen in *Stella Dallas* (1937), directed by King Vidor, with a script by Mason and Heerman based on the novel by Olive Higgins Prouty. Stella (played by Barbara Stanwyck) is vulgar, ambitious, touching, and obnoxious all at once, as the woman whose ambition gets her from the wrong side of the tracks, but who still sacrifices enormously for the daughter she adores. Early on, the screenwriters establish her character: "She looks at her reflection in broken mirror above sink. Certainly SHE thinks better of herself than to throw herself away."

When she meets Stephen (John Boles), the man who will take her away from her sordid surroundings, she explains, "So then they all got the idea at my business course I was—well, different—and that's no good because you can't get along with the people you got to live with if you're different—what are you smiling at?" And Stephen answers, "You *are* different." Then Stella, "You mean that? Because it's so important to me. I mean—being different...more important to me than, well, being anything—[with sudden exaltation]." And she gives a radical, rebellious speech about motherhood: "Tell me, why is it doctors an' nurses an' husbands seem to be the only ones who know anything about this maternity business? Don'tcha think a mother learns anything in that little room you wheel 'em into? (raised eyebrows of satire) Or is that just the kindergarten class? Lemme tell you I picked up quite a little education in here—an' it wasn't outa books either (a little snort) Experience!" Later she turns convincingly (some would say soppily) into a self-sacrificing mother, though she never loses her déclassé mannerisms and speech.

Of all the screenwriting teams in Hollywood, perhaps the best known and "purest" is that of Garson Kanin and Ruth Gordon. Their screen stories were all original, they never worked under contract, no one rewrote their scripts, and they worked closely with the director of their films, George Cukor, a friend. (So that when there are changes from screenplay text to film, at least we know the writers must have had a hand in.) Together, they wrote only four films, but of course those four are classics: *A Double Life* (1948); *Adam's Rib* (1949); *The Marrying Kind* (1951); *Pat and Mike* (1952). Kanin has said that the two argued as they wrote together, and became tired of this, so they stopped writing as a team.

Ruth Gordon with Garson Kanin, Spencer Tracy,
and Katharine Hepburn

Gordon on her own wrote *The Actress* (1953). Based on her
autobiographical play *Years Ago*, it starred Spencer Tracy and Teresa
Wright as her parents and Jean Simmons as a young, rambunctious
Ruth, and won her a Writers Guild nomination. In the *New York
Times*, Bosley Crowther observed: "They say that Ruth Gordon, who
wrote it, both as a film and a play, was fondly recounting her own
girlhood and her dewy eyed longings toward the stage, in which she
ran counter to her father, who was shocked, incredulous and
confused. That could be. The simple little story of a high-school girl's
push to overcome the stubborn resistance of Papa rings quaintly and
adequately true." An actress and writer, she was often leading lady
on the Broadway stage, though perhaps her parts in the films
Rosemary's Baby (1968) and *Harold and Maude* (1972) are most
familiar for today's audiences. The irrepressible Gordon also wrote a
number of unconventional memoirs: *Myself Among Others, My Side,
An Open Book,* and *Shady Lady,* as well as plays and journalism for
The Atlantic Monthly.

In an interview in *Backstory 2,* Kanin notes that she was a published writer long before he was, and says of Gordon, who died in 1985:

> Her strength was always tremendous, tremendous theatrical expertise. She knew more about the theater than anybody that I ever encountered in my life. And she, being a very great actress, could recognize the strengths and the weaknesses in a role, so that she wouldn't allow a part in any of our films to be anything less than a wonderful acting part. Not only the female roles, but especially the female parts—it was almost as though she was going to act them herself. Was it a good enough part? Was the part boring? Was it consistent? Was it flat? Did it lack variety or humor? And she always stuck with that idea of what was going to make a good part. That was a tremendous strength in writing films....
>
> Moss Hart used to say, "In a collaboration, there's always a sitter and a walker. One guy sits at the typewriter and the other guy walks. In the case of Ruth and me, we used to talk, talk, talk, talk endlessly, and then after the talking I would put it down on paper. Then, after it was done, she would go over it and revise it extensively. Or sometimes there would be scenes which she had dreamed up or created, and she would do the first draft of those.
>
> (pp. 106–7)

Earlier in the interview, he had said:

> In real life we never quarreled at all. But when we were writing together, we quarreled incessantly. It's part and parcel of the profession, which is why I don't collaborate, because I don't have the energy or the time or the *patience* to go through quarrels, disagreements, fights, and compromises. I could never be induced to collaborate again.
>
> (p. 97)

Gordon says in her memoir *An Open Book* that Raymond Massey's wife, Dorothy, whom she obviously admired, was "the

Butterick pattern for the Katharine Hepburn part in Garson's and my screenplay of *Adam's Rib.*" So we do know that the concept for much of Amanda Bonner came from Gordon. And here is the dilemma of the film—the shooting of a husband by his wife when she catches him in an act of infidelity, as cogitated over by Amanda in the beginning of the movie, as they are driving:

AMANDA

All I've been trying to say is this. Lots of things a man can do and in society's eyes it's all hunky-dory. A woman does the same things—the same, mind you, and she's an outcast.

ADAM

Finished?

AMANDA

No. Now I don't blame you personally, Adam, because this is so.

ADAM

Thank you. That's large of you.

AMANDA

It's not your fault. All is say is why let this deplorable system seep into our courts of law, where women are supposed to be equal?

ADAM

If anything, females get advantages!

AMANDA

We don't want advantages! And we don't want prejudices!

ADAM

Don't get excited.

AMANDA

What did she do? She tried to keep her home intact.

ADAM

That's right. By killing her husband.

AMANDA

She didn't kill him.

ADAM

She tried to. She missed.

AMANDA

What if he were a woman and she were a man—that's
right—what if Mr. Attinger was Mrs. Attinger and Mrs.
Attinger was Mr.—uh—

ADAM

Attinger?

AMANDA

Yes—Mr. Attinger. What then? Go ahead.

[*She turns the radio on. The market reports drone on. He
turns it off again.*]

ADAM

I can't follow your line.

AMANDA

Scot-free. She'd go scot-free. That is *he* would. Lennahan
did!

And a bit later, in the middle of dictating to her secretary Grace,
Amanda suddenly stops and says "Grace—What do you think of a
man who is unfaithful to his wife?" Grace's answer is (indulgently):
"Not nice." Amanda, "Now, what about a woman who is unfaithful
to her husband?" Grace (outraged): "Something terrible." Then,
Amanda, still dictating, "I again urge you to study and consider
United Zinc Co.—[*She suspends the speech, turns into the room
again*] A boy sows a wild oat or two, the world winks. [*The phone
rings*] A girl does the same—scandal."

And as the summations are being made, Amanda instructs the
jury to imagine Mrs. Attinger as a man:

...Think of her as a man sitting there, accused of a like
crime [Think!]"

[*And, of course, in some unaccountable way, Mrs. Attinger
becomes a man. He has her face and physical position, but
he is a man, nevertheless. A man named Mrs. Attinger.*]

The jury is transfixed.

There is an apt use of the dissolve technique, and of the
movement of the heads turning, as described in the filmscript.

[*Again the heads switch in unison.*]

Close Shot—Mr. Attinger

AMANDA'S Voice: And suppose him a woman.

Medium Shot—the Jury
[*They are finding this a bit harder to do. But they try.*]

Close Shot—Mr. Attinger

AMANDA'S VOICE: Try. Try hard.
[MR. ATTINGER *changes into a woman, dressed as* MRS.
ATTINGER *is dressed now, including the hat* ADAM
bought.

A bit later Amanda sums up:

Full Shot—the ROOM
[*The* JURY, *to say nothing of the subjects involved,
have been somewhat shaken by the experiment.*]

AMANDA

Now you have it. Judge it so. An unwritten law stands
back of a man who fights to defend his home. Apply the
same to this maltreated wife and neglected mother. We ask
you no more. Equality! [*Another sip of water*] Deep in the
interior of South America, there thrives today a civilization,
far older than ours, a people known as the Lorcananos,
descended from the Amazons. In this vast tribe, members
of the female sex rule and govern and systematically deny
equal rights to the men—made weak and puny by years of
subservience. Too weak to revolt. We look upon this
condition as a fantasy, a comic opera, and yet, how long
have we lived in the shadow of a like injustice?

Seemingly impromptu and witty, this is quite a speech, and
concept, to put forward in a comic movie. The whole idea of the
matriarchy seemed shocking enough when it was reactivated by
feminist groups in the early seventies. It must have seemed even more
radical in 1949, but the lesson here seems to be that humor helps a
lot. Perhaps the seventies feminist movement could have picked up
that hint from this film.

Fay Kanin was married to Garson Kanin's screenwriter brother,
Michael, and their film work together includes *Sunday Punch* (1942),
My Pal Gus (1952), *Rhapsody* (1954), *The Opposite Sex* (1956), and
Teacher's Pet for which they received an Oscar nomination for best

screenplay in 1958. And like Ruth Gordon and Garson Kanin, Fay and Michael decided to end the working relationship eventually and opt for the marriage instead. "We decided we would have to keep the working collaboration or the marriage. We decided on the marriage," Kanin told *People* magazine in April 21, 1980. Kanin also wrote Broadway plays, some on her own (like *Goodbye, My Fancy*) and some with her husband (like *Rashomon* and the musical *The Gay Life*). She segued from film work into writing movies for television, including the Emmy Award winning *Tell Me Where It Hurts* (1974) and the adaptation of C. D. B. Bryan's *Friendly Fire* (1977), the story of an accidental Vietnam death of an American soldier being shot by his own forces.

Kanin was also the first woman president of the Academy of Motion Picture Arts and Sciences (excluding Bette Davis's one month stint during World War II), serving four consecutive terms, and for years was active in the Writers Guild. She has said that she knew from an early age that she wanted a career in the movie industry, and—though from a small upstate town, Elmira, New York—transferred from Elmira College to the University of Southern California. Upon graduation she got a job at RKO as a $25-an-hour-reader through the help of story editor Robert Sparks. "I walked on dead and live sets, invaded the cutting rooms, snooped in the music department, made friends in publicity. I worked all day and stayed on at night." (Fact Sheet on Fay Kanin, Museum of Modern Art). She also met Michael Kanin at RKO, where he was working as a screenwriter.

Like Gordon, another actress who started out in the performing end and then became a scriptwriter was Frances Goodrich. Perhaps best known for her coauthorship of the play *The Diary of Anne Frank* (as well as the screen adaptation in 1959), Goodrich wrote many highly successful films in the thirty-year range in which she wrote scripts with her third husband, actor-turned-writer Albert Hackett. (She was actually his second wife, the ninety-four-year-old Hackett told this writer during a February 1994 interview at his apartment in New York City.)

Some of the films Goodrich wrote with Hackett include *Penthouse* (1933); *The Thin Man* (1934); *Naughty Marietta* and *Ah! Wilderness* (both 1935); *Rose Marie* and *After the Thin Man* (both 1936); *The Firefly* (1937); *Another Thin Man* (1939); *The Hitler*

Frances Goodrich

Gang and *Lady in the Dark* (both 1944); *It's a Wonderful Life* and *The Virginian* (both 1946); *The Pirate, Summer Holiday* and *Easter Parade* (all 1948); *In the Good Old Summertime* (1949); *Father of the Bride* (1950); *Father's Little Dividend* (1951); *The Long Long Trailer, Give a Girl a Break,* and *Seven Brides for Seven Brothers* (all 1954); *Gaby* (1956); *A Certain Smile* (1958); *The Diary of Anne Frank* (1959); and *Five Finger Exercise* (1962).

Goodrich was born in 1891 in New Jersey and went to Vassar College. She met Hackett when they were both acting in the theater and they married in 1931. While she and Hackett were appearing in a stock company as actors, she showed him a play script she had written. They rewrote it together and ended up with the play *Western Union* (although it apparently didn't get produced until 1937). Their second, *Up Pops the Devil* (1930), was bought by Paramount and ultimately filmed as Bob Hope's *Thanks for the Memory* later in 1938. At this point they were hired by MGM as staff writers.

"The studios took care of everything," said Hackett contentedly, who also added that he has no idea as to the whereabouts of their scripts. "You handed them in and that was that."

Their method of writing was to write separately (though in the same room), exchange drafts, and then criticize. "Scream is more like it," Goodrich told Ron Bowers in an interview published in *Films in Review* in October 1977. "Albert is a very, very gentle human being and I am the one who screams." This is how Goodrich described their method to the *New York Sunday News* (May 27, 1956):

Each of us writes the same scene. Then each looks at what the other has done, and we try to decide which of us has done the better. We advise each other and then go back at it again. We argue but we don't quarrel. When a scenario or a play is finished, neither of us can recognize his own work.

This setup is corroborated by a look at their office in the apartment where Hackett now lives with his third wife. The office, where Goodrich (who died in 1984) and Hackett worked when in New York, overlooks Central Park and is preserved as if the two of them were still there writing. There are two desks with typewriters, paper, pens, and pencils sitting about. Hackett was particularly proud to show a photograph of the statue of Anne Frank that is in the middle of a town square in Amsterdam. Mementos on the wall include cartoons of the two of them writing. Goodrich's is notable for an enormous ashtray filled with cigarette butts.

Though the pair did musicals, more serious work such as *Anne Frank*, and even a Western, *The Virginian* (along with two other cowriters, Howard Estabook and Edmund Peremore Jr.), it was *The Thin Man*, the adaptation of the Dashiell Hammett novel, which really established the team at MGM. "Hammett had written those wonderful characters and their relationship," Goodrich told Bowers, "and we just took it from there."

Indeed the two former actors were familiar with the bantering, sophisticated tone of the late twenties and thirties plays, and this was perfect for the lighthearted detective series, for which they wrote the first three—and the most successful—of the six-film series starring Myrna Loy and William Powell. When asked by Mark Rowland in an interview in *Backstory* if Nick and Nora were based as much on them as on the Hammett characters, Hackett replied, "No, not any more than usual. You do put a lot of yourself in scenes. But those were the sort of scenes you'd have written in the theatre."

Goodrich also admitted, "Credit must also be given to director Woody Van Dyke, who said, 'I don't care anything about the story; just give me five scenes between those two people.' We did and it was filmed in sixteen days." And she added that Van Dyke made them feel very much a part of the film, consulting the writers about casting, allowing them to see the rushes, and so forth. Perhaps this explains the artlessness of the atmosphere and dialogue.

Though Nora doesn't accompany Nick on the more dangerous aspects of his detective work, she would very much like to and always tries very hard to join in. They are definitely a team: it is said the first loving and sophisticated marriage on screen. Nick and Nora are partners, really, a relationship which must have mirrored some of Goodrich's experiences; not just her working relationship with Hackett, but perhaps some of the more progressive elements of an earlier marriage too.

Nora is a witty and spirited woman with gumption who gives as good as she gets, though she is from a privileged background and married to a fellow with "low-life" connections. Nick: "It's my dog and my wife." Nora: "You might have mentioned me first." When the gentleman of a couple tips his hat to them, Nora replies to Nick's query, "You wouldn't know them darling. They're respectable."

Typical of the devil-may-care, ironic attitude of the Charleses: When one of his cronies asks Nick, "What's the idea of the kid?" (their cinematic son, Nickie, a year old in the 1939 *Another Thin Man*), Nick coolly answers, "Well, we have a dog, and he was lonesome." He turns to Nora. "Wasn't that the idea?" When Creepsie the Crook looks at the baby, saying, "Just trying to see who he looks like," Nick rejoins offhandedly, "Anyone I know?"

While being overnight guests, Nora puts the baby in an open dresser drawer to sleep, and of course Asta the dog has his sleep drawer too, in a parallel one across the room. Nick says about the baby, "I hope it doesn't get to be a habit. It might be a little inconvenient when he grows up."

After doing *The Thin Man* scripts and musicals for Jeannette MacDonald, the team took a break from MGM and went back to New York, where they wrote another play, *The Great Big Doorstep* (1942). Hackett returned to acting for a while, and then "when the money ran out we went to Paramount where we did *The Hitler Gang* for director John Farrow and the film version of *Lady in the Dark*. We had a wonderful time with *Lady in the Dark*. Then Mitchell Leisen [the director] came in. He was being analyzed at the time—had been for six years. He brought in his woman analyst and they rewrote the whole thing. He even dropped the most important song, 'My Ship,' which contained the theme of the film."

Even so, the main character, played by Ginger Rogers in the movie, still comes through as a strong female figure typical of the forties. A magazine editor, she says at one point that she has "despised girls who only thought of love and marriage as a career." (Though of course one of the points of the film is to reveal her more glamorous nature to herself through a dream sequence.) And she says as she visits a psychiatrist:

I've clung desperately to my work to see me through the days—to sort of steady myself and—well, now that's beginning to go! I've lost the power of making decisions. I hesitate over the simplest things. That's why I'm here.

One of the team's most successful films was *Father of the Bride,* directed by Vincente Minnelli. By that time they had returned to MGM. Of the script, Goodrich has said, "That was fun; we used the characters from the book by Edward Streeter and held to the book because we knew Spencer Tracy was a wonderful comedian and Joan Bennett was wonderful as the mother. We then did the sequel [*Father's Little Dividend,* 1951] and they wanted another, but...that was the end of that."

Surprisingly, Goodrich somewhat disclaimed the film version of *The Diary of Anne Frank,* which won the duo a Pulitzer Prize as a play:

> We were not keen on it as a picture...we really didn't want to do the picture at all. We felt we had done the play and we were satisfied with it, but we didn't see how you could get inside those walls for the motion picture. And also, George Stevens was a difficult man. Stevens liked to make a star, and that was the real problem. The girl, Millie Perkins, was someone nobody could make a star. Stevens kept rewriting it and kept us there watching the rushes until Twentieth Century Fox got furious and we went off salary. Then we were on again, then off, and Stevens couldn't have cared less. It was a shame because it could have been an important picture.

Goodrich and Hackett were working in Hollywood at MGM in the fifties during the blacklist scare. Goodrich said that the two of them were called into the office of an MGM executive, L. K. Sidney, and asked to write a letter which would exempt themselves from any kind of trouble in that regard. "He had dossiers on us," said Goodrich. "Mine was three pages long and Albert's was two. He said, 'If you don't write a letter, I'm afraid we'll have to tear up your contract.' So, we went to a lawyer and that was all we had to do—call his bluff—and we never wrote any letters."

(Above quotes both from *Films in Review,* p. 466)

Goodrich was active in the formation of the Screen Writers Guild, served on its board in the thirties, and as its secretary in 1937. This is how she described the atmosphere during the Guild's early years:

The pressure at MGM was relentless. They had the big boys, you know, McGuinness, Rogers, Mahin, and Patterson McNutt.... The "Four Horsemen" went around all the time, day after day, talking to writers, particularly the young writers, the ones who were just starting, warning them about the upcoming vote. So we proselytized, too. We walked around that lot and so did Lilly Hellman, and we talked to the young kids who were not aware of the problem but only on our lunch hour, so that no one could ever say we had used studio time for union activities. And we couldn't do our proselytizing on the phone, of course, because Thalberg's boys were always listening in.

(*The Hollywood Writers' Wars*, p. 65)

As a working professional, and an independent woman, Goodrich was writing plays in the twenties and earning her living as an actress. Interestingly, after a first marriage to a movie actor, Robert Ames, ended in divorce, she married the writer Hendrik Willem van Loon in 1927. They maintained separate apartments. This used to be called a "companionate marriage," though Goodrich had downplayed this aspect in a typically no-nonsense way. As quoted in the *New York Daily News* (May 27, 1956), she had earlier said: "I know that he [van Loon] can work best when alone, and that he courts interruptions as an excuse not to work. Then, of course, he gets awfully angry because his schedule is not up to expectations." And she seems to have been the driving force in the Goodrich-Hackett team. (By all accounts, Hackett has always been shy and soft-spoken.)

The image of cool, couth, and confidence is to be found in spades in the work of, and in the public image of, the husband and wife screenwriting team of Phoebe and Henry Ephron. They were originally playwrights living in New York, and their first big success was the 1943 play *Three's a Family*. After a move to California in the mid-forties the two wrote *Bride by Mistake* (1944); *Always Together* (1947); *Look for the Silver Lining* (1949); *The Jackpot* (1950); *On the Riviera* (1951); *Belles on Their Toes* and *What Price Glory?* (both 1952); *There's No Business Like Show Business* (1954); *Daddy Long Legs* (1955); *Carousel* (1956); *Desk Set* (1957); and *Captain New-*

man, M.D. (1964), for which they were nominated for an Academy Award.

Phoebe Wolkind went to Hunter College, and she met her future husband, Henry Ephron, when they were both counselors in a summer camp. (Is this the inspiration for one of the married couples briefly interviewed in Nora Ephron's *When Harry Met Sally...* who say they met while counselors at a summer camp?) After college, she became a secretary to Gilbert Miller, a well-known theatrical producer, and she and Ephron married in 1934. Shortly thereafter, they started collaborating on plays. And the experience of living in a New York apartment with their first child, Nora, became the basis for *Three's a Family.* It was such a hit that they were invited by Twentieth Century Fox to come to Hollywood to write scripts, and Henry Ephron reports in his book *We Thought We Could Do Anything* that their salary at Fox was $750 a week, and their royalties on the play between $500 and $600. (The couple would return to the Broadway stage and presumably much greater royalties two decades later writing such plays as *Take Her, She's Mine* and *My Daughter, Your Son.*)

An article about Phoebe Ephron, at the time of the play, declared:

> Because of her experience as a secretary, Phoebe has found that almost none of her friends believe she actually had a creative hand in *Three's a Family.* (Ephron did admit, however, that it took her three years to learn to write and really polish play dialogue.) But as further proof, she said that *Three's a Family,* which eventually was published as a novel, was also based in part on her own aunt who was a dentist. Her aunt's husband ran the household, did the cooking, and took care of the children. (from an unsigned and undated news clipping in the Billy Rose Theater Collection at Lincoln Center)

Though she was not writing, strictly speaking, screwball comedies, Phoebe Ephron's films sometimes have this edge, as can be seen in a bit of dialogue on page 84 of the script from her 1956 film about the songwriting team of DeSylva, Brown, and Henderson, *The Best Things in Life Are Free,* cowritten with William Bowers.

FADE IN

EXT. WILLIAM FOX STUDIO—HOLLYWOOD—DAY

From a high angle to show gate with lettered identity.
(NOTE: *Suggest we shoot the old South Gate at 20th
Century-Fox.) We move in to show a crowd of costumed
extras walking on the lot—sailors, Egyptians, Turkish
dancing girls, Cossacks, Swiss yodelers, Hawaiian hula
dancers.*

CLOSER ANGLE—DOLLY SHOT—DAY

to reveal Lew [composer Lew Brown], *dressed in a loud
sport shirt, two-tone shoes and bulky checkered plus-fours,
walking among the extras. A* COSSACK *comes up alongside
him. The Cossack, noticing Lew's attire, looks him over
carefully from top to bottom. Lew grows self-conscious.*

> COSSACK
> [*in perfect English*]

What picture are you in?

> LEW
> [*furious*]

I'm not in any picture. I'm writing songs for one. Can I
help it if this's how songwriters dress out here?

And the film's repartee always seems urban and sophisticated, no
matter what the setting. In *Desk Set* it's clear New York is the location,
in any event. When Gig Young barges in on an actually innocent tête-
à-tête of Spencer Tracy and Katharine Hepburn, he halfheartedly
apologizes, "I suppose I should have called first," to which Tracy
replies, "Yes, do that next time." Young says, "I never thought
anyone would be here," and Hepburn snaps, "Thanks." Or during
the Christmas office party, "There are eighty-five calories in a glass of
champagne." The rejoinder, "I can get it in my neighborhood for
sixty-five." In fact, *Desk Set* is a very boozy film, as befits the time:
1957, and that era's concept of "office fun." A character is described
as being "like one of those men who've just switched to Vodka." In

Daddy Long Legs, which came out in 1955, "Let's have another martini" is the reaction when Fred Astaire tells his adviser that the French orphan he wants to adopt is an eighteen-year-old girl.

This is all meant naturally to convey an air of conviviality (not to promote alcohol, though indeed the couples' alcoholism has been discussed in print since that time) as the Ephron comedies have an air of frothiness, perfect for a performer like Astaire. He can get to say, when presented with a large sheaf of letters from his charge, "For a moment I was afraid there was a baby in there." And, when dancing with an athletic looking type at a college dance and she asks if she's leading too much, he: "Up until now I think it's a tie."

Phoebe Ephron in interviews sounded publicly a bit like her characters. In 1958, she told the *New York Times,* "I don't go in the kitchen very often except for ice cubes for a drink. We have a cook for the cooking and a nurse for the children. I've been a full-time screenwriter since 1943, and I put in a full day at the office." The *Times* writer saw her as "slim, vivacious, witty, able to pass for Rosalind Russell." Her daughter, Delia, has described her as "powerful and opinionated," in the *New York Times* (February 16, 1992) and said that she and her sisters were the only ones in Beverly Hills who had a working mother so controlling that she chose their courses in high school.

Another well-regarded writing team of the forties and fifties— though not husband and wife—were Betty Comden and Adolph Green, former nightclub performers (along with Judy Holliday) who started to write their own material, they have said, because you had to pay royalties to use other people's. They went to Hollywood in the forties as performers even though Hollywood really didn't know what to do with them, and their musical comedies are still considered top of the line. Their films include *Greenwich Village* (as performers) (1944), *Good News* (1947), *The Barkleys of Broadway* and *On the Town* (both 1949), *Singin' in the Rain* (1952), *The Band Wagon* (1953), *It's Always Fair Weather* (1955), *Auntie Mame* (1958), *Bells Are Ringing* (1960), and *What a Way to Go!* (1964). They became contract writers at MGM in 1947.

After their initial brush with Hollywood in the mid-forties, they went back east and dashed off a Broadway musical called *On the Town* with Leonard Bernstein. Hollywood came calling again.

Betty Comden

About this period, and dispelling any possible myths, Comden says, "We had an office in a big administrative building that they used to call 'The Iron Lung.' It was a bleak office and we went to work every day about nine o'clock. People always think you go to Hollywood, whee! Playing tennis! Wow! But we worked very hard. All the writers worked very hard. And we worked evenings, too. Almost around the clock." Adolph Green said, "When Betty and I are at our best as writers, the quality that seems to come across is spontaneity." Comden: "Almost improvisation." Green: "Which is not improvisation. It's very tough work." (*Backstory 2*, pp. 78, 83)

In the spring of 1994 Comden and Green were still performing (at a theater in Sag Harbor, New York) and Comden spoke about their years together over dinner in a chic restaurant—her choice—in the theater district of Manhattan. It seemed every luminary in the spot knew and was happy to greet her. Beautifully coifed and wearing a striking pantsuit with long pearls and scarf, the seventy-seven-year-old never dropped a beat in meeting and greeting.

She said that during her years in Hollywood—at the Arthur Freed unit where Freed, a producer, headed up musicals at MGM—she was very much protected against any kind of discrimination against herself as a woman writer, and in fact gave it very little thought at the time. "When you're in the middle of something, you don't really have time to theorize about it, or about the work you're doing." The work and the money were shared equally by herself and her partner, she said, and she was not necessarily used for women's roles, or a woman's point of view.

She did allow, though, that she had a special relationship with her husband, a businessman (now dead), who was supportive of her. "I've had a career all my life. My husband, Steven Kyle, was a totally enlightened man, interested in what I did and a supporter of Adolph and me. Sometimes he would come out to California for a while while we were working, and so did each of my two children. Or I would go back to visit. But it wasn't easy. It never is." Comden added that she and Green (who is married to musical comedy star Phyllis Newman) never permanently lived in California, being called out to work when there was a project, and staying only for the duration of the project and then returning to New York.

She also said that as a team the two were the first to introduce the concept of singers and dancers not performing on a stage in a musical, but actually being out in the streets. "The studio people said, 'What? These characters are going to sing and dance in the streets?' We wanted to show them in the setting of everyday life."

The Algonquin wit Dorothy Parker came to Hollywood in the thirties and stayed through the forties with her younger husband Alan Campbell as her writing partner. Her attitude toward her work swung from "There is no sinking to mediocrity in Hollywood. This *is* their best," to an admonition that, when "in the act of writing, it really is impossible to condescend to the material." She enjoyed the large amounts of money made, and—it is said—spent it lavishly.

Scripts the two wrote together include *Suzy, Three Married Men, The Moon's Our Home* (coauthors) and *Lady Be Careful* (all 1936); *A Star Is Born* and *Woman Chases Man* (both 1937); *Sweethearts* (1938); *Trade Winds* (1939) with a third writer, Frank Adams; *Weekend for Three* (1941); and *The Fan* with Walter Reisch and Ross Evans (1949). The 1937 *A Star Is Born,* for which the two received an Academy Award nomination, is considered their best film together. With Joan Harrison and Peter Viertel, Dorothy Parker wrote *Saboteur* in 1942. *Smash Up: The Story of a Woman Alone,* the 1947 Susan Hayward film, was based on a story by Parker and Frank Cavett with a script done by others, and *Queen for a Day* (1950) is also based on her stories. Parker also contributed dialogue—along with Campbell and Arthur Kober—to Lillian Hellman's screen adaptation of *The Little Foxes,* whose title she had originally suggested.

A contemporary husband-and-wife writing team still going strong is that of Harriet Frank Jr. and Irving Ravetch, who have been active since the 1940s and first collaborated on James Cagney's *Run for Cover* in 1955. In 1957 they wrote the critically acclaimed *Long Hot Summer* starring Paul Newman and Joanne Woodward. It was the first of many successful collaborations with director Martin Ritt resulting in films which have increasingly had—with Ritt, anyway—a socially conscious, left-wing orientation. They did *The Sound and the Fury* (1959) with Yul Brynner; *Hud* (1963) with Paul Newman—an adaptation of Larry McMurtry's novel *Horseman, Pass By*—which earned the writers and the director Oscar nominations and the film four Academy awards; *Hombre* with Newman again in 1967; and *Conrack* with Jon Voight in 1974.

Norma Rae (1983), which won a Best Actress Oscar for Sally Field and an Oscar nomination as Best Picture, was the story of labor organizing in a Southern factory; *Murphy's Romance* (1986) was also with Field and James Garner; and *Stanley & Iris* (1990) with Jane Fonda and Robert De Niro is the story of illiteracy among adults. Though themes of social change are treated, there is no didacticism; there are lighthearted lines, for instance, in *Hud,* as Newman says to Patricia Neal, his father's housekeeper who has escaped his clutches, "I'll always remember you, honey. You're the one who got away." Or when Norma Rae tells her kid not to eat hot dogs, "There's red dye in there and all sorts of things you don't want to know about." Or the witty end of *Murphy's Romance,* when Garner finally tells his real age—sixty—in a voice-over at the very conclusion of a movie where he fought to show his quirky worth to Sally Field in contrast to her more gadfly former husband.

In press notes to *Stanley & Iris,* Harriet Frank is quoted as saying,

> We had wanted very much to make a story about illiteracy because we feel that it's one of the great destroying factors among America's young people. It's terribly necessary that we be aware of how important it is to read, to write, to be able to command jobs, to be able to rise above a painful environment and move ahead in the world.

And about *Hud,* after a *Hud* screening at a graduate screenwriting seminar at the UCLA Film and Television Archive, Frank said,

> I felt at the time that it was interesting to say that an antihero comes very attractively packaged... both of us felt that it was important to say that that kind of personality, which is not totally un-American, should be packaged that way, and that Paul [Newman] was the perfect actor to play it, because he has that duality of great physical beauty and presence, as lots of American villains do.
> > (an undated mailing announcement from UCLA in the MOMA file on Frank and Ravetch)

Both graduates of UCLA and California residents from an early age, Frank and Ravetch became writers at MGM, where they met and married. Frank, who like Mary McCall appended the Jr. to her name, was originally from Oregon, and is also a novelist. Ravetch hails from Newark, New Jersey. In addition to the above films with Ritt, the team wrote *The Dark at the Top of the Stairs* and *Home From the Hills* (both 1960); *House of Cards* and *The Reivers* (both 1969); *The Cowboys* (1972); and *The Spikes Gang* (1974).

About their writing methods, Ravetch said, "During the first ten years of our married life we wrote separately. We lived in a little apartment. Harriet made me my breakfast, she kissed me good-bye, I took my little briefcase, I walked down the hall about ten feet and went into a bedroom, and she did the same.... One day, we decided let's try... let's stay together... why this parting? this painful parting? So we stayed together that day and it worked very well for us. We've been together ever since.... It's been a sheer delight." (Undated UCLA flyer in Ravetch file at MOMA)

One other contemporary husband and wife writing team which comes to mind is Renée Taylor and Joseph Bologna, whose original screenplay was the basis for the witty 1971 film *Made for Each Other*, about a couple who meet at an encounter session and fall in love.

Taylor and Bologna are actor-playwrights who have been writing material since the late sixties (*Lovers and Other Strangers* is probably their best-known play, a quartet of cartoon-like comedies for which they also did the filmscript in 1970). They have based their characters on each other and their friends. (Though their friends never recognized themselves in their work, Taylor told the *New York Times* on October 6, 1968.) Taylor told the *New York Daily News* that unlike other writing teams, she felt collaborative work was good for their marriage. "We love writing comedy. That's what has kept us together, thinking everything is funny no matter what it is" (October 2, 1988).

5

The Exception That Proves the Rule

Though you may have to look far and wide to find interesting scripts by women in the fifties, or new women entering the screenwriting business, there is the outstanding exception of Ida Lupino. In 1949, after seventeen years of screen acting which she deemed a failure, she turned to other Hollywood endeavors. She had cowritten and produced a film for television, and this gave her incentive to create her own company, Emerald Productions, later known as The Filmmakers, with Collier Young, her husband at the time.

The first film for the new outfit was *Not Wanted* in 1949, the story of an unwed mother, with a script by Lupino and Paul Jarrico. She produced it and completed the direction of the film when the credited director (Elmer Clifton) fell ill, and the next year, in 1950, she coscripted and directed *Never Fear*, about a dancer who contracts polio. In the same year she took on the same tasks for *Outrage*, the story of a rape, and provided the same service for *The Hitchhikers* in 1953. She then cowrote *Private Hell* in 1954, a film directed by Don Siegel. (Other films she had a hand in but did not write are *Hard, Fast and Beautiful* and *On the Loose*, both in 1951; *Beware My Lovely* in 1952; and *The Bigamist* in 1953.)

Some of these topics alone, and the naturalistic style of her films—even if they have an occasional upbeat ending—are enough to make Lupino something of an anomaly in the 1950s. She has said that "if I could stay home and write screenplays and lyrics, I'd do it. But I direct simply because it's a livelihood. I have no alternative" (an interview with Marjorie Rosen, 1973). So her reasons for directing are not the same as a number of other screenwriters: i.e., to maintain control of the production. In another interview in 1972, Lupino said, "Frankly, I was more interested in getting stories together than directing. Our company did stories back then that were very daring. You name it and we did it, but it was in good taste. [My films] were not only about women's problems, they were definitely about men's too."

This was one reason that the feminist revival of interest in women's films that took place in the early to mid-1970s had some difficulty in placing Lupino—at first a happy find—in a convenient feminist format, especially since some of her heroines are passive and victimized, as they probably were in the "real" life they depicted. Sometimes aware of what's happening to them, and sometimes not, the "ordinary women" are often trapped in documentary-like city streets or a home for unmarried mothers, making for a tense atmosphere in a naturalistic milieu.

In *Outrage*, Ann (played by Mala Powers) is being stalked by a man but it seems that she has outrun and avoided him. Racing toward a vehicle for her getaway, she is trapped. Here is the stark (but not offensive) description of her entrapment:

> *She sobs with frustration, pulls hard at the door handle*
> *and slips. As she slips, her elbow hits the truck horn. It*
> *blares out loud and angry. She tries to stop it, but it too is*
> *stuck. She starts out the other door, trips, hits her head*
> *against the running board and falls to the ground half*
> *unconscious.*

> MED. SHOT—*Man. Hearing the sound of the horn, he*
> *rushes toward the truck where Ann is hiding.*

> EXT. BEDROOM WINDOW—IN NEARBY TENEMENT

> OVER SHOT *can be heard sound of the truck horn. A*
> *sleepy-eyed man in pajamas gets up, goes to the window,*
> *slams it shut.*

REVERSE SHOT—FROM ANGLE OF WINDOW AS WE SEE:

LONG SHOT—SHOOTING DOWN—*the truck yard as the man moves toward the truck, the sound of the horn continues.*

NOTE: *The foregoing sequence will, of course, be shot in a highly impressionistic manner so as to offend good taste at no time. It should be pointed out that the two people are never photographed in close proximity.*

DISSOLVE THRU SOUND OF HORN TO SHRILL SOUND OF CLARINET HITTING HIGH NOTE:

EXT. STREET—NIGHT

BLURRED LONG SHOT—*From Ann's* ANGLE. *The clarinet sound comes over as the* SHOT *becomes clearer. It is a* LONG SHOT *of Nick's Place, a cheap bar a block away with a flickering neon sign in front. The clarinet solo is from a jukebox record in the bar.*

MED. SHOT—*Ann struggling down the street toward the beckoning neon lights of Nick's Place. She walks as if coming out of paralysis. Her clothing is disheveled.*

MED. CLOSE SHOT—ANN. *A bleeding scratch on her face. Her hair is matted. She sobs weakly and hysterically, almost whimpering. A dazed, almost drunken look about her face. She reaches into her handbag, finds a handkerchief, dabs at the scratch on her cheek. Her sobs subside. She draws in her breath and starts down the street, towards a telephone booth outside Nick's Place. She enters booth, fumbles in her purse for a nickel.*

Later in the film she nearly kills a young man with a wrench who she perceives is also trying to rape her, though in fact he just wants to kiss her. But the movie has somewhat of an upbeat ending, as a courtroom scene "forgives" everyone because the rapist—whose neurosis hadn't been treated—had been let loose upon society. A fifties belief in the fixability of all things, but just the fact that this rape is depicted in naturalistic detail is significant.

Between 1949 and 1954, Lupino wrote and directed six features while continuing her career as an actress, but because of small, non-studio budgets, she was forced to shoot exclusively on location and use relatively unknown actors. Besides unwed motherhood and rape, she treated the theme of bigamy in a realistic way. And none of her heroines are in the glamorous mold at all; rather the reverse. Waitresses, factory workers, and bookkeepers who drift into trouble or have trouble thrust on them, they are very far from the glamorous heroines of the thirties or the assertive women of the forties. And light years from Hollywood.

Because they were too startlingly realistic to be great commercial successes at the time, or even to be widely distributed, it is only in the past few years that her films and Lupino's work as writer, director, and producer have received much attention.

6

The Contemporaries
Hen's Teeth in a Mare's Nest

The scarcity of women screenwriters today is made even more evident when compared to other high-paying, competitive professions where even glass ceilings have left some room at—at very least—the near top. There are a few names which come to mind: Joan Didion *(True Confessions, Play It as It Lays)*, Vicki Polon *(Girlfriends)*, Joyce Corrington *(Planet of the Apes)*, Leslie Dixon *(Outrageous Fortune)*, Kathryn Bigelow *(Blue Steel)*, Callie Khouri *(Thelma and Louise)*, Nora Ephron *(Heartburn, When Harry Met Sally...)*, Melissa Matheson *(E.T.)*, Elaine May *(Such Good Friends, Ishtar)*, Gloria Katz *(American Graffiti, Indiana Jones and the Temple of Doom)*, Barbara Benedek (cowriter of *The Big Chill*).

But it's a handful, really, when talking about more than two decades. ("All two of them?" was the reaction this journalist got placing a call to Callie Khouri's agent, requesting an interview and explaining I was working on a book on women screenwriters.) Also, most of the contemporary women writers are very much outside the Hollywood system in one way or another, even in a time when allegiances are more to agents and agencies than to the large studios. Many of them are independents or—in some cases—have used writing as a stepping stone to directing, as Elaine May, Kathryn Bigelow, and Nora Ephron have done.

184

Unlike during the early years of films, few of these women entered the movie business as an actress, though a number came from journalism or related fields. Didion and Ephron were already names when they started to write scripts; Khouri was working as a video producer in Los Angeles when she wrote her "spec" script; Leslie Dixon put in her time at a number of low-level jobs just to be in Los Angeles and soak up the atmosphere of the movie business before attempting her first on "spec." (Elaine May is one exception: she was first a comedienne, with her partner Mike Nichols. And Barbra Streisand is another, as cowriter of *Yentl* (1983), a movie she also produced, directed, and starred in—the first woman to do all of this, according to the film's publicity material.)

Streisand wrote *Yentl* with British screenwriter Jack Rosenthal, a British Academy Award winner for Alan Parker's first film, *The Evacuees*. But Streisand was most publicly notably "stiffed" by the Academy of Motion Pictures Arts and Sciences: she was nominated in no category. She even took it on the chin to the extent that Isaac Bashevis Singer, from whose story the film was adapted, "interviewed himself" in the question and answer format on the front page of the Arts and Leisure section of the Sunday *New York Times* (January 29, 1984). Calling *Yentl* a "splashy production [with] nothing but a commercial value," complaining that "Miss Streisand is always present, while poor Yentl is absent," he also cleverly compares Streisand's newly happy ending to an imagined change in *Anna Karenina* where she marries an American millionaire instead of committing suicide. In the interview Singer admits that he did write a script for Streisand, which was rejected. It is also worth noting that—despite Streisand's obvious clout in the movie business—it still took her over a decade to mount the production.

One of the earliest "name" women screenwriters in recent times is Eleanor Perry, who was nominated for an Academy Award for her screenplay for *David and Lisa* in 1971. An outspoken voice in the late sixties and early seventies about the very few women in positions of power in the film business, Perry also wrote *Ladybug, Ladybug* (1963), *The Swimmer* (1964), *Last Summer* (1969), *Diary of a Mad Housewife* (1970), and *The Man Who Loved Cat Dancing* (1973). And Truman Capote's *Trilogy* (1969), with Capote, based on three of his short stories. She has shared credit with three other writers on *The Deadly Trap* in 1972 and with Richard Harris (not the actor) for *The*

Lady in the Car With Glasses and a Gun (1970). With the exception of *Lady, The Deadly Trap,* and *The Man Who Loved Cat Dancing,* all of Perry's films were directed by her second husband, Frank Perry. Interestingly (though I have no idea why or what this means) all but one are adaptations.

Originally from Cleveland, and with a master's degree in psychiatric social work, she wrote some thrillers under a pen name, short plays on mental hygiene and eventually in 1958 a full-length play, *Third Best Sport,* based on one of her thrillers, with her first husband, Leo Bayer. The play made it to Broadway, and Perry never made it back to Ohio.

She met and married Frank Perry, the director, and started working with him as a team. She wrote, he directed. *David and Lisa* was their highly acclaimed film made from Dr. Theodore Rubin's novel about two emotionally disturbed teens, and her script for *Diary of a Mad Housewife,* made in 1970 and starring Carrie Snodgress, became a feminist classic. Perry told the *New York Times* in 1973, "Today I would write it differently. Today I would carry it one step further, to show Tina liberating herself, but not through a man. She'd get a job, or go back to school, or whatever women do to liberate themselves."

And she was vocal in that interview, as in others, about women's roles in film and in the film business: "It seems women are always getting knocked up, killed, or raped, and those are men's fantasies we're seeing, right? There is not one woman head of a studio, and I hope to live to see that." (Perry died of cancer in 1981.) But she also said,

> I like men. Now is not the time to do what they do. What's the point of turning around and doing to them what they do to us? Why don't we have mixed crews where everybody is just a person? I belong to two oppressed groups, writers and women. I don't want to oppress men just because we've been oppressed.

Perry also complained that she was discriminated against in her work on the modern Burt Reynolds Western *The Man Who Loved Cat Dancing.* "I thought for a while I was being oppressed as a writer. I'm used to that. Writers are the low men on the totem pole in the whole Hollywood hierarchy.... [then] my associate kept implying that I didn't know Westerns, as though there was something mystical about Westerns, that only jocks can write Westerns.... I can write this sagebrush crap; I know the proper curse words." Other writers were assigned to the script, says Perry, men to do the "sagebrush crap." Layers upon layers of writers were used, she says, and this is the reason for the mess the script turned out to be, and the negative reviews the film received.

She was a leader of a feminist protest group at the 1972 Cannes Film Festival at which a group of women sprayed red paint over three breasts of a nude woman in a poster advertising Fellini's *Roma* and also carried a sign which said "Women Are People, Not Dirty Jokes." It is difficult today, though fun, to remember or imagine the zeitgeist that made those feelings and pranks possible.

Possibly more in tune with our age is Perry's comment—which is echoed by writer-director Nora Ephron—that the power aspect of moviemaking is pure fun. Ephron calls it giddy. Perry called it heady. "I've decided from now on that I want to be coproducer on the films that I do. I like that clout, that power... I've seen my movies shake up people, and make them cry. It's a heady feeling, it's just fabulous... a joyful human experience."

The writing-directing path for women today was somewhat cleared by the talented Elaine May, who started as an actress and became a touted comedienne in the brilliant satirical team of Nichols and May. After they split up, May began writing and directing for the screen, specializing in satirical comedy. May adapted *Such Good Friends* (1971) under the pseudonym Esther Dale from Lois Gould's novel and was a coscreenwriter (with Warren Beatty) for *Heaven Can Wait* in 1978. She was also an uncredited cowriter of *Tootsie* in 1982. May scripted and directed *A New Leaf* in 1971 and *Mikey and Nicky* in 1976, and directed *The Heartbreak Kid* in 1972. And she wrote and directed, with Beatty, the 1987 bomb *Ishtar*. She has a reputation in the movie business as a script-doctor—a function we have seen other women writers perform.

In an interview that May gave at the New School for Social Research in New York in 1975, here are her somewhat bitter comments about writing a movie script:

I wanted to see if I could get away with it. And they cut it out.

Right to the throat. I mean, they do not cut out the peripheral stuff. They cut out exactly what you wrote the thing for. (pause for effect) They know, somehow.

In doing the first movie, *A New Leaf,* I realized it was quite an insane industry. And I was new enough to know it. You would not be able to open a fruit stand that way. I mean, they would laugh you out of town....

I think there are problems with certain subjects because they're not considered commercial, but not because they're considered controversial. I think it's a very funny country now. Anything that will make money, no matter what it is, they will put on. If Hitler were alive today, as somebody said, I guarantee you, twenty million at the box office.

You just take a chance. You experiment, and you fall on your ass. The world does not offer it to you, no. This country does not offer it to you. It's a bad setup for people who are in the arts. It's really hard to work here. Mike Nichols once said that if you have a career, your career is diametrically opposed to your work. And that's true. It's like a credit rating. I mean, you just are really terrified if you miss a phone bill, because you know that someplace there's a computer that's recording it all and that someone will call up and it'll give you a bad rating. And that's a very hard atmosphere to go ahead and experiment in. So you just say, after a while, forgive me, "Fuck it. I'll do it anyway."

It's a funny thing to sit down and write or direct a movie. It really doesn't seem like life, which to me is really like working at Florsheims. You're doing this peculiar thing which is you're writing a script. And then you're doing this funny thing on a set with a seventy-five-man crew. And no matter what you say about it, it's that strange thing that everyone makes fun of: Hollywood. It's the same thing with writing. You sit at a typewriter, and somebody's actually going to pay you...

I guess it's sort of like you feel: Will they find out? I don't think it's that you enjoy it so much, as that it's something that's in your mind that you are going to impose or inflict on an enormous amount of people, and get paid on top of it. And every once in a while you think, "Well, gee, I'm getting away with it." But not because you enjoy it, but because it's better, God knows, than a lot of other things. It's not wild fun. But what is? What is?

It's very long, hard work to direct a movie. Actually, the only thing you need—you don't need talent—you just need an enormous amount of stamina and physical endurance, and I'm very strong for my size. It's actually a rather tedious way of making a living. But not as bad as working at Florsheims.

May's comic sensibility has been compared to Woody Allen's with its fascination with the interdependence of neurotic characters. Its dark side shows people selling each other out, though the tone is still humorous. May has said, "You can kill somebody straight or you can kill them funny. Funny is closer to life.... Humor is just a way of looking at things. You can look at it this way and it's a disaster. And you can look at it this way, and it's funny."

Nora Ephron had been a well-known humorous journalist and novelist when she made the "switch" to screenwriting (and since that time to directing as well). Ephron said that after her marriage to *Washington Post* reporter Carl Bernstein broke up, she found herself back in New York from Washington with two tiny babies to support. "I couldn't go running all over town as I would have liked to do and carry on reporting the way I used to," she said in an interview given in her apartment on New York's Upper West Side in the fall of 1993. With characteristic acerbity, she observed, "I couldn't afford to live on a journalist's salary in Manhattan anyway and still be able to pay the baby-sitter."

Tall and slender, with short dark hair, and dressed in slacks and the casual but expensive-looking silky wrap layers—the rich "schmatas" of the movie business—the attractive fifty-two-year-old said that for many years she had resisted going into the movie business. Her parents were screenwriters Phoebe and Henry Ephron, and she grew up as the eldest of four sisters ("Nora was her father's favorite," observed Catherine Turney) mainly in California. Poised and very much in control of the interview, a spot she's been in many times, on both sides, Ephron still spontaneously broke in and broke up (laughing) at times, as one thought would lead to another and she

Nora Ephron

would refocus the topic and the conversation. And when that happened her hands would fly into descriptive images—running quickly with her thoughts—almost as if they had their own will and life away from a very collected posture. Occasionally, Ephron would look at them as if to say, "There they go again."

Ephron went to Wellesley College after high school in California. Her 1962 college reunion is satirized in her humorous essay, "Reunion" (most recently printed in *Nora Ephron Collected*), in which she nails down the attitude of smug moderation—"What Wellesley wanted was for us to avoid the extremes, to be instead that thing in the middle. Neither a rabid careerist nor a frantic mama. That thing in the middle: a trustee"—in the college's attitude, and measures it against some of the changes in the women's movement of the early seventies.

Ephron then worked at the *New York Post* and *New York* magazine before becoming a columnist at *Esquire*, writing mostly on women's topics. Possibly her best-known lighthearted essay is "A Few Words About Breasts," first written for *Esquire* in 1972, which concludes about women who complain that their breasts are too large, "I have thought about their remarks, tried to put myself in their place, considered their point of view. I think they are full of shit." Other pieces are "On Never Having Been a Prom Queen," "Baking Off" (about a Pillsbury Bake-Off Contest), "Dorothy Schiff and the *New York Post*," and an essay which characteristically ends with a recipe for "Nora Ephron's Beef Borscht." The pieces, which are acerbic but not sour, are collected in *Wallflower at the Orgy, Crazy Salad, Scribble Scribble,* and—*Nora Ephron Collected.*

"I didn't want to be a screenwriter or live in California," said Ephron. "When I was a teenager I wanted to be Dorothy Parker. I wanted to be a journalist in New York. And I was that for a while: the newspaper, magazines. Then all of a sudden in the late seventies—I guess it was really in 1976—it seemed that everybody in New York was writing a script. And [ironically] I'm nothing if not a follower."

Ephron said her first script was turned into a movie for television, something she now cringes at when she sees it (a woman's caper, which she definitely did not want to discuss any further).

When I was married and had a tiny baby and was pregnant with another it was convenient for me to write scripts. I couldn't go off and do journalism. It was simply the wrong year to go gallivanting around. I wrote something for Paramount that never got made. A good draft for *Compromising Positions* that never got made. I had been hired by Warners to do a comedy and then my marriage [to Bernstein] ended. And it was a miracle that I was writing movies. I couldn't go back to journalism. It was like a door slammed.

Ephron had been married first to humorist Dan Greenberg, then to Bernstein, of the *Washington Post* Bernstein and Woodward Watergate team—her Washington years—and is now married to *New York* magazine journalist Nick Pileggi, also an author and occasional screenwriter (for Martin Scorsese's *Goodfellas*, based on Pileggi's book about crime, *Wiseguy*).

The film that brought her into national prominence as a screenwriter in 1983 was Mike Nichols's *Silkwood*, a coauthorship with writer Alice Arlen which told the story of real-life activist Karen Silkwood (played by Meryl Streep), who protested the radiation coverup at the Kerr-McGee plant and who was (probably) assassinated for her efforts and belief. Ephron said that her experience as a journalist made her a natural choice to do the script for *Silkwood*, and she credits Arlen with having taught her a great deal about structure ("Alice studied film at Columbia," Ephron observes). And she says that, because they were women, they were in fact another obvious choice.

Ephron suddenly, and in a very direct way, says:

Look, I have no idea why there are so few women screenwriters today. But I will tell you one thing. It's not that the studios conspire to not have good parts for women. It's that if women don't write movies then there simply aren't going to be that many good parts. [Later she qualified this to say a number of male writers can write for women, such as Lawrence Kasdan and James Brooks.] It's not that the roles for men are so great...there's just more of them.

As examples of what she means, Ephron cited the films *JFK*, *Bugsy*, and *Malcolm X*.

Kevin Costner's wife, Annette Bening, Mrs. Malcolm, all had the same small role. "I never see you. You're never home. Why don't you ever come home?" I thought to myself, "Gee, this is great. This is apparently all Oliver Stone or Spike Lee can ever imagine a wife saying to her husband." No woman would write that part and have it that hackneyed, that clichéd.

Ephron also says she had experienced no direct prejudice against her because she is a woman:

Though I have experienced some blatant examples of age-ism, there's never been a moment when I heard someone say, "Let's get a guy writer." In fact I have said those words but not because I believe there's any difference in ability. For instance on a project that Alice and I were working on for Richard Gere and Michelle Pfeiffer. So that Richard would not feel that she and I would weight it for Michelle. It's not a conscious thing, but it happens. Like when I was writing *When Harry Met Sally...* and Harry was based on Rob [Reiner, the director]. There was a brief time I was off the film and I came back and there were suddenly sixteen scenes about Harry. Then I had to even it out.

In the world of fiction, men write about men and women write about women. It's very rare that you get a Henry James who writes about women. So why should it be any different in writing for movies?

Heartburn, which also starred Meryl Streep, is Ephron's 1985 adaptation of her own bitterly humorous novel which detailed the breakup of her marriage to Bernstein because of his affair with the wife of a Washington diplomat. *This Is My Life* (1990) began her coauthorship with her sister, Delia, and was Ephron's first feature film direction (it received mixed reviews), and *Sleepless in Seattle* continued that writing partnership in 1993, with Ephron's second feature film direction: a success all round. "Everything fell into place with *Sleepless,*" said Ephron. "The cast of my dreams. A very fast shoot. And the movie went through the roof. I'm sure I'll pay for it the rest of my life."

Ephron continued,

> I love working with Delia. We spend some time together
> writing, some time apart. [Delia Ephron lives in California.]
> We put together an incredibly detailed outline with a huge
> amount of dialogue. It usually takes about three weeks. Then
> we separate and each takes a section. We send it to each
> other by fax or Federal Express, and then we get together
> again.

Ephron said that once she starts the actual process of directing, as
with *This Is My Life* and *Seattle* and two projects in the works, she no
longer can write or work on the script. "I know Woody Allen can do
it, but I can't. There is always the moment when I say, 'Get me the
writer.'" Ephron said that *Sleepless,* the 1993 romantic comedy with
Tom Hanks and Meg Ryan, was not just a critical but also a
commercial success that enabled her to put together the deal for her
current project, a movie which she will also direct, about a suicide
hotline on Christmas Eve. Again, Delia Ephron is the coauthor.

And *Sleepless* has brought her a great deal of media attention;
talk show appearances in addition to the usual articles, awards from
women's magazines such as *Glamour,* and of course offers to speak at
film seminars like those held at the Museum of Modern Art. About
directing, in general, Ephron has said, "It's better to be in charge than
get screwed. Your role as a screenwriter is to get screwed, man or
woman."

She said that—though she originally had a strong antipathy to
the movie business—once you see your words on paper become a
reality, you're hooked.

> I never wanted to be in the business when I first started
> writing scripts. It was "Thank God these people are paying
> me because it's keeping everything afloat." I would write
> movies for nine months and then my novel for three months.
> Back to movies for nine months, and so forth. I kept thinking
> "I'm just doing these movies to pay the rent."
> But then one of them got made. *Silkwood.* And once one
> of them gets made it puts a different kind of hook into you.

Then it's not about writing screenplays. It's about making movies. And making movies is fun.

Most of the time, anyway. Because with *Silkwood*, with Mike Nichols [the director], I was involved with all aspects. Characters, costumes. That's the giddy part. That's the fun part. Watching this *thing* that had been on paper suddenly come to life.

Ephron also went on to say—in a spurt of honesty rare in the film industry—that there is also the excitement of being a part of a large commercial enterprise, even if it may only be a temporary one. "You turn up somewhere and there are ten Winnebagos on the street and it's because you wrote one hundred and twenty pages. Never mind the coffee, never mind the doughnuts. Then you get to go to the dailies. When Alice [Arlen] had to go to jury duty, for instance, the producer wrote her a letter saying she couldn't go because she was an important figure in a $14 million corporation. And [feigned but amused amazement] it's true!" On the topic of money, though she did not say this, her fee for a script is reputed to be in the high six figures.

Cookie was written in 1989 with Alice Arlen and directed by Susan Seidelman. *When Harry Met Sally* also in 1989, and *My Blue Heaven* in 1990, both written by Ephron on her own. But whether her scripts are coauthored or not, there are still a number of distinguishing concerns and stylistic motifs running throughout. In an interview in *New York Newsday* (July 19, 1989), Ephron said about *Cookie,* "As a woman screenwriter, my job is not to write some idealized woman, but to write women who are real, whatever they are like, who are lovable or not lovable, but who are at least as comprehensible and as complicated as men are in the movies."

This is surely true of *Silkwood* as well, which gives a warts-'n'-all picture of a sometimes difficult, erratic but exciting woman who has a rocky but inevitable growth of consciousness about her lowly guinea pig-like status at the nuclear plant she works at. We stay on her side, though sometimes it's as hard for us as her housemate Dolly (Cher) and lover Drew (Kurt Russell), both of whom love her. And she can be a real pain at work, snitching people's food and mocking it, taking notes (for the union) on everything folks say.

In speech and thought the characters are true to their rural Southwest, a world not native to Ephron or the other filmmakers but captured nonetheless. The main characters are realistically multi-faceted: Dolly and her frustrated love for Karen, which doesn't keep her from pointing out her faults; the perfectly drawn labor union organizer played by Ron Silver, well-meaning but arrogant and—ultimately—making the end justify the means, even if that means is some human hurt.

A certain class of working poor has been caught: with the self-effacing determinism of those who already see themselves as losers. As in the dialogue when Drew and Karen are trying to convince Dolly, who is resisting them and lolling in bed, to take a long, boring car trip to see Karen's kids:

DREW

You comin'?

DOLLY

No. What's to do down there?

DREW

Nothin'.

DOLLY

O.K. I'll come.

Or when Dolly tells Karen of her feelings for her in some deceptively simple-seeming language:

DOLLY

I love you Karen.

KAREN

I love you too.

DOLLY

I don't mean I love you too.

KAREN

I know that's not what you mean. But it's what I mean.

In Ephron's other films, you could make a very good case for the intrusion of her own persona into the female characters she has created, at least in her contemporary comedies. All writing is autobiographical of course, even if it's not "all copy."

Ephron's interest in and metaphorical use of food is well known. As in *Heartburn*, an over-easy example perhaps, since the lead is Rachel Samstat, a food writer, and a clear alter ego for Ephron in her Washington years. Rachel (Meryl Streep) fantasizes about the food she will cook for and serve various men the minute she meets them, her wishful way of bonding them to her.

With Mark (her husband-to-be in the movie and a stand-in for Carl Bernstein) it's "pot roast and potato pancakes and apple sauce." Mark (Jack Nicholson) queries, "With little lumps from real apples?" to which Rachel answers a resounding "Yes!" When Rachel sees the young blond man in the subway who will eventually rob her therapy group, her mental fantasy is "I made your favorite dinner, lasagna...Rocky, Randy, Joe Bob." Detective O'Brien, the policeman who eventually returns Rachel's ripped-off engagement ring, sparks the fantasized dream sequence in making his "favorite dinner of boneless loin of pork with little apples and onions and potatoes." He is thought of as Dennis, Kevin, Colin, or Brendan. For the darkskinned (Middle Eastern?) man she runs into outside her father's building in New York on Broadway it's "curried goat."

Rachel's last words before going into labor are:

> Just put the lamb on for thirty-five minutes, turn it once, and baste it with the stuff in the pan.

And even the film script directions are laden with food, food which tells us about the taste, and class, of the characters:

> [*Arthur is plugging in a long extension cord to a blender. Rachel is fussing with a tableful of food—there are fresh tomatoes and basil, a perfect roast chicken and cold string beans.*]

And it is a peek into Ephron's life: we are way beyond even Manhattan recognition here, such as the fact that the subway robber carries a Balducci's bag. Rachel's father's apartment courtyard in the film script is a near replica of where Ephron lives now:

As Rachel walks out of her father's entry into the
courtyard. There are two fountains splashing. Rachel wipes
her eyes as she crosses the courtyard.

EXT.   Broadway—DAY

As Rachel turns to walk uptown to Zabar's.

At the time the movie came out there were various reports that part of their divorce settlement included a stricture from Bernstein that Ephron tone down some of the script to protect their mutual children—boys. And indeed the kids have been changed to girls in the film script. Other reports had it that perhaps the film was not as successful as it might have been because Ephron's usual sting was missing. (See especially the February 1992 *Vanity Fair* for more.)

Nor is *Heartburn* the only film in which food plays a prominent part; in *When Harry Met Sally*, Sally's food obsessions are used to indicate her character, a type of self-analysis Ephron offers in her introduction to the published film script:

So I began with a Harry, based on Rob. And because Harry was bleak and depressed, it followed absolutely that Sally would be cheerful and chirpy and relentlessly, pointlessly, unrealistically, idiotically optimistic. Which is, it turns out, very much like me. I'm not precisely chirpy, but I am the sort of person who is fine, I'm just fine, everything's fine. "I am over him," Sally says, when she isn't over him at all; I have uttered that line far too many times in my life, and far too many times I've made the mistake of believing it was true. Sally loves control—and I'm sorry to say that I do too. And inevitably, Sally's need to control her environment is connected to food. I say inevitably because food has always been something I write about—in part because it's the only thing I'm an expert on. But it wasn't my idea to use the way I order food as a character trait for Sally; well along in the process—

third or fourth draft or so—Rob [Reiner] and Andy [Shein-
man, the coproducer with Reiner] and I were ordering lunch
for the fifth day in a row, and for the fifth day in a row my
lunch order—for an avocado and bacon sandwich—consis-
ted of an endless series of parenthetical remarks. I wanted the
mayonnaise on the side. I wanted the bread toasted and
slightly burnt. I wanted the bacon crisp. "I just like it the way I
like it," I said, defensively, when the pattern was pointed out
to me—and the line went into the script.

> (*When Harry Met Sally*, intro.
> New York: 1990, x–xi)

Indeed, the line comes just after Harry satirizes Sally's behavior:

HARRY

You don't see that. [*mimicking her*] "Waiter, I'll begin with
the house salad, but I don't want the regular dressing. I'll
have the balsamic vinegar and oil, but on the side, and
then the salmon with mustard sauce, but I want the
mustard sauce on the side." "On the side" is a very big
thing for you.

SALLY

Well, I just want it the way I want it.

Sally, like the Meg Ryan character in *Sleepless in Seattle* (and like
Ephron), is a journalist. In *When Harry Met Sally*, she works at the
News; in *Sleepless in Seattle* she works at a Baltimore paper.

And in *This Is My Life*, the concerns of a working mother having
to occasionally leave her kids—something which Ephron herself
needed to do in making the film—is apparent. "All this stuff about
quality time and how kids are happy if their mother is happy—that's
all nonsense. They just want you to be there," said Ephron, just as
Dottie Ingels says in the film. "If your kids have to choose between
you being away and being happy and committing suicide in the next
room, they'll choose suicide in the next room." Just as wittily, Ephron
has said in interviews that they'll all find out later in therapy if any
permanent damage was done to her sons in the ten weeks she spent
on location making *This Is My Life* in Toronto.

Sibling rivalry is the movie's other motif, a sharply observed one that the two sisters—Nora and Delia—must have had a good chuckle over (or something else) while writing. Here are directions in the script, directions pretty clearly written by someone who has been there (it's hard to think that an only child would write this):

> *Erica is still irritated. The truth is Erica is always a little irritated in the manner of 1.) teenage girls 2.) girls whose sisters are cuter than they are 3.) older sisters who never quite get over the fact that their younger sisters were born.*

One of the appeals of Nora Ephron movies is undoubtedly a kind of wish fulfillment fantasy for those who would like to constantly travel on the Eastern shuttle like Rachel Samstat, be part of the movie business like Dottie Ingels, or a member of the intelligentsia of *New York* magazine and book writers:

MARIE

"Restaurants are to people in the eighties what theater was to people in the sixties." I read that in a magazine.

JESS

I wrote that.

MARIE

Get outta here.

JESS

No, I did. I wrote that.

MARIE

I never quoted anything from a magazine in my life. That's amazing. Don't you think that's amazing? And you wrote it.

JESS

I also wrote, "Pesto is the quiche of the eighties."

MARIE

Get over yourself.

JESS

I did.

MARIE

Where did I read that?

JESS

New York magazine.

HARRY

Sally writes for *New York* magazine.

MARIE

Do you know, that piece had a real impact on me. I don't know that much about writing, but...

JESS

Look, it spoke to you, and that pleases me.

MARIE

It had a wonderful, unique—is the word "style"?

JESS

If you say that's the word, that's the word.

MARIE

I...I mean...I really have to admire people who can be as...as...articulate...

JESS

Nobody's ever quoted me back to me before.
(*When Harry Met Sally*, pp. 58–59)

The sense of place, New York place—as in the scene with Harry and Sally in the Egyptian "wing" of the Metropolitan Museum of Art—is formidable. And at times heavy with class indications: affluent liberals who probably choose to live in Greenwich Village or the Upper West Side of Manhattan. In *This Is My Life,* in a scene most explicit in its directions, the script directions say, "EXT. WEST END AVENUE—DAY" or "OUTSIDE THE CALHOUN SCHOOL"—a grammar school in the West 70s. And shopping: "Mia, Erica, and Opal going down the aisle at Fairway [a well-known New York grocery store] while Mia picks out obscure vegetables." (Though one presupposes this will change some as the scope of more of Ephron's films gets broader: the Richard Gere/Michelle Pfeiffer film is a period piece about a World War II nurse, for instance.)

And an occasional phrase, or concept, comes up again in different scripts. There is for instance the anecdote that the character Dan tells in the therapy group in *Heartburn.*

DAN

When the dog goes to the bathroom in the house, I hit him. But sometimes the dog goes to the bathroom in the house because he's sick. I hit him anyway, because he doesn't know I know he's sick.

EVE

What are you talking about?

DAN

Rachel.

EVE

Rachel?

RACHEL

Who's the dog?

DAN

You are.

EVE

What?

RACHEL

I am? I'm the dog?

In *When Harry Met Sally,* in the final fight scene between the leads toward the end of the film, at the wedding of their friends Jess and Marie:

HARRY

Why can't we get past this? I mean, are we gonna carry this thing around forever?

[*Sally stops, whirls around to face him.*]

SALLY

Forever? It just happened.

HARRY

It happened three weeks ago.

[*Sally looks at him disbelievingly.*]

HARRY
[*Cont'd*]

You know how a year to a person is like seven years to a dog?

SALLY

Yes.

[*Harry throws up his hands as if it's self-explanatory.*]

SALLY
[*Cont'd*]

Is one of us supposed to be a dog in this scenario?

HARRY

Yes.

SALLY

Who is the dog?

HARRY

You are.

SALLY

I am? I'm the dog?

This leads eventually to the slap across the face in the kitchen of the hotel where the wedding is taking place.

Probably the most important paradigmatic similarity of Ephron's urban heroines, however, is the romantic-sexual paradox of contemporary women. That is, the squaring of the romantic yearnings of middle-class, or upper middle-class women brought up to want one thing (sometimes romance, sometimes marriage, and now—inevitably too—a profession), while men have been conditioned to something else (sex and a fear of commitment).

But the unifying element of all Ephron's scripts is an original take on the familiar that makes it easy for the viewer (or the reader) to "get in." It's the kind of thing that can be seen in an essay about why "we" never use the living room: the other rooms are used—the sleeping, eating rooms, while the unused though very pretty living room looks on in snobby awareness of the social status the apartment's inhabitants do not have.

> But what can you do in a living room? Tell me. I really want to know. I know what to do in a charcoal gray and pink breakfast nook, but the only thing I can think of to do in a living room is living, and I clearly don't have a clue as to what that consists of, especially if you rule out eating, sleeping, working, and swimming. I'm sure that some people are good at it, whatever it is. They probably lie around in a marginally useful way. They probably contemplate life. They probably

have servants and drinks before dinner and coffee table books. They probably think of themselves as civilized.

My living room sits in my apartment, a silent snobbish presence, secretly contemptuous that I don't know what to do with a room that has no clear function. I'm sure it wishes I were more civilized; I'm positive it hopes that someday I will grow up and spend a little more time in it. And some day I will. Some day when I am very old. By that time I will be no good at all at eating, sleeping, working and swimming, but I won't mind, because I will finally have found a use for the living room. It is obviously the perfect place in which to die.

> ("Why We Never Use the Living Room,"
> *Nora Ephron Collected,* New York: 1991,
> pp. 198–99)

So that even when writing about a more rarefied existence than most movie viewers know—such as the luxury of being a newspaper reporter in *Sleepless in Seattle* who can drum up an assignment to go "interview" (i.e., meet) a fantasy figure inspired by a voice on a radio—there is always the gemütlich touch. Meg Ryan plays the reporter, engaged in the beginning of the film to a fairly dull fellow with a lot of irritating allergies. The allergies are the point of entry.

It's Mark's going out to buy more socks to replace the ones lost in domestic disorder in *Heartburn* that hint at his affair. We all know from socks even if the Watergate Hotel is not within our purview. And Rachel's recognition scene about his extramarital activities takes place at the hairdresser's. She leaps up only "half blown out" and leaves the shop. Whether cheated on or not, we've all—women that is—been heavily worked over at the salon.

The wit, or the comedy, is accessible. You, we (millions of viewers) can "get in."

Of her own writing or work habits, Ephron has said that when she is writing she aims at writing five pages a day. And..."If I finish by 9:30 A.M., I quit for the day." It generally takes her ten to twelve weeks to do a script, she said. This schedule, which sometimes seems to be adhered to in a private office and sometimes not, appears to be something she has derived herself and not picked up from her parents, the playwrights-turned-screenwriters Phoebe and Henry

Ephron. "They went off to the studio and had an office at Fox for most of my childhood," says Ephron.

There were a number of screenwriters in the forties who were women, agrees Ephron. "In the 1940s, when my parents went out there [to Hollywood], there were women writers but they were mostly married to men writers.... Some were friends of my parents, like Fay and Mike Kanin, or the Hacketts [Frances Goodrich and Albert Hackett]. I don't know that much about it, but I would say that there were some. Then there weren't any, paralleling all of America, right? After World War II? When women were pushed out of the job market."

Of Henry Ephron's book *We Thought We Could Do Anything* about his marriage to Phoebe, the Hollywood years, their family and life together, Ephron said, "Some of it is true. Not all." Upon being pressed, Ephron said that parts about her parents' marriage and careers may be true, but some of the facts about the daughters were a bit confused: "They got us mixed up. Which child did what. And almost nothing about me in the book is true."

Though the Ephrons (Sr.) wrote plays together before collaborating on scripts, Nora Ephron says, speaking for herself,

I don't think you can collaborate on an original. There's just a moment when you have to sit down and make it up out of whole cloth. It's not about negotiating or collaborating with someone else. It's got to be personal in some way.

But if you're working from a fact-based thing, like the Karen Silkwood story, or from a book like the Meg Wolitzer's [*This Is Your Life*], then it's great to have a writing partner. Because you're already collaborating from the beginning.

About the current proliferation of screenwriting classes, seminars, and "writers' boot camps" which have cropped up across the country, Ephron said she has little opinion, except to observe that there are a number of screenplays out now which are, in her opinion, "overly structured." (Many of these classes suggest a writing paradigm or specific pattern.) "I thought about *The Crying Game*," she said, "and how you really couldn't diagram that. And how lucky it was that something like that got through." Instead, she suggests:

I believe the best training anyone can have for screenwriting is journalism—it's the cleanest, simplest writing; I'm not referring to dialogue, but to things such as set description. The continual question of journalism—What's the point of this scene? What are we trying to get to? Where is the truth here? My advice would be not to do it until you're older. One of the best things about journalism is that I spent almost twenty years seeing and doing things, not just going to the movies but covering political conventions, trials, even a war. This may not be evident in my work but the point is it is. It's very much a part of who I am as a person. I don't know what happens to people who start writing screenplays in their twenties because it seems to me that they're not going to see enough to write movies about. But on the other hand, they may have better imaginations than I have. Still, I think being a journalist is the best writing training there is.

Joan Didion is another best-selling writer (*Slouching Towards Bethlehem, A Book of Common Prayer, After Henry,* essays in *The New Yorker,* the *New York Review of Books,* and many other periodicals) whose alienated, sometimes apocalyptical personal vision has permeated the scripts she's worked on. With her husband, writer John Gregory Dunne, Didion has written scripts for *The Panic in Needle Park* (1971), *Play It As It Lays* (1972, on her own and adapting her own novel), *A Star Is Born* (1976), and *True Confessions* (1981, adapted by Didion and Dunne from Dunne's novel).

Originally from California, though she worked as a magazine editor in Manhattan after graduating from college, Didion now lives in New York though she has often divided her adult life in moving back and forth between the two coasts. Though she would not define herself as primarily a scriptwriter, she moves easily in this world via her reputation and connections. She's also worked as a script doctor.

Another more egalitarian but riskier approach to writing for the movies today is the method of writing a "spec" (on speculation) script in the hopes that it will capture the attention of an important agent, or producer, or at least get sold so the writer can get a credit. This was the route taken by Callie Khouri, though hers is a perhaps unusual story in that—Cinderella like—her first effort won an

Academy Award for screenwriting: the script for *Thelma and Louise* (1991) with Susan Sarandon and Geena Davis, the first mainstream female road movie and of course the first big hit with an angry, feminist, anti-male tone.

Khouri had been working as a producer of rock videos in Los Angeles, and was writing her script in her spare moments. This process, while she was working full-time, took about six months, with some work being done on the set as she was producing, and some at night. Khouri said that she had written the script in longhand, and then would come in after hours at work to use the computers and put it into script format.

According to an interview in *American Screenwriters:*

> One night I was coming home from a shoot, and I had just gotten off the Freeway and I pulled up in front of my house and parked the car. And I turned off the engine, and I thought, two women go on a crime spree. That was about December 1987. And I just sat there in the car because of that phrase. I liken it to being hit in the head by a two-by-four. That's what it felt like.
>
> (ed. by Karl Schanzer and Thomas Lee Wright, New York: 1993, pp. 124–25)

Khouri also told the *New York Times* (June 5, 1991) that the original idea expanded to a jotting in her notebook in which she wrote: "Screenplay idea: two women go on a crime spree. They're leaving town, both leaving behind their jobs and families. They kill a guy, rob a store, get hooked up with a young guy."

She also said that *Thelma and Louise* was a conscious effort to counter what Khouri saw as Hollywood's tendency to limit women's roles to easily identifiable types such as "'bimbos, whores and nagging wives. I did want the movie to be fun, and for people to laugh,'" she told the *Times*. "'But I also wanted, as a woman, to walk out of the theater not feeling dirty and worthless, for a change, not feeling like I had compromised the character of women, because that is one area where women really get short-changed in movies. So many times you go to the movies, and what woman up there would you want to be? None of them.'" But Khouri had more personal reasons for writing the script, as she described them to the *Village Voice* (July 28, 1991):

In order to get my karma straight about women, I had to write this script. When you become known in the business for producing videos that more often than not have naked women writhing in front of the camera for no reason and to not such interesting music, you eventually have to look at what you're doing.

Khouri said her producing partner, Amanda Temple, showed the script to Ridley Scott (*Alien*), who liked it right away and went on to direct it, and that she was pleased because "he did not want to change the ending, and he had enormous sensitivity for the characters' dialogue, their phrasing."

Khouri was thirty-three at the time of the movie's release, and familiar with the world of working-class Southern women represented by Thelma and Louise, who are supposed to be from Arkansas in the film. Khouri is from Paducah, Kentucky, and majored in drama at Purdue University. Odd jobs she worked at in Nashville include waitressing at restaurants and bars and receptionist and salesclerk positions; she has said that she was closely acquainted with the world of her main characters.

"From the way she writes, you could tell she knew these characters inside out," said Geena Davis, who played Thelma in the film, to the *New York Times*. "I know that if I needed to find out the color of the toothpaste Thelma used, I could call Callie and she would know."

Though this was Khouri's first effort, she knows how to establish character quite well, right off, with the innovative device of showing a close-up shot of each woman's suitcase. Louise has talked Thelma into taking the trip with her, and Louise's final instructions to her on the telephone are, just before she picks up Thelma from her house where she lives with her stereotypically male chauvinist husband Darryl:

LOUISE

And steal Darryl's fishin' stuff.

THELMA (V.O.)

I don't know how to fish, Louise.

LOUISE

Neither do I, Thelma, but Darryl does it, how hard can it be? I'll see you later. Be ready.

[*They both hang up.*]

INT—THELMA'S BEDROOM—CLOSEUP—SUITCASE ON BED—
DAY

Going into the suitcase is bathing suits, wool socks, flannel pajamas, jeans, sweaters, T-shirts, a couple of dresses, way too much stuff for a two-day trip. REVEAL *Thelma, standing in front of a closet, trying to decide what else to bring, as if she's forgotten something. The room looks like it was decorated entirely from a Sears catalogue. It's really frilly.*

INT—LOUISE'S BEDROOM—CLOSEUP—SUITCASE ON BED—
DAY

A perfectly ordered suitcase, everything neatly folded and orderly. Three pairs of underwear, one pair of long underwear, two pairs of pants, two sweaters, one furry robe, one nightgown. She could be packing for camp. REVEAL *Louise. Her room is as orderly as the suitcase. Everything matches. It's not quite as frilly as Thelma's, but it is of the same ilk. She is debating whether to take an extra pair of socks. She decides not to and closes the suitcase. She goes to the phone, picks it up and dials. We hear:*

ANSWERING MACHINE (V.O.)

Hi. This is Jimmy. I'm not here right now, but I'll probably be back 'cause...all my stuff's here. Leave a message.

[*Louise slams down the phone. A framed picture of Louise and Jimmy sits on the table next to the phone. She matter-of-factly slams that face down, too.*]

(*Thelma and Louise* filmscript, p. 5)

So we quickly know something about each woman's tempera-ment, and also a bit about their personal lives: Thelma has an obnoxious, none-too-bright husband whom Louise hates, and Louise has a boyfriend whom she is angry with, someone who—according to his answering machine message—has a bit of an attitude problem.

Structurally, too, Khouri has shown that she has conquered the action genre. By page 26 of the script, the two women have hit the road, there has been a scene in a bar, an attempted rape (of Thelma, in the parking lot), and Louise has killed the would-be rapist.

It has been said that Khouri refused to modify the tone of her script or make it less full of outrage; or to make her portraits of men any less one-sided: Here is her answer to those accusations, "You can't do a movie without villains. You have to have something for the heroines, or anti-heroines, to go up against, and I wasn't going to contrive some monstrous female." (*New York Times*). And here is Khouri's portrait of the script's first really nasty man:

[*Louise starts to back away, but the gun is still close to his face. His pants are undone in the front. She is still backing away with the gun raised. Thelma is inching away as well.*]

LOUISE [*cont'd*]

Just for the future, when a woman's crying like that, she's not having any fun.

[*Louise lowers the gun and stares at him for a second. Then she turns and walks away. Thelma does, too.*]

HARLAN
[*angry, pulling up his pants*]

Bitch. I should have gone ahead and fucked her.

[*Louise stops in her tracks.*]

LOUISE

What did you say?

HARLAN
[*smiling, arrogant*]

I said suck my cock.

[*Louise takes two long strides back toward him, raises the gun and* FIRES *a bullet into his face. We hear his body* HIT *the gravel parking lot.* LOUISE'S POV. *The car behind him is splattered with blood.*]

(p. 20)

Khouri told *American Screenwriters:*

> After *Thelma and Louise* I have to work harder to keep the writing pure. It's not that I don't feel as strongly about it; I think I second-guess myself more. It's harder to get myself into the moment than it was with *Thelma and Louise*. First of all, when I was writing *Thelma and Louise* I felt that I was writing a story that hadn't yet been told; I really felt like I was doing something new. I don't know if writers ever have the luxury of having that experience twice.
>
> So I feel I'm in a period of development as a writer. That first one was my gift, and from everything on it's just going to be really, really, hard work. And I'm going to have to find the ways to do that.... In many ways *Thelma and Louise* was divine inspiration.... And so there was an intensity to it that I may never experience again.
>
> I'm working on a Southern family saga now. A story about two sisters who come from a very traditional family. One of the sisters is married and a Junior League type and has always been the dutiful, good daughter. The other daughter works for the father; she's very, very business-oriented.

(pp. 130–31)

Another woman who has worked in the "buddy" genre—a female adaptation of the old male form—is Leslie Dixon, who may be said to have been the first to do so in contemporary times in her 1987 film *Outrageous Fortune,* starring Bette Midler and Shelley Long. In her early thirties when the assignment came her way, Dixon had been working at odd jobs in Los Angeles in order to have a flexible schedule and turn out scripts. Her first script had been sold by a small agent, and she was hired to rewrite another script.

Two producers, Robert Cort and Ted Field, had the idea for a female buddy comedy and had hired several writers, but with no luck.

They called in Dixon. "I went away and thought about it," Dixon told the *New York Times* (January 17, 1987), "and realized that one of the problems with all the drafts they had commissioned was that time and again they had hired men to write them. And that shouldn't necessarily be a problem, but these particular men did not have a feminine sympathetic side of their nature and couldn't get into a woman's frame of mind. Robert and I worked out the story, and he was delightful to do that with because he has a grossed-out, disgusting sense of humor exactly like mine." Dixon went on to say that, though the script was set up with Disney, very few changes were demanded in her script: "All the crude and raunchy stuff, the shocking moments survived."

After this film, Dixon and her husband, Tom Ropelewski, did a rewrite on Blake Edwards's *Blind Date* (1987) and a number of other rewrites. She also did the script for *Overboard* (1987), a poorly received comedy with Goldie Hawn and Kurt Russell, and worked on *Big Business* (1988). "*Overboard* was a writing assignment." Dixon said in a 1993 interview in *American Screenwriters*. "For me to complain about how [it] turned out is a little silly, because how good can any movie with amnesia as a central plot device ever be?...I contractually had to work on *Big Business*—identical twins switched at birth. I am the queen of dopey premises that get handed to me. A studio head once told me, 'Stop breathing life into corpses.'" (p. 205)

This, however, is Dixon's recipe for success in the movie-writing business, as the spritelike young woman with long brown hair defined it during press interviews in California for *Outrageous Fortune*:

> The first thing that you have to do is move to Los Angeles. Otherwise, chances are nothing will ever happen to you. Something in the atmosphere here tells you what kind of movies are being made. It's impossible to find these things out if you live elsewhere, like the Middle West, or even New York. The next thing you have to do is read a lot of scripts, preferably scripts that are going to be produced.
>
> And the first thing that I did was to try to write a role that an actor would want to play. So in my first script, I wrote the lead so the actor would have four different roles to play because I figured that would appeal to some actor's ego.

(That script was sold to Columbia Pictures, and had the title *A.K.A.,* though again—to this writer's knowledge—it was not made. The "bought but not produced" syndrome is a common one in the film industry, and may still make for an exceptionally lucrative deal.) Dixon also told the *New York Times:*

I noticed that I had developed a fantasy about myself as a writer [at twenty-six] as opposed to actually doing it, and that I better put my fanny in a chair and get on with it. I finally summoned up the bad taste to move to L.A.

I did not know a living soul. I just worked at demeaning, low-paying, depressing, semi-skilled jobs, like word processing, where I would do as little as I possibly could and take time off to work on a script and read lots and lots of scripts.

But being on the outside of the business is like you're on the outside of this medieval moat and everyone else is inside the castle. And you need just that first point of contact into the big-time Hollywood regime—making friends with a particular development executive at a studio, or a successful screenwriter who says, "I'm going to give your script to my agent." But you need to hit something like that, and suddenly you're in the castle with everybody else and it's easy from that point.

Another point of entry into the film writing business has been to go to film school, and this is what writer-director Kathryn Bigelow did in the late seventies at Columbia University's Graduate Film School. She made the independent film *The Loveless* (1982) in New York, and—a native Californian—she taught at the California Institute for the Arts in 1983. At that time she got a writing and directing deal at Universal, through the help of writer-director Walter Hill. Bigelow told the *Village Voice* (Nov. 22, 1988), "I was teaching B filmmakers because I liked them, and I'd invite directors up to class. Walter Hill came. I showed him *The Loveless,* and he asked what I'd like to do next and gave me a development deal." Bigelow has said that her favorite directors are, along with Hill, the action directors Sam Peckinpah, George Miller, and James Cameron.

Her biggest success to date has been *Blue Steel,* the 1990 thriller with Jamie Lee Curtis as a rookie cop. It was produced by Ed Pressman, the well-respected filmmaker who has gone out on a limb for a number of new and innovative writer-directors such as Oliver Stone, Brian De Palma, and Terence Malick. Pressman has been quoted as saying, "When I saw *Near Dark* [Bigelow's 1987 film], I saw a really original sensibility which could take a convention and turn it around. It's provocative that she's a woman doing genre, but it's only interesting because her films work. The kinds of films directors make are often embodied in their physical presence. Kathryn has a strong magnetic presence that galvanizes people and inspires confidence." (*Village Voice*, Nov. 22, 1988)

It's clear, though, that for Bigelow writing is mainly the means to a cinematic end; i.e., her film and its direction. In an interview about *Blue Steel*, Bigelow told the *New York Times* (March 11, 1990), "It wasn't until I began to write on spec, when you become a sort of gladiator because you own the property and you're able to control the outcome of it, that I made it work for me here [meaning Los Angeles]."

Judith Rascoe, the scriptwriter for the adaptation of *Who'll Stop the Rain* in 1978, *Eat a Bowl of Tea* in 1989, *Havana* in 1990, and *The Ruth Etting Story* (in preproduction at the time of this writing), seems to have taken both time honored routes to get into the movie business: getting a writing reputation, and also taking an entry level job. A producer saw one of her short stories published in the *Atlantic Monthly* and called her about making it into a film; and she also went to Los Angeles after completing her course work for a Ph.D. at Harvard and took a job as a reader at a studio.

One of the ironies—or perhaps it proves the point—is that the woman who is the most prolific and most produced of all contemporary screenwriters is a German Jew, who grew up in Nazi Germany, was educated in London, married an East Indian, and spent nearly twenty years in India before moving to New York City (or at least spending three-quarters of her time there) in the late 1970s. This may not have been her intent—for she had none in this direction anyway—but her productivity and success have been completely outside the industry establishment, or the mental state of Hollywood. (Though with her recent successes this has changed with a business deal with Walt Disney Pictures.)

She is Ruth Prawer Jhabvala, the novelist and screenwriter who has written or cowritten nearly all the Merchant-Ivory films, whether they are original scripts or their highly touted literary adaptations. She started her partnership with the team—James Ivory, an American director, and Ismail Merchant, an Indian producer who had known Jhabvala's husband—in 1963. "We are in the *Guinness Book of Records* for film team longevity," the gregarious Merchant once said with a laugh.

A highly regarded though not widely known novelist and short story writer who lived in India with her Indian architect husband and three daughters, Jhabvala was first contacted by Merchant in 1951 to do a film of her novel *The Householder* (others include *The Nature of Passion, Esmond in India,* and *Travelers*). One perhaps apocryphal version is that Merchant, in search of the rights to *The Householder,* and knowing of Jhabvala's reticence, disguised his voice and telephoned long distance, pretending to be Jhabvala's mother-in-law in Bombay announcing a surprise visit.

The persuasive Merchant did convince her, not just to sell the rights but also to do the script. And since that time Jhabvala worked in 1965 with James Ivory on an original screenplay for *Shakespeare Wallah* as the first of their many collaborations, an award-winning film about a troupe of East Indians performing Shakespeare across India.

This was followed by *The Guru* (script by Jhabvala and Ivory) in 1969, *Bombay Talkie* (Jhabvala and Ivory) in 1970; *Autobiography of a Princess* (sole credit by Jhabvala) in 1975; *Roseland* (Jhabvala) in 1977; *Hullabaloo Over Georgie ând Bonnie's Pictures* (Jhabvala) in 1978; *The Europeans* (Jhabvala, from the Henry James novel) in 1979; *Jane Austen in Manhattan* (Jhabvala) in 1980; *Quartet* (Jhabvala, from the Jean Rhys novel) in 1981; *Heat and Dust* (Jhabvala, from her own novel) in 1983; *The Bostonians* (Jhabvala, from the Henry James novel) in 1984; *A Room With a View* (Jhabvala, from the E. M. Forster novel) in 1986; *Mr. and Mrs. Bridge* (Jhabvala, from the Evan S. Connell novel) in 1990; and *Howards End* (Jhabvala, from the E. M. Forster novel) in 1992.

Perhaps it is significant that the recent films from Merchant-Ivory which have not used Jhabvala have not been that critically well-received or commercially successful: *Maurice* (1987), *The Deceivers* and *The Perfect Murder* (both 1988), *Slaves of New York* (1989), and *The Ballad of the Sad Cafe* (1991).

Ruth Prawer Jhabvala with James Ivory and Ismail Merchant

The trio—director Ivory, producer Merchant, and writer Jhab-vala—started working out of a Manhattan townhouse during a period which coincided with what Jhabvala has described as a kind of homesickness and a feeling of being overwhelmed by India, a condition also treated in her novel *Heat and Dust.* In an interview in the *New York Times Magazine* in 1983, Jhabvala said about India:

> In the beginning, I adored the summers; I loved that extreme heat after being so cold in wartime England. Then it became more and more difficult. India sucks the marrow from your bones, only you're not aware of it. You can't live in a completely alien place. I got very homesick for Europe. It was a homesickness that was so terrible, so consuming. And the only place that reminded me of the Europe that I once knew was New York. To anyone of my generation, Europe now does smell of blood.

Their first movies made in New York were *Hullabaloo Over Georgie and Bonnie's Pictures,* and *Jane Austen in Manhattan. Roseland*—the story of three interlocking stories about lonely people whose passion for dancing led them to the old Roseland Dance Hall on West 52nd Street in New York—received attention at the New York Film Festival and did well commercially in 1977. The adaptations which followed, of *The Europeans* and *The Bostonians,* were critically praised.

Most acclaimed was the first real hit, *Heat and Dust* (1983), starring Julie Christie and the adaptation of Jhabvala's own prize-winning novel which won the Booker Prize (the most significant literary award given in England), and her script won the British equivalent of an Academy Award. *A Room With a View* (for which Jhabvala won an Oscar for screenwriting in 1986), which cost $3 million to make, grossed more than $60 million worldwide and put the team effort into a whole new light in the eyes of the movie business establishment. (Less known is the fact that Jhabvala and director John Schlesinger collaborated on the script for *Madame Sousatzka* in 1988.)

The well-liked *Howards End,* another Forster adaptation by Jhabvala, catapulted its female star, Emma Thompson, into national prominence in the United States, though *Remains of the Day* (1993) was actually scripted by Harold Pinter (an agreement which was already in the works when the decision to make the film came about). As of this writing Jhabvala has adapted *Portrait of a Lady,* the Henry James novel, for Disney Pictures, with which Merchant-Ivory has formed a business alliance, and there is a project in the works, also with Disney, about Thomas Jefferson's visit to Paris.

Especially the Disney connection must seem curious for the austere and publicity shy Jhabvala, born in 1927 in Cologne, who survived Nazi Germany by escaping with her family to London. She started reading and writing intensively in high school, she said, adding that her favorite subjects were the lower middle classes of the British:

> I wrote about them in the stories, plays, unfinished novels that I turned out in a relentless stream all through those school years. Not really having a world of my own, I made up for my disinheritance by absorbing the world of others. The more regional, the more deeply rooted a writer was, the more I loved them: George Eliot, Thomas Hardy, Charles Dickens. Their landscapes, their childhood memories became mine. I adopted them passionately. But I was equally passionate to

adopt, for instance, the landscapes of Marcel Proust, of James Joyce, of Henry James, of the great Russians—Tolstoy, Dostoevsky, Turgenev, Chekhov. It was as if I had no senses of my own—besides no country of my own—but only theirs.

> (from her talk "Disinheritance," before the Scottish Arts Council after receiving its Neil Gunn Fellowship. This is the only time that Jhabvala has spoken about her personal history publicly. Quoted in *The Films of Merchant Ivory,* New York: 1991, p. 20.)

Jhabvala's father committed suicide in the late 1940s in despair over the discovered details of his forty-some relatives lost in concentration camps. Soon afterward she married her Indian architect husband, in part, she has said, for his cheerful stoicism in the face of adversity. They made their home in India, and there she raised three daughters, all of whom are now grown and live in California, India, and England. Her husband maintains his practice in India, and Jhabvala spends three-quarters of her time in New York, with much visiting back and forth.

As a fiction writer—surprisingly—Jhabvala's themes have been social, not political, ones: the ambiguities, tensions, and mysteries of middle-class India in contemporary times, the perennial theme of the European fascination with the continent; all with a cool, ironic tone. She is compared to Chekhov, Jane Austen, and E. M. Forster. In this country, her fiction appears in *The New Yorker.*

The transition to scriptwriting was both difficult and easy, she told the *New York Times* in 1977 in an interview about *Roseland.*

> In a novel, there's not that much dialogue—it's far more indirect. You don't have to put everything in the mouths of your characters. But in a screenplay you have to say so much. You have to dramatize it. But I always had had a lot of dialogue in my early novels. It was never a problem. It's the thing that comes easiest to me, and I suppose dramatic situations do, as well. So I suppose in a way I was a natural screenplay writer, dramatist, or something.

Still, she said, her first experience in screenwriting—adapting her novel *The Householder*—was not so easy.

The cutting was a lot because I didn't know how long the script was supposed to be and I wrote far, far too much dialogue. I didn't realize at the time how far two words can go on the screen—so much farther than on the page. The actors' expressions and all sorts of things help out, so you really need just half a sentence written. I think we really didn't cut down quite enough. I cut three sentences to one, but I should have cut them to half. It took years before I could really get my writing down to a half sentence.

She also has said that she had been long interested in the movies of European and American directors, having watched them at film society screenings in London and New Delhi. And after agreeing to work on *The Householder,* she read all the books on the art of screenwriting (not too many, she recalls) she could get her hands on at the local Indian libraries.

And perhaps because—paradoxically—she is a writer herself she has been quoted as saying that the screenwriter approaching a literary "masterpiece" for adaptation should probably not do so with any great reverence. "You must not even think of the writer, dead or alive," she told the *New York Times* (March 3, 1992). "The first rule is not to be reverent. The only thing is to be disrespectful. What you aim for when you adapt a novel is not the detail but the ambiance, the whole atmosphere, the idea of people of living in a certain way."

In adapting, Jhabvala says that once a project has been decided upon, director James Ivory will give a copy of the book selected with certain passages underlined that he definitely wants in the film. She says that she ignores most of his suggestions. "I give the draft to him, and then he says what he doesn't like, which is almost everything. I go back and do another one, and that he likes a little bit more." Ivory corroborates:

It's a step-by-step thing....We decide what we want to emphasize in the script, and I tell her what my favorite scenes might well be, or are, if she's adapting a book. If it's from a book then I mark up the book, so that she knows the favorite things of mine that I wouldn't want to lose. I would want to make something of them. She usually agrees, though she doesn't always.

Then she writes her script, and I never see it. I have no idea what she's doing. She's off somewhere doing it, maybe she's off in India. She comes back with this mess of papers, all scotch-taped together. Then I read it and I start shouting: "No, no, this isn't what I wanted," and "Why have you left out such and such a thing?" and "Are you crazy?" And this will go on for an hour or two, and then we sort of redo it, with me trying to push things I want, and she agreeing to some of it. And that's it, that becomes the screenplay. And then, usually before we begin shooting, it goes through another kind of slight metamorphosis; it alters before shooting, and then it alters during the shooting.

(quoted in *The Films of Merchant Ivory*, by Robert Emmet Long, pp. 23–24)

Jhabvala says that wherever she is, which is usually at home in her apartment in Manhattan (a floor in the Merchant-Ivory building where business takes place and the filmmakers also live), her mornings are devoted to writing, which is done in a plain school notebook. And she usually starts at ten A.M.

She generally does not go on the film set, nor, she says, does she care to, she told the *New York Times* in 1977.

I don't want to be there when they're filming. I don't want to know what's happening. At that stage, I'm not really inter-ested at all. There's nothing I can do. [She has also said that she has no interest in casting either.]

I don't understand what's going on. There's so much confusion, turmoil, uproar and all sorts of things. I just don't want to know. So whatever they come out with they come out with. But then I get into it again when they go into the editing room and I can see again what can come out. And I can see what mistakes I made, what mistakes they made, and I can see what we should do to correct them.

At the moment, Jhabvala is probably best known for her script for *A Room With a View*. In truth, Jhabvala has written a script close to both the spirit and the letter of the book, with some small changes of structure and detail. But unlike a lot of literary adaptations, it doesn't somehow seem dutiful, in the least bit careful, or—worse yet—stodgy.

Room is a straightforward adaptation—that is, it is chronologically straightforward, beginning when and where the novel begins and ending when and where it ends (in Italy, at the Pension Bertolini) with only a few changes, some omissions, and a couple of fittingly "in the manner of" Forster-like additions. Though naturally it could not be possible to have a whole novel in a film, it does seem as if no significant section or speech has been left out. (*A Room With a View* is not a massive work, in any event.)

A few "cinematic" alterations come to mind, like the fact that when her fiancé Cecil Vyse (Daniel Day Lewis) in the film plants his first awkward kiss on her and his pince-nez glasses get caught between them, Lucy Honeychurch (Helena Bonham Carter) flashes back in the movie to the moment when George Emerson (Julian Sands) impetuously and romantically kisses her suddenly in an open field in Italy. Just as about three-quarters of the way into the film there is a flashback showing how Cecil met the Emerson father and son in a gallery, rather than the novel's way of explaining it through conversation. And Lucy and George have a discussion of a possible romantic motivation for Charlotte Bartlett's (Maggie Smith) getting the couple together, which occurs at the end of the movie as they are happily honeymooning at the end of the novel. In the film this is shown instead in a quick cut to Charlotte alone in bed in England, wistfully reading a letter from Lucy.

But the script is remarkably free of cinematic devices, unless you count the fact that the Miss Alans, Catherine and Teresa, have their room and hair decorated in cornflowers in the film (larger and more eye-catching?) rather than the more discrete violets of the novel. And it's poppies in the film rather than the river of violets that Forster describes.

George is a bit more playful in the film, as we see by the addition of his question mark formed by peas that he puts on his plate and turns to Lucy. Still, this preserves the spirit of philosophical inquiry that is a part of George; and this is emphasized in the question mark hung on the back of a portrait in his room. He's definitely more active and attractive, though, than in the novel, where his character is shown to be brooding at times.

But the novel-film similarities are striking without seeming self-consciously so, or portentous, a charge which has been brought against some of the Merchant-Ivory adaptations.

This is how the novel begins in the dining room of the house. "The Signora had no business to do it," said Miss Bartlett, "no business at all. She promised us south rooms with a view close together, instead of which here are north rooms, looking into a courtyard, and a long way apart. Oh, Lucy!" The film starts off in the bedroom (where it's clear that Jhabvala knows the film is going to end up in the tradition of same scene at beginning and end—in this case with a happier concluding atmosphere). And here is the Bartlett speech from the film:

> This is not at all what we were led to expect. I thought we were going to see the Arno. The Signora distinctly wrote south rooms with a view and close together. Instead of which she's given us north rooms with no view and a long way apart. She had no business to do it. No business at all.

The film then moves us down the staircase to the dining room, where the cast of characters—including George and Mr. Emerson (Denholm Elliot)—and the conversation is quite the same as in the novel. In the book, Mr. Emerson says, " 'This is my son, his name's George. He has a view too.' 'Ah,' said Miss Bartlett, repressing Lucy, who was about to speak. 'What I mean,' he continued, 'is that you can have our rooms, and we'll have yours. We'll change.' "

The women refuse out of a sense of propriety, and Mr. Emerson goes on, " 'But why?' he persisted. 'Women like looking at a view; men don't.' And he thumped with his fists like a naughty child, and turned to his son, saying, 'George, persuade them.' 'It's so obvious they should have the rooms,' said the son. 'There's nothing else to say.' "

In the film, with an efficient way of showing Mr. Emerson's free-thinking, romantic nature, here is his speech taken from the novel: "Why shouldn't you have them? Women like looking at a view. Men don't." And then there is the character-revealing Jhabvala addition to Mr. Emerson's speech; an addition which is indeed very Forster-like:

> It's ridiculous, these niceties. They go against common

sense. Every kind of sense. I don't care what I see outside.
My vision is within. [*thumping his chest*] *Here* is where the
bird sings. *Here* is where the sky is blue.

There are a few structural changes in the early Italian sequence.
Miss Lavish (Judi Dench) takes Lucy for a walk with a Baedeker in
the novel, describing the smell of the streets, eventually losing her.
Whereas in the film it's Charlotte who is taken along, and Charlotte
who reacts by holding her handkerchief over her mouth. In the novel
perhaps an explanation is needed as to why Lucy is alone, running
into Mr. Emerson, in the church. But in the film she just appears, and
to a modern-day audience it does not seem untoward.

The fight in the square with the Italian youth killed is very much
the same in both film and novel. In the novel, "He frowned; he bent
toward Lucy with a look of interest, as if he had an important
message for her. He opened his lips to deliver it, and a stream of red
came out between them and trickled down his unshaven chin." In the
film the Italian's blue eyes are shot from above, making a nice
contrast with the red blood, as he passes out at Lucy's feet. And the
swirling camera indicates her subsequent fainting.

Many of the important speeches are kept, of course: such as
Reverend Beebe (Simon Callow) saying, after listening to Lucy play,
"If Miss Honeychurch ever takes to live as she plays, it will be very
exciting—both for us and for her," a speech repeated much later in
the novel by the Reverend to Cecil Vyse at a most inopportune time:
i.e., the moment just before Cecil tells him that he and Lucy are
engaged.

And the observation of Cecil's mother that sums up the difference
in their two families is cleverly picked up and used in the film; Mrs.
Vyse, happily, about Lucy: "She's purging off the Honeychurch
taint." Just as much of George's speech to Lucy is retained, that Cecil
"wants you for a possession like an ivory box."

In the movie, it actually is the meddling Charlotte who straightens
things out with Mr. Emerson just as Lucy is about to escape
everything connected with her broken engagement and go to Greece:
it's Reverend Beebe in the novel. But perhaps this is because it will
give Maggie Smith, as Charlotte, a chance to say to Lucy's mother, as
they drive off in the carriage, in the wonderfully arch, sonorous tone
only Smith can muster: "The plans for Greece may change."

Mr. Emerson's most poignant speeches are kept intact in the film, however, and they are of course the ones which touch, and change, Lucy's heart: He defends his son's behavior, which is described as abominable by Lucy, "Not 'abominably,'" was the gentle correction. "He only tried when he should not have tried." And: "My dear, I am worried about you. It seems to me that you are in a muddle. Take an old man's word; there's nothing worse than a muddle in all the world." And at the end of the speech the narrator says, quoting the speech which is retained in the film, "Then he burst out excitedly: That's it; that's what I mean. You love George. You love the boy body and soul." And in the film he goes on to tell her that she has deceived everyone: George, Cecil, her family, and most of all herself.

The discussion about her possible deception takes place in the novel with Reverend Beebe having reentered the room, but it is clearly more cinematic, and dramatic, to have Mr. Emerson making his heartfelt, but gentle, accusations to Lucy one-on-one.

Omitted from this last scene is the rather complicated worry Mr. Emerson has that his son may have "gone under" in despair at the loss of Lucy's love, somewhat in the way his wife went downhill. Not that George too will die, but that there will be no joy in his life. On screen, this obviously would have seemed a bit maudlin, and so it was probably a good decision to leave this out.

Also left out of the novel overall is the first person point of view, or, more properly, the subjective state of each character's feelings. It is left, instead, up to each actor to convey his or her feelings. Nor are there full letters in the movie, as there are in the book.

It's not possible to tell if the engraved looking "placards" and titles that divide certain scenes in the film were Jhabvala's idea, but— except for the chapters three and four in the novel—they correspond nearly exactly to the chapter titles in the book and do work well in giving an ironic sense of the coming scene, such as "Lying to George" (chapter 16), "Lying to Cecil" (chapter 17), and "Lying to Mr. Beebe, Mrs. Honeychurch, Freddy and the Servants" (chapter 18). (One is reminded of June Mathis's suggestion not to avoid titles in your film if using them will work well.)

In *Heat and Dust* Jhabvala has adapted her own work. It's a clever announcement of the movie's theme of the clash of the two cultures, British and Indian, as a tape recorder is rather offhandedly played back ostensibly to see if it is working. Harry (Nickolas Grace) is being interviewed by Anne (Julie Christie) about her great-aunt Olivia, and he tells her, "She was outraging two conventions: those of her own people and those of the Indians, which are if anything even stronger."

It also picks up a kind of secondary motif on the comparison of two generations of women: today's supposedly freer woman, as played by Julie Christie as Anne, and the more impulsive actions of her grandmother and her cousin, Olivia in the film, played with fetching sensuality by Greta Scacchi.

HARRY

I suppose women have changed. It's not like it was. Your grandmother carrying on in Paris. Olivia in India. My goodness, they were romantic. They were all for love and that sort of thing. You've got better things to do, I daresay.

ANNE

Oh, I don't know.

Olivia's character is established quickly in the film, using the device of two story lines, though mostly it's the earlier generation we see. Olivia is unconventional, gleeful, prone to improprieties. She doesn't want to go away for four months during the terrible Indian heat like the other English matrons do; she wants to see an "entertainment" that is designed strictly for men during a social function which mixes the British and the Indians; in a foreshadowing of her bad judgment, she walks through a door behind which there are three men—including the Nawab, or Indian prince, to whom she is attracted—and they are not pleased at her intrusion. And, as the only woman taking part, she plays with childish joy at the Indian game of first to sit down on a pillow. She also tells the Nawab that she doesn't really like horses—that British obsession—that much, and he says he thought not. She is not, in short, a proper memsahib.

The Indian attitude toward English women—the more stolid kind—has already been established as the prince tells a joke about a jockey mistaking an English woman for a horse. And in case we are in any doubt about the differences in cultures, there are the cross-cuts to his mother looking spitefully pleased as Olivia spits out some Indian treats into her handkerchief, as well as Harry's warning Olivia that she is out of line: the Nawab's mother is not receiving Olivia.

Because of distribution problems *Heat and Dust* (the title refers to the permeating and stultifying atmosphere of the terrible Indian heat) was not as widely seen in the United States as in Europe, but it was highly acclaimed in Europe. For this viewer, it is Jhabvala's finest film script.

Other women screenwriters must be mentioned, even if they have been a bit elusive or difficult to research. Jay Presson Allen, who many must think is a man when they read her screen credits, wrote *Marnie* (1964), *The Prime of Miss Jean Brodie* 91969), *Cabaret*, and *Travels With My Aunt* (both 1972), *Prince of the City* (1981), and *Never Cry Wolf* (1983), among others. Carole Eastman wrote *Five Easy Pieces* (1970) and *The Fortune* (1975); Gloria Katz wrote *American Graffiti* (1973) and *Indiana Jones and the Temple of Doom* (1984); Melissa Mattheson, *E.T. The Extraterrestrial* (1982, the largest grossing film of all time; Barbara Benedek, *The Big Chill* (1983) with Lawrence Kasdan, prefaced by some creative television work like "Mork and Mindy," "WKRP in Cincinnati."

Nancy Dowd's script for Paul Newman's *Slap Shot* in 1973 was considered by some too realistically vulgar in its hockey language to have been written by a woman; she also wrote the original script for *Coming Home*, the 1978 film with Jane Fonda and Jon Voight for which she eventually shared Oscar credit with screenwriter Waldo Salt. Joan Micklin Silver started writing educational films before moving into feature writing and directing (*Hester Street* in 1975; *Bernice Bobs Her Hair* in 1977; *Chilly Scenes of Winter* in 1979; *Crossing Delancey* in 1988, all adaptations). Claudia Weill, the documentary filmmaker, coauthored the story for *Girlfriends* with Vicki Polon in 1978, but Polon wrote the script. And Weill eventually moved on to directing.

Their story should be told in another whole chapter in another whole book. Did they enter the business through an independent effort or is a female networking system springing up which would mirror the early days of movies after all?

There are some indications that a tentative system may be starting, or that the patrilineal ice is beginning to break up a bit. Caroline Thompson, who was born in 1956, scripted *Edward*

Scissorhands in 1990 and cowrote *The Addams Family* in 1991, got her first break through the filmmaker Penelope Spheeris (known most for the 1981 documentary *The Decline of Western Civilization*). Thompson moved to Los Angeles after college, wrote an unusual novel which a friend got to an agent at ICM (International Creative Management) who got it to Spheeris. According to Thompson, "...she loved it and immediately responded to it and wanted to make it into a movie. I agreed *if* I could cowrite the script with her so I could learn about scriptwriting." (*American Screenwriters,* p. 232) Thompson said that they got a deal at MGM, though the movie never got made, and that at least gave her a reputation as someone who had a unique vision.

The unsettling truth is, however, that the film industry is no longer open in the way it once was, the structure formed by the women's solidarity of the early years has been undermined as those women died, and the hegemony of the male writer—cashing in all the chips—has held firm since the end of World War II.

7

Afterword

My original intent for this book was to have a chapter analyzing the progress of women screenwriters in the international community, but that too must be a subject for another study, one which tries to determine if the same pattern is evident for these women as for their American counterparts. But they at least deserve a litanylike listing: Colette, *Maedchen in Uniform* (1932), *Lac-Aux-Dames* (1933), and *Divine* (1935); Marguerite Duras, *Hiroshima Mon Amour* (1959); writer-director Lina Wertmuller, *The Seduction of Mimi* (1972), *Love and Anarchy* (1973), and *Swept Away* (1975); Suzanne Schiffman, *Fahrenheit 451* (1967), *Day for Night* (1973), and *The Last Metro* (1980); Penelope Gilliatt, *Sunday Bloody Sunday* (1972); Nelly Kaplan, *Le Regard Picasso* (1967) and *Au Bonheur des Dames* (1979); Margaretta von Trotta, *A Free Woman* (1972); Maggie Greenaway, *The Ballad of Little Jo* (1993).

One description seems to be common to all the women writers discussed here, and as usual June Mathis figured it all out right away in "Wave Length of Success":

A scenario writer's life becomes just one scene after another. Before she is through with one story she is thinking and planning for the next. This is why it is difficult for the amateur to break in. The trained writer understands the needs of the studio, is familiar with the pet ideas of the studio executives.

229

Occasionally a well-known playwright or author breaks into the business and succeeds and learns to live the irregular, hectic life, but the majority of them throw up their hands and declare the whole motion picture industry and all connected with it to be impossible, and they go back to their former work.

We may as well let June Mathis have the last word. She would have wanted it that way.

Select Bibliography

American Screenwriters, eds. Karl Schanzer and Thomas Lee Wright (New York: Avon Books, 1993).

Backstory: Interviews With Screenwriters of Hollywood's Golden Age, ed. Patrick McGilligan (Berkeley, Cal.: University of California Press, 1986). *Backstory 2: Interviews With Screenwriters of the 1930s and 1940s*, ed. McGilligan (Berkeley, Cal.: University of California Press, 1990).

Basinger, Jeanne. *A Woman's View* (New York: Alfred A. Knopf, 1993).

Beranger, Clara. *Writing for the Screen* (Dubuque, Iowa: W. C. Brown, Co., 1950).

Cary, Gary. *Anita Loos* (New York: Alfred A. Knopf, 1988).

Coffee, Lenore. *Storyline: Reflections of a Hollywood Screenwriter* (London: Cassell, 1973).

Eels, George, and Stanley Musgrove. *Mae West* (New York: William Morrow, 1982).

Ephron, Henry. *We Thought We Could Do Anything: The Life of Screenwriters Phoebe and Henry Ephron* (New York: W. W. Norton & Co., 1977).

Ephron, Nora. *Crazy Salad* (New York: Random House, 1975)

————. *Heartburn* (New York: Alfred A. Knopf, 1983).

————. *Scribble Scribble* (New York: Alfred A. Knopf, 1978).

————. *When Harry Met Sally* (New York: Alfred A. Knopf, 1991).

Film Writers Guide. ed. Kate Bales (Beverly Hills, Cal.: Lone Eagle Press, 1988).

Films For, By, and About Women. ed. Kaye Sullivan (Metuchen, N.J.: Scarecrow Press, 1980).

Gabler, Neal. *An Empire of Their Own: How the Jews Invented Hollywood* (New York: Doubleday, 1988).

Gordon, Ruth. *My Side: The Autobiography of Ruth Gordon* (New York: Harper & Row, 1976).

————. *Ruth Gordon: An Open Book* (Garden City, N.Y.: Doubleday & Co., 1980).

————. *Shady Lady* (New York: Arbor House, 1981).

231

Hamilton, Ian. *Writers in Hollywood 1915-1951* (New York: Harper & Row, 1990).

Higham, Charles, and Joel Greenberg. *Hollywood in the Forties* (New York: Paperback Library, 1970).

Jacobs, Lewis. *The Rise of the American Film* (New York: Teachers College Press, 1968).

Klein, Carole. *Gramercy Park: An American Bloomsbury* (Athens, Ohio: Ohio University Press, 1967).

Latham, Aaron. *Crazy Sundays: F. Scott Fitzgerald in Hollywood* (New York: Viking Press, 1970).

Long, Robert Emmet. *The Films of Merchant Ivory* (New York: Harry N. Abrams, 1991).

Loos, Anita, with John Emerson. *Breaking Into the Movies* (New York: James McCann Co., 1981).

————. *A Girl Like I* (New York: Viking Press, 1966).

————. *Kiss Hollywood Good-by* (New York: Viking Press, 1974).

Marion, Frances. *How to Write and Sell Film Stories* (New York: Covici, Friede, 1938).

————. *Off With Their Heads!* (New York: Macmillan, 1972).

Ramsaye, Terry. *A Million and One Nights* (New York: Simon and Schuster, 1926).

Schwartz, Nancy Lynn. *The Hollywood Writers' Wars*. Completed by Sheila Schwartz (New York: Alfred A. Knopf, 1982).

Walker, Alexander. *The Celluloid Sacrifice* (New York: Hawthorn, 1967).

Women in Film: An International Guide ed. Annette Kuhn with Susannah Radstone. (New York: Fawcett Columbine, 1990).

Index

233

Man Who Loved Cat Dancing, The,
59, 186–87
Marion, Frances, 4, 6, 7–8, 22–36,
27, 45, 48, 80, 88, 93, 155
Marsh, Mae, 6
Mason, Sarah Y., 4, 154–58
Massey, Dorothy, 160–61
Massey, Raymond, 160–61
Matheson, Melissa, 184
Mathis, June, 4, 6, 7–22, 19, 45,
225, 229–30
Matriarchy, 164. *See also* Feminism
Mattheson, Melissa, 227
May, Elaine, 184, 185, 187–89
Mayer, Louis B., 33, 92, 100, 106,
114, 138
Mayo, Archie, 76
Meehan, John, 144
Meet Me in St. Louis, 126, 131, 132
Men and Women, 53
Merchant, Ismail, 216, 217
Merchant-Ivory films, 62, 216, 218,
223
Meredyth, Bess, 4, 6–7, 10, 14, 20,
28, 36–42, 37
Merkel, Una, 68
Metro-Goldwyn-Mayer. *See* MGM
Metro (studio), 9, 10, 59, 64, 93, 152,
155
MGM, 9, 28, 34, 64, 93–94, 99–100,
111, 139, 152, 171
Midler, Bette, 212
Midsummer Night's Dream, A, 111,
125
Mildred Pierce, 140
Millard, Oscar, 126
Miller, Alice D. G., 4, 6, 7, 43–45,
45–46
Miller, Alice Duer, 4, 7, 44, 60, 68
Miller, Charlotte, 149
Miller, George, 214
Miller, Gilbert, 172
Millionaire's Double, The, 12, 14, 21
Min and Bill, 35
Minnelli, Vincente, 170
Mission Road Studio, 92
Mission to Moscow, 83
Mix, Tom, 45, 58, 110
Moby Dick, 13, 14, 39–42
Montgomery, Robert, 48
Moore, Colleen, 147
Morris, Chester, 68

Morris, Gouvenor, 55
Movie business, 5, 6, 68, 79
Muir, Jean, 111, 113
Murfin, Jane, 4, 6, 44, 48, 80,
147–48, 155
Murphy's Romance, 178
Murray, Mae, 62
Musgrove, Stanley, 68
Myers, Carmel, 20
My Son, My Son, 98–99

N

Naldi, Nita, 17, 18
National Velvet, 126
Neal, Patricia, 178
Networking, 6, 28, 227–28
Never Fear, 180
New Dark, 215
Newman, Paul, 177, 178, 227
Newman, Phyllis, 176
New York Hat, The, 11, 46
Niblo, Fred, 20, 43
Nichols, Mike, 185, 187, 188, 192
Nicholson, Jack, 197
Night After Night, 76
Norma Rae, 178
Norris, Frank, *McTeague,* 22, 24
North Star, The, 80–82, 83
Not Wanted, 180
Novak, Kim, 64
Novarro, Ramon, 20

O

O'Brien, Margaret, 131
O'Hara, George, 41
O'Hara, John, 131
O'Hara, Maureen, 85, 86, 144
O'Neill, Eugene, *Anna Christie,* 34
O'Neill, Frank, 44
Orczy, Baroness, *Leatherface,* 43–44
Ouspenskaya, Maria, 86
Outrage, 180, 181–82
Outrageous Fortune, 212, 213
Overboard, 213

P

Pagano, Jo, 139
Paramount (studio), 9, 73, 76, 79

PHOTO CREDITS

Grateful acknowledgment is offered for permission to reprint the following material:

Page 19, June Mathis, from Museum of Modern Art Film Stills Department; pages 24–25, from *The Complete Greed of Eric von Stroheim*, by Herman Weinburg (New York; Arno Press, 1972); page 27, Frances Marion and Mary Pickford, courtesy MOMA Film Stills; script reproductions from *The New York Hat*, *The Millionaire's Double*, and *Sea-Beast*, courtesy MOMA Department of Film; page 26, Greta Garbo in *Anna Christie*, courtesy of Turner Classic Television; page 37, Bess Meredyth, courtesy MOMA; page 50, Clara Beranger, courtesy of Billy Rose Film and Theatre Collection at Lincoln Center; pages 69. 72, Viña Delmar, Anita Loos, and Jean Harlow, from the collection of Jerry Vermilye; page 77, Mae West, from the collection of Allan J. Wilson; page 89, Lenore Coffee, from the Billy Rose Film Collection; page 109, Mary McCall Jr., courtesy of [her daughter] Sheila Benson; page 143, courtesy of Catherine Turney; page 130, Sally Benson, courtesy of Billy Rose Film Collection; page 132, Judy Garland in *Meet Me in St. Louis* from Turner Classic Television; page 150, Marguerite Roberts, courtesy of Billy Rose Collection; page 166, Frances Goodrich, courtesy MOMA; page 175, courtesy of Betty Comden; page 217, Ruth Prawer Jhabvala, with Merchant and Ivory, courtesy MOMA.

All other reprints are from files at the Billy Rose Film and Theatre Collection at Lincoln Center.

ABOUT THE AUTHOR

Marsha McCreadie has written two books on women and film, both published by Praeger: *Women on Film: The Critical Eye* (1983), a study of women film critics, which won a Choice Outstanding Academic Book Award and the Dartmouth College Award for Best Dramatic Criticism; and *The Casting Couch and Other Front Row Seats* (1990), a collection of her film reviews and other articles. From 1983 to 1988 she was the film critic at the *Arizona Republic,* and she has published articles on film topics in *Film Comment, American Film,* the *Village Voice, Premiere,* the *New York Times,* and other periodicals and film journals. She has taught at Rutgers University, and holds a doctorate from the University of Illinois in Urbana-Champaign.

Most recently, she has reviewed independent films for the Bergen County *Record* in New Jersey. Ms. McCreadie lives in New York City with her husband, Bob Keller, who makes sets for film and television. And she wishes that her scripts were half as terrific as the ones written by the women in this book.